Science and Theology

Science and Theology

The New Consonance

edited by

Ted Peters

Westview Press
A Member of the Perseus Books Group

Published in 1998 in the United States of America by Westview Press, 5500 Central Avenue, Boulder, Colorado 80301-2877, and in the United Kingdom by Westview Press, 12 Hid's Copse Road, Cumnor Hill, Oxford OX2 9JJ

A CIP catalog record for this book is available from the Library of Congress.
ISBN 0-8133-3258-3 (hc.) ISBN 0-8133-3259-1 (pbk.)

The paper used in this publication meets the requirements of the American National Standard for Permanence of Paper for Printed Library Materials Z39.48-1984.

10 9 8 7 6 5 4 3 2 1

Contents

Acknowledgments

The preparation of this book was made possible by the John Templeton Foundation, which, in conjunction with the Center for Theology and the Natural Sciences at the Graduate Theological Union in Berkeley, California, has been sponsoring the CTNS–Templeton Foundation University Lectures on campuses in North America and around the world.

The intellectual purpose of the CTNS–Templeton Foundation University Lectures is twofold. First, the lecturers explore the presence or absence of a spiritual dimension to the natural world as discerned through the scientific enterprise. Second, the lecturers explore the mutual interaction between disciplines in the growing field of Theology and the Natural Sciences. Speakers chosen for the lecture series have on some occasions been research scientists reporting on their work, with theologians serving as respondents. On other occasions theologians have offered presentations with scientists responding. The chapters in this book written by Charles Townes, Nancey Murphy, and Wolfhart Pannenberg were originally delivered as part of this series.

I would like to thank my colleagues at CTNS for their indispensable counsel, aid in manuscript preparation, and ongoing encouragement: Anne Bade, Kirk Bingaman, Peter Hess, Ann Hubrig, Bonnie Johnston, Stan Lanier, Norris Palmer, Richard Randolph, W. Mark Richardson, Robert John Russell, Fred Sanders, Kathryn Smith, Catherine Thompson, Kirk Wegter-McNelly, and Carl York. I would also like to thank Fran Schapperle of the John Templeton Foundation for her collegiality and leadership.

Ted Peters
Berkeley, California

Introduction

Despite the popular image of an alleged warfare between science and religion, a closer look will reveal a more peaceful yet exciting confluence of interests if not a growing sense of partnership between scientists and theologians. One form this more peaceful cooperation takes is *hypothetical consonance*. As the first chapter will indicate, this book is an exploration in hypothetical consonance—that is, an attempt to uncover the domain of inquiry shared by science and theology.

With the term *consonance* we are looking for areas of correspondence or connection between the understanding of nature discerned scientifically and the understanding of the world as God's creation discerned theologically. In the strongest sense of the word, "consonance" means full accord or harmony. It would be too much to say that the current state of the dialogue between science and theology consists of total accord or total agreement regarding the role that God plays as the world's creator and redeemer. These two fields remain quite different in their approaches and different in the scope of their knowledge. Yet, if we use the term "consonance" in a milder or weaker sense, it might be fruitful for seeing connections. In its milder form consonance functions as a hypothesis: If there is only one reality and if both science and theology speak about the same reality, is it reasonable to expect that sooner or later shared understandings will develop? Both science and theology pursue truth; and even though the methods differ, each of the two disciplines should eventually be able to recognize some level of truth reported in the other.

With the term *hypothetical*, then, theological assertions about the absolute mystery we call "God" become subject to critical evaluation in light of data gained from the natural sciences. Scientific knowledge should inform and sharpen theological truth claims. In addition, scientific thinking reflects upon itself and asks philosophically to what degree the positing of the idea of God grants greater illumination for understanding the natural world in which we live.

Over the past few decades we have been finding that within the domain of scientific research and reflection the question of transcendence—the question for which the idea of God provides an answer—has arisen. To ask the question of what transcends yet participates in nature is for science to share a domain of questioning with theology. This by no means constitutes a proof for God's existence. Rather, it raises the hypothesis: Would acknowledging the existence of a God who creates and continues to participate in the world of nature illuminate more of what we perceive about reality?

Whether in the strong or weak sense of the term, hypothetical consonance makes the assumption that there is one God and one cosmos. This means that, in the long run, science and theology are attempting to understand reality. This assumption is raised to the level of a hypothesis so that we embark on a research program consisting of dialogue between disciplines that seek confirmation or disconfirmation. Rather than a religiously dogmatic approach, the theologian here must be open to a dialogue that may confirm or disconfirm the God hypothesis. Rather than a secularly dogmatic approach, the scientist here must be open to a dialogue that may confirm or disconfirm the God hypothesis. We may fall short of proving conclusively the God hypothesis; yet intellectual progress can in principle be made if working with the God hypothesis yields greater illumination—that is, greater explanatory adequacy—than working without this hypothesis. Hypothetical consonance constitutes a disposition toward dialogue that looks for intellectual fruitfulness.

Let me make clear that this method does not constitute a proof for the existence of God. Rather, by working with the idea of God, we ask whether theology and science in concert provide greater illumination and understanding of the reality in which we live than we would have if we worked with one or the other discipline alone or with the two independently.

The chapter authors in this volume include a Nobel Prize–winning physicist, a renowned evolutionary theorist and former president of the American Association for the Advancement of Science, and other natural scientists. They reflect on the questions of transcendence and of value raised by scientific research. I include here also the thoughts of Pope John Paul II along with other theologians who engage scientific thinking with theological concerns and reflections. Works by hybrids, individuals who are trained in both theology and a scientific discipline, who carry on both sides of the dialogue within their own minds, are also included. The authors may not uniformly agree with one another; yet each in his or her own way engages science and theology in a tough-minded exchange aimed at fostering new insight and furthering discussion.

The first chapter, "Science and Theology: Toward Consonance," by the book's editor, does two things. First, it provides a road map pointing out different directions now being followed by the science-religion interaction. The chapter identifies eight different ways that scientists and theologians relate, or fail to relate. It acknowledges that one of the optional ways is warfare, that some persons in fact presume that natural science and religious reflection are engaged in mortal battle. Yet, warfare is not the only way. Other more peaceful options are available. Consonance is one of the more peaceful paths one may follow. Second, this chapter stresses that potentially the most fruitful frontier of the science-theology interaction is the search for consonance. It recognizes various forms of hypothetical consonance at work in the methodological commitments of a number of scholars such as Nancey Murphy, Wentzel van Huyssteen, Wolfhart Pannenberg, Thomas Torrance, Arthur Peacocke, John Polkinghorne, Robert John Russell, and Philip Hefner.

The remainder of the book is divided into two large collections of essays, the first of which is "Physics and Faith." As we think about the history of the interaction between science and theology during the final third of the twentieth century, we note three overlapping phases in the movement toward increased interaction. The initial phase resulted from a reassessment of the character of scientific method during the 1960s, wherein the philosophers of science relativized, historicized, and subjectivized the presumed objectivity of scientific research. By relativizing alleged objectivity in science, the methodological discussion placed the natural sciences into conversation with other humanistic disciplines such as theology that were also wrestling with the relativity of human knowing. This methodological phase gave way to the physics phase, wherein the mind-busting questions raised by relativity theory, quantum mechanics, sub-atomic indeterminacy, and Big Bang cosmology led physics beyond itself to metaphysics. The God question began to arise from within physics, as Paul Davies and others have dramatically documented. Whether at the level of the smallest reality such as a sub-atomic particle or at the level of the largest conceivable reality such as the Big Bang cosmos, the physical world is much more mysterious to us today than it was a century ago. The more we learn, the more mystery we uncover. Physics prompts faith questions. So, here in this book, we turn to the physicists.

The author of Chapter 2, "Logic and Uncertainties in Science and Religion," is physicist Charles H. Townes. Now in active retirement from the University of California at Berkeley and still pursuing research in microwave spectroscopy and infrared astronomy, Nobel Prize winner Townes is the co-inventor of both the maser and the laser. Here in this chapter he tells us the story of the insight—what one might call a religious experience—that led to the laser. Although he does not use the term "consonance" with much frequency, Townes here presses for increased consonance and beyond to actual cross-relatedness between natural science and religious reflection. Science listens carefully to nature. Nature gives voice to beauty, and beauty to meaning and purpose. Even if the language of the scientist may seem lifeless or deadening to the ear of the poet, the scientist himself or herself is often sensitive to the immensity of space, the complexity of the material world, and the inherent beauty of nature. There is more to nature than what science can interpret; and it takes a duet of scientist and poet for us to hear nature singing its true song.

Chapters 2 and 3 have something in common. Both are personal reflections by physicists. Chapter 3, "From Physicist to Priest," is an intellectual autobiography, previously published in *Dialog, a Journal of Theology*, by John Polkinghorne. After beginning a career as a professor of mathematical physics at Cambridge, Polkinghorne studied theology, became ordained an Anglican priest, and has served until recently as President of Queens College at Cambridge. His 1994 book, *The Faith of a Physicist*, is being widely read in the university community. In this chapter he develops one of the important themes of his thought: Epistemology models ontology. Polkinghorne believes that the human mind and material nature—the "world stuff"—are coordinated. Nature speaks to the human mind, and we understand what nature says. This makes this physicist priest a realist, a critical realist. Applied to theology, statements about God refer to a reality, to God. For the Cambridge scholar, realism in science is consonant with realism in theology.

We turn from autobiographical reflections to a more scholarly mode of presentation. In the fourth chapter physicist Paul Davies asks, "Is the Universe Absurd?" Davies is a popular writer. In best-selling books such as *God and the New Physics* and *The Mind of God* he has shown how the very study of the natural world at the quantum level leads to questions about spirit, questions about the divine dimension of reality. In this essay he asserts that the universe is ordered in a rational and lawlike manner; that nature is contingent—that is, it could have been otherwise; that nature is intelligible to the human mind; that nature's lawfulness is completely dependable; and that nature includes chance, indeterminism, creativity, and life. Davies goes on to recognize the legitimacy of asking questions such as: Where did the laws of physics come from? Why these laws? Could these laws come from the mind of God? Davies admits that these questions do not reside within the domain of physics proper; yet the field of physics presses beyond its own methodological fences to ask such metaphysical questions. To refuse to ask such questions tacitly grounds the world in absurdity. Yet, the world need not be thought of as absurd. It could be thought of as meaningful and purposeful. Without giving in to any quick theological fix regarding God, Davies declares that we should press the questions of meaning and purpose with openness and humility.

Questions regarding nature's intelligibility combined with the intelligibility of theological claims continue to be raised in Chapter 5, "Does the 'God Who Acts' Really Act in Nature?" by Robert John Russell. Russell is a hybrid—that is, both a physicist and a theologian. He asks whether it is intelligible to speak of special providence, to speak of God acting in natural events. He answers affirmatively. Russell, who founded the Center for Theology and the Natural Sciences at the Graduate Theological Union in Berkeley, says that we can understand special providence as the objective acts of God in nature and history and we can understand these acts in a non-interventionist manner consistent with science. In the centuries since the Enlightenment, especially since David Hume's rejection of miracles, we have more or less assumed that the laws of nature are fixed and that God does not intervene. Oh, yes, God may be present to human subjectivity as it interprets nature, the liberal theological tradition has assumed; but we have also assumed that we cannot speak about divine actions as interventions that override the laws of nature. What is needed is a noninterventionist understanding of God's acts in the world, and employing new insights gained from quantum physics, Russell offers us such an understanding.

In Chapter 6, "Theology, Cosmology, and Ethics," philosophical theologian Nancey Murphy advocates that universities teach *subjunctive theology*—that is, they should teach the natural sciences and social sciences *as if* there exists a creating and loving God. In contrasting the now passing modern world with the now arriving postmodern consciousness, Murphy points out that the customary distinction between fact and value—wherein facts are assigned to the natural sciences and values are assigned to the humanities and to theology—has in effect excluded talk about God from the modern intellectual world. With postmodernity, Murphy wants to revive intelligible God-talk. A relentless foe of reductionism, Murphy diagrams a holistic hierarchy of the sciences by showing how certain disciplines incorporate more basic disciplines in order to deal with nature at more inclusive levels. Chemistry, for example, incorporates physics to deal with chemical reactions. Biology incorporates both physics and chemistry to deal with life. Ethics and theology are disciplines that incorporate all the underlying physical fields into holistic schemes in order to deal with human ecology and with God. It makes sense to think of God as creator in relation to all that is; and to think of God relating to the most comprehensive whole makes additional sense. All this leads to ethics, not as an autonomous set of morals or values but as an integrated outcome of our relationship to God and to nature. In short, a university curriculum should teach the natural sciences *as if* God's existence matters and *as if* human action has value.

At this point the book moves into phase three of the movement toward increased interaction between science and religion, namely, theological questions arising out of evolutionary theory and genetic research. This section is titled "Evolution, Ethics, and Eschatology." Oh yes, because of the war fought between evolutionists and fundamentalists in the 1920s, we might say that this issue has been around for a long time. Yet, what is happening now has some new features. On the theological side, the long history of genetic mutation and natural selection has become tacitly accepted, virtually as fact. Although the focal issue has to do with whether or not purpose lies inherently in the developmental process, most theologians seem willing to surrender this as well. At least methodologically, neither the scientists nor the theologians demand that we see purpose within otherwise random natural processes. Yet, nature can certainly have a purpose, a divinely appointed purpose. How might this be the case? How should we understand human nature in light of our evolutionary past and God's promise for an eschatological future?

Purpose exists as long as purposeful beings such as human beings exist. With the advance of the frontier of genetic research, we can foresee that molecular biology may give the present generation of scientists the technological power to alter the evolutionary development of future generations of *Homo sapiens*. Even if evolution in the past was without purpose, the impartation of human purposes may now change that. This raises ethical questions: Should we try to guide our own future evolution? Or should we restrain our technology and simply yield our future to random natural processes? If we become pro-active, which direction should we go? Can we appropriate visions of God's promised new creation—in which "death will be no more; mourning and crying and pain will be no more" (Rev. 21:4)—to guide our bio-tech planning?

In Chapter 7, "So Human an Animal: Evolution and Ethics," Francisco J. Ayala asserts that human nature is continuous with the rest of the living world, a continuity established by the process of evolution. An evolutionary biologist and former President of the American Association for the Advancement of Science, Ayala argues here that human culture derives from, yet goes beyond, its biological origin. After outlining the grand story of human evolution, he argues that our exalted ethical judgments are themselves a product of evolution but that they transcend biological determinism. Human history, replete with social and religious traditions, transcends the biological history that gave it birth. He concludes by saying that science provides us with something necessary for understanding our place in nature, but science alone is inadequate to complete the task of comprehending the meaning of human existence. Like Davies in physics, Ayala in biology shows the limits of the scientific method and the need to add philosophical and theological inquiry.

Chapter 8, "Human Life: Creation Versus Evolution?" raises the question of whether we have to choose between evolution with purpose or without purpose. Munich theologian Wolfhart Pannenberg acknowledges that despite its difficulties, the theory of evolution provides the most plausible interpretation of what is known about the history of organic life on earth. Yet, appeal to strictly natural selection as a mechanism without purpose seems to clash with theologies of creation wherein God works purposefully through natural processes. Must these be alternatives, or could we affirm both? Pannenberg wants to affirm both. In a mood of consonance, he contends that creative self-organization in the process of life's evolution since the transition from inorganic to organic matter corresponds to the blowing of the divine wind—that is, to the Spirit of God—as we understand it in Scripture. This movement of the divine Spirit ultimately promises the overcoming of all perishableness, as we have seen it in the resurrection of Jesus Christ. Pannenberg offers a Christian account of evolution that looks beyond the present stage toward the eschatological resurrection of the dead, to communion between God and creation.

Pope John Paul II, in cooperation with the Vatican Observatory and the Center for Theology and the Natural Sciences, convened a symposium of scholars at the Vatican during the summer of 1996 to analyze carefully the theological implications of the theory of evolution. In October of that year he delivered an address to the Pontifical Academy of Sciences on this subject. Chapter 9, "Evolution and the Living God," presents the core of that message. The pope shows confidence in the dialogue between science and theology by affirming that "truth cannot contradict truth." The pontiff emphasizes that the concept of evolution is much more than merely a hypothesis. It is a significant theory—or, perhaps better, a set of several theories—and the pontiff says that the theologian must be informed by what we learn from the natural sciences. In particular, the church's theologians should draw out the implications of evolution for our understanding of humanity, for Christian anthropology. Following Pope Pius XII, John Paul II combines evolutionary science with dogmatic commitment: if the human body takes its origin from pre-existent matter, the spiritual soul is immediately created by God. The latter, the divine act of imparting to each of us a soul, is the ground for human dignity. In Chapter 10, "Evolution and the Human Person: The Pope in Dialogue," astronomer and Vatican Observatory director George Coyne, S.J., spells out the immediate context and historical significance of these papal reflections.

Chapter 11, "Biological Evolution and the Human Soul: A Theological Proposal for Generationism," continues the discussion begun by Pope John Paul II and George Coyne. The author, Anne M. Clifford, C.S.J., interprets the pope as reserving certain truths for the domain of revelation that remain untouched by scientific research, in particular the special creation by God of each individual soul. Clifford, who teaches theology at Duquesne University, contends that biblical anthropology understands the human being as an undivided whole; and this implies that we need to see more continuity and less discontinuity between evolutionary theory and theological anthropology. It is too simple to consign the body to natural selection and the soul to divine action. The body needs the soul, because the soul is life-giving, eternally life-giving. Recognizing that there is a close and pervasive unity between body and soul, Clifford develops the concept of *generationism*. Believing generationism to establish consonance between science and theology, Clifford argues that *Homo sapiens*—in both body and soul—are inextricably bound to the evolutionary process. Human dignity is grounded in God's call to us through the human soul to transcend our biological origin and orient ourselves toward our divinely appointed destiny.

Philip Hefner in Chapter 12, "Biocultural Evolution and the Created Co-Creator," provides the reader with a manifesto of sorts. It presents Hefner's anthropology as a window through which we can view nature as a whole. Hefner, the director of the Chicago Center for Science and Religion, describes the human being as the created co-creator. The created co-creator acts on behalf of all of nature to stretch the various systems of nature beyond mechanistic determinism into the mode of freedom and, thereby, enables them to participate in God's purposes. On the one hand, the human race has been created through the evolutionary process. On the other hand, culture deriving from the evolutionary leap into freedom gives evidence that the human being is a *creator* as well. The rise of technological civilization and the rise of religion demonstrate that human culture, though dependent upon its evolutionary history, has transcended the determinism of its past. Human freedom and creativity and the emergent process of self-defining mark the present and the future. The fact that the created co-creator has appeared is a statement about what nature itself has come to, what nature itself is capable of, and what nature has allowed to appear. Set within a theological context, Hefner can affirm that God works through nature, through biocultural evolution, in the ongoing creative process. Jesus Christ—who is free, intentional, and loving—becomes the paradigm for understanding human beings as fully embedded in nature and fully participating in God's ongoing creative activity.

In Chapter 13, Oxford professor Arthur Peacocke provides us with "A Map of Scientific Knowledge: Genetics, Evolution, and Theology." Like Nancey Murphy in an earlier chapter, Peacocke squares off against reductionism and constructs a holistic hierarchy of the sciences. That the whole is greater than the sum of its parts is the foundational assumption of holism. Applied to the sciences, more inclusive disciplines such as biology cannot be reduced to component parts such as chemistry or physics. There is something to life that is not reducible to chemical or physical equations. Nor can studies of human culture be reduced to biology. Climbing still higher, this means that the subject matter of theology, namely, God and the world, cannot be explained exhaustively by scientific analysis of any parts of the world. Theology builds upon, but is not reducible to, what we know about nature through scientific research. Peacocke, himself both a geneticist and a theologian, examines behavioral genetics, sociobiology, and the cognitive sciences and places them within the context of a more inclusive theological anthropology. The upshot of the work of both Murphy and Peacocke is that the various fields, including the various natural sciences and theology, are provided with a way to engage in dialogue that maintains the integrity of each discipline.

In Chapter 14, "The Greening of Science, Theology, and Ethics," Audrey Chapman provides a rationale for integrating science, theology, and ethics. The urgency of what is called the "environmental crisis" is calling us to a united front. If theology is foundational to ethics, and if theology is uninformed or contradicted by what is known through science, then our ethical foundations will crumble. So Chapman, who directs the Program of Dialogue between Science and Religion at the American Association for the Advancement of Science in Washington, presses the discipline of theology to seek consonance with science. To move toward consonance she recommends interface, dialogue. She notes how twentieth-century views of nature emphasize relationality and the connectedness of all dimensions of nature. This complements the theological view of the world as God's creation; and it readies us for dealing with the ecosphere, wherein systems approaches alert us to the complex ways in which all things ae related and connected. Chapman admonishes us to become scientifically informed regarding specific environmental issues and problems, and to integrate what is learned scientifically with a theological vision of our ethical responsibility.

The final chapter, 15, "Evolution, Tragedy, and Hope," brings evolutionary theory into conversation with Christian eschatology. It brings nature's past into conversation with God's future. The chapter's author, John Haught, does not expect evolutionary theory all by itself to give an adequate theological account of nature's meaning; but he does expect theology to do so. Haught, a Georgetown University systematic theologian, thinks of God as both *kenotic love* and the *power of the future*. When viewing evolutionary history through lenses clarified by divine revelation, theology can see levels of meaning that are invisible apart from such revelation. At the center of this revelatory lens is John 3:16, "God so loved the world that he gave his only begotten Son." The world cannot be understood for what it is apart from understanding the Son-giving love of God. Nor can it be fully understood apart from God's promise of ultimate redemption, the eschatological redemption that will include the resurrection of the dead. Creation needs to be viewed in light of the still outstanding new creation. Haught believes that a neo-Darwinian biology could live quite comfortably within the eschatological vision of ultimate reality.

Thinking in terms of the Stimulus-Response pattern of Pavlov's dogs, it would appear that most of our authors take science as the stimulus and theology as the response. Perhaps this is inescapable in our era. The frontiers of serious scientific research are moving like a wildfire across prairie grass. Just monitoring the advance takes effort, yet it is rewarding effort.

In addition, these are tough times for theologians. Legacies of the warfare between science and religion still abound. Movies such as *Contact*, based on the work of scientist Carl Sagan, continue to depict stereotypical images of religious people as narrow-minded, dogmatic, and obstructionist. Theologians whose imaginations have been liberated and whose curiosity propels them to pursue ever more interesting topics find themselves virtually invisible in today's cultural climate. So, at least part of the motive for pursuing consonance is that of pursuing credibility, although it would be far too simplistic to reduce the enterprise to this peripheral concern. More central is the fact that what is happening in scientific research these days is downright exciting, and theologians are just as excited as the scientists. The world is becoming bigger, more mysterious, more awesome, and more beautiful. Appreciating God's creation is becoming more complex and more enticing.

Even with this, some are not waiting to respond to a specific scientific stimulus before advancing a theological position. Here in this volume we find Robert John Russell, Nancey Murphy, Wolfhart Pannenberg, Arthur Peacocke, and to some extent John Haught placing science and theology in consonance and then placing theology in the leadership role. What we know about God, say these scholars, helps illuminate what we know about nature through science. Science alone is not enough. Revelation from God casts nature in a new light and leads us toward a more adequate understanding of its reality. This is a courageous move. It promises further excitement for the future of scholarship.

Chapter One

Science and Theology: Toward Consonance

TED PETERS

"A passionate new battle over religion and science," was the way the *New York Times* opened its front page article describing the church leaders' misdirected stand against patents in genetics and biotechnology.[1] Note two things here. First, the interaction between science and religion is front page news. Second, the interaction is described with a military metaphor, as a battle. The battle metaphor probably reflects the image bequeathed us a century ago by A. D. White in his notorious book, *A History of the Warfare of Science with Theology*.[2] But is it accurate to sum up the relation between these domains of knowing as warfare? Not everyone would picture it this way. "The idea of a long-standing war between science and religion is a historical fiction invented in the late nineteenth century," writes Margaret Wertheim.[3]

It appears to me that warfare is part of the picture; but it is not the whole picture. Science and religion relate to one another in a variety of ways, and all of them together fill out a much larger picture. The task of this chapter will be to describe some of the different ways in which these two fields of human endeavor relate in our era, and to give special attention to one peaceful alternative, namely, hypothetical consonance.[4]

In the meantime, a correlate to the warfare metaphor may be useful here: revolution. We are not in a war right now, but we might be witnessing a revolution. The revolution metaphor adds complexity and nuance so that it is no longer accurate to see science and theology merely as pitched enemies. The revolution is being led by an unpredicted and astounding intellectual trend, namely, the reasking of the God-question within the orbit of scientific discussion about the natural world. The raising of theological questions within the scientific camp does not fit neatly into the warfare model.

In addition, the pre-revolutionary situation from which we are now emerging ought not be described as a situation of constant war either. Rather, it is better described as a truce—that is, for decades we have worked with the assumption that a border should separate what we know about the natural world through science and what religious thinkers say about the transcendent reality, God.

Since the Enlightenment we have pretty much assumed that these two represent separate domains of human knowing. We have erected a high wall of separation between church and laboratory. Yet, now as the revolution is beginning to take hold, this is increasingly recognized as most unfortunate. It is unfortunate because we all are aware that there is but one reality. So sooner or later we will become dissatisfied with consigning our differences to separate ghettos of knowledge.

The pre-revolutionary separatists and the revolutionary scientists asking the God question still represent only part of the picture. There is another group of quiet revolutionaries who since the 1960s have been looking for parallels, points of contact, consonance, crossovers, and conflations. Their emerging new discipline as yet without a name is studying developments in natural science—especially physics and the life sciences—and is engaging in serious reflection on various loci of Christian doctrine. Scientists and theologians are engaged in a common search for shared understanding. The search is not merely for a shared discipline. They are not looking merely for rapprochement between separate fields of inquiry. Rather, scientists and theologians are aiming for increased knowledge, for an actual advance in the human understanding of reality. Until a name comes along, we will refer to this new enterprise as *Theology and Natural Science*.

In this chapter I will briefly outline eight different ways in which science and religion are currently thought to be related.[5] I will note that the dominant view—the truce by separation view—in academic circles is what I label the "two-language theory," but I will go on to point out that the advancing frontier is taking us in the direction of hypothetical consonance. Then I will turn to the central methodological issue, namely, the classic concern for the relation between faith and reason. Rather than sharply contrasting what we can know by faith and what we can know by reason, current scholars such as Nancey Murphy and Wentzel van Huyssteen are maximizing the overlap. Along the way I will note the work of some of the more important scholars in the field of Theology and Natural Science: Ian Barbour, Wim Drees, Langdon Gilkey, Philip Hefner, Nancey Murphy, Wolfhart Pannenberg, Arthur Peacocke, John Polkinghorne, Robert John Russell, and Thomas Torrance. I will then conclude with my own observations regarding the merits of hypothetical consonance and the value of making a theological interpretation of nature so that we can see the natural cosmos as divine creation.

Eight Ways Science and Theology Battle and Make Peace

How should science and theology relate? Not everyone sees it the same way. If we extend the metaphor of warfare, we can see that relations vary from pitched battle to an uneasy truce.

Scientism

What I identify as "scientism" is sometimes called "naturalism" or "scientific materialism" or "secular humanism." Scientism actually fits the warfare model. As a point of view, it seeks war with total victory for one side. Scientism, like other "-isms," is an ideology, this one built upon the assumption that science provides all the knowledge that we can know. There is only one reality, the natural, and science has a monopoly on the knowledge we have about nature.[6] Religion, which claims to purvey knowledge about things supernatural, provides only pseudo-knowledge—that is, false impressions about non-existent fictions.

Earlier this century British philosopher and atheist Bertrand Russell told a BBC audience that "what science cannot tell us, mankind cannot know." At mid century astronomer Fred Hoyle argued that the Jewish and Christian religions have become outdated by modern science. He explained religious behavior as escapist, as pursued by people who seek illusory security from the mysteries of the universe.[7] Later Jacques Monod would assert that "objective knowledge is the *only* authentic source of truth" and that modern science now replaces ancient religious explanations.[8]

Physicists Stephen Hawking and Carl Sagan have teamed up to assert that the cosmos is all there is or was or ever will be, and to assert that there was no absolute beginning at the onset of the Big Bang. Why no beginning? Had there been an absolute beginning, then time would have an edge; and beyond this edge we could dimly glimpse a transcendent reality such as a creator God. But this is intolerable to scientism. So, by describing the cosmos as temporally self-contained, Sagan could write confidently in the introduction to Hawking's *A Brief History of Time* about "the absence of God" on the grounds that there is "nothing for a Creator to do."[9] In the warfare between science and theology, scientism demands elimination of the enemy.

Scientific Imperialism

This position is scientism in a slightly different form: rather than eliminating the enemy, scientific imperialism seeks to conquer the territory formally possessed by theology and claim it as its own. Whereas scientism is atheistic; scientific imperialism affirms the existence of something divine but claims knowledge of the divine comes from scientific research rather than religious revelation. "Science has actually advanced to the point where what were formerly religious questions can be seriously tackled . . . [by] the new physics," writes Paul Davies.[10] Physicist Frank Tipler, claiming that quantum theory combined with Big Bang and thermodynamics can provide a better explanation than Christianity for the future resurrection of the dead, declares that theology should become a branch of physics.[11]

According to Margaret Wertheim's interpretation, Stephen Hawking would belong to this second category. Even though he denies that there is anything for a God to do, he proceeds to invoke divine imagery and God-talk to proffer his ideas about physics. "He [Stephen Hawking] seems to want it both ways—at the same time pushing God out of the universe altogether and invoking him as the constant subtext of his work."[12] By knowing the laws of nature, the scientist can know the mind of God, so to speak. "He [Stephen Hawking] writes about a deity as if he were telling the reader about a clever older brother, someone whom he admires but whose achievements are well within his own range of comprehension. . . . Hawking and his god are almost on the same level."[13]

Shifting away from physics to genetics, we note that evolutionary psychologists—alias sociobiologists—claim to be scientific and also claim to be able to explain religion better than religion can. E. O. Wilson defines *sociobiology* as "the scientific study of the biological basis of all forms of social behavior in all kinds of organisms, including man."[14] Religion is a form of social behavior, therefore, it has a biological explanation. After committing himself completely to scientific materialism, Wilson contends that "every part of existence is considered to be obedient to physical laws requiring no external control. The scientist's devotion to parsimony in explanation excludes the divine spirit and other extraneous agents. Most importantly, we have come to the crucial stage in the history of biology when religion itself is subject to the explanations of the natural sciences."[15]

Kin to religion is morality. Evolutionary biologists believe they can explain that too. Ethical values are rooted in biology, specifically in the selfish gene which seeks relentlessly to replicate itself through human procreation.[16] "People tend to pass on the sorts of moral judgments that help move their genes into the next generation," writes Robert Wright, "and there's definitely no reason to assume that existing moral codes reflect some higher truth apprehended via divine inspiration or detached philosophical inquiry."[17] E. O. Wilson and Michael Ruse put it this way: "Morality, or more strictly, our belief in morality, is merely an adaptation put in place to further our reproductive ends. Hence the basis of ethics does not lie in God's will. . . . [Rather, it is] an illusion fobbed off on us by our genes to get us to cooperate."[18]

In sum, the option we call "scientific imperialism" presumes that theologians give at best only an inadequate account of their religion, perhaps even a misleading one when they refer us to God. Natural science is ready to explain religion better, ready to explain the supernatural naturally.

Ecclesiastical Authoritarianism

Appeal to the authority of the church's revelation is the defensive tactic followed by some in the Roman Catholic tradition who perceive science and scientism as a threat. Presuming a two-step route to truth in which natural reason is followed by divine revelation, theological dogma is here ceded authority over science on the grounds that it is founded on God's revelation. The middle of the nineteenth century was an anxious time for the Church of Rome. The Enlightenment had opposed authority in the form of dogma and clerical power. The rise of democratic institutions was accompanied by a cultural impatience with traditions rooted in the ancient past. The industrial revolution was providing new wealth and new economic power beyond the fences of the church yard. Armies were marching to take away the papal states and estates. And, most importantly, the natural sciences were taking over university life and knocking the queen of the sciences, theology, off her throne. This was a period in which the church felt it was under siege.

In 1864 Pope Pius IX promulgated *The Syllabus of Errors*, wherein item 57 stated it to be an error to think that science and philosophy could withdraw from ecclesiastical authority. This was followed in 1870 with the First Vatican Council, declaring the holder of the papal office to be infallible in matters of faith and morals. A century later the Second Vatican Council dropped the defenses by declaring the natural sciences to be free from ecclesiastical authority and called them "autonomous" disciplines (*Gaudium et Spes*: 59). Pope John Paul II, who has a serious interest in fostering dialogue between theology and the natural sciences, is negotiating a new peace between faith and reason.[19]

Scientific Creationism

Sometimes called "creation science," scientific creationism is not a Protestant version of church authoritarianism even though it is frequently so mistaken. The grandparents of today's scientific creationists were fundamentalists, to be sure, and fundamentalism appealed to biblical authority in a fashion parallel to the Roman Catholic appeal to church authority. Yet, there is a marked difference between fundamentalist authoritarianism and contemporary creation science. Today's creation scientists are willing to argue their case in the arena of science, not biblical authority. They assume that biblical truth and scientific truth belong to the same domain. When there is a conflict between a scientific assertion and a religious assertion, then we allegedly have a conflict in scientific theories. The creationists argue that the book of Genesis is itself a theory which tells us how the world was physically created: God fixed the distinct kinds (species) of organisms at the point of original creation. They did not evolve. Geological and biological facts attest to biblical truth, they argue.

Scientific creationists typically include in their list of theological commitments the following: (1) the creation of the world out of nothing; (2) the insufficiency of mutation and natural selection to explain the process of evolution; (3) the stability of existing species and the impossibility of one species evolving out of another; (4) separate ancestry for apes and humans; (5) catastrophism to explain certain geological formations, e.g., the flood explains why sea fossils appear on mountains; and (6) the relatively recent formation of the earth about six to ten thousand years ago.[20]

When establishment scientists try to gain quick victory over creationists, they do so by dismissing them. Stephen Jay Gould, the colorful Harvard paleontologist, says the very term "scientific creationism" is meaningless and self-contradictory.[21] Although the battle between scientific creationists and established scientists appears to be all-out war, this is not the case. The creationists, many of whom are themselves practicing scientists, see themselves as soldiers within the science army.[22]

A fascinating chapter in the larger story of the battle between evolution and creation is the one being written by University of California law professor Phillip E. Johnson. Without defending creation as a religious commitment, he attacks Darwinian evolutionary theory with an internal critique by saying that it is less than fully scientific. As a lawyer analyzing scientific evidence, he contends that Darwinians have presumed a dogmatic defense of materialistic naturalism—that is, the theory that posits leaps in evolutionary development from mere chemicals to bacterium and from bacterium to humanity is an unproven assumption betraying an underlying commitment to materialistic naturalism. The Darwinian dogma expressed as the so-called "fact of evolution" is in effect an anti-religious prejudice that precludes honest scientific consideration of possible falsifying evidence.

"Prejudice is a major problem," Johnson writes, "because the leaders of science see themselves as locked in a desperate battle against religious fundamentalists, a label which they tend to apply broadly to anyone who believes in a Creator who plays an active role in worldly affairs." But by rhetorically asking who is calling the kettle black, Johnson accuses the Darwinians of being religious, of being narrowly dogmatic and unwilling to consider evidence that might challenge their cherished theory. "Scientific organizations are devoted to protecting Darwinism rather than testing it, and the rules of scientific investigation have been shaped to help them succeed."[23]

Without taking sides in this debate, I'd like to point out a subtlety. The mood here is that of warfare between science and religion, a retaliation against scientific imperialism. Yet, note the weapons. Johnson believes he is defending true science against narrow religion. The trick is to see that Darwinism counts as narrow religion, not true science. From Johnson's point of view, the warfare is between true science and pseudo-science.

The Two-Language Theory

Keeping science and religion in separate domains might appear to be the way to establish a truce with an enduring peace. This is because it respects the sovereign territory of both science and theology and because it is advocated by highly respected persons in both fields. Albert Einstein—remembered for his remark that "science without religion is lame and religion without science is blind"—distinguished between the language of fact and the language of value. "Science can only ascertain what *is*, but not what *should be*," he once told an audience at Princeton; "religion, on the other hand, deals only with evaluations of human thought and action." Note the use of "only" here. Each language is restricted to its respective domain.

Stephen Jay Gould calls this the NOMA principle, for "nonoverlapping magisteria." He says, "The net of science covers the empirical universe; what it is made of (fact) and why does it work this way (theory). The net of religion extends over questions of moral reasoning and value." These two have their separate domains; they do not overlap. "To cite the arch cliches, we get the age of rocks, and religion gets the rock of ages; we study how the heavens go, and they determine how to go to heaven."[24]

A theologian of neoorthodox and liberal persuasion, Langdon Gilkey, has long argued for the two language approach. Science, he says, deals only with objective or public knowing of *proximate* origins, whereas religion and its theological articulation deals with existential or personal knowing of *ultimate* origins. Science asks "*how*?", while religion asks "*why*?"[25] What Gilkey wants, of course, is for one person to be a citizen in two lands—that is, to be able to embrace both Christian faith and scientific method without conflict.[26] To speak both languages is to be bilingual, and bilingual intellectuals can work with one another in peace.

Nancey Murphy points out that the two language position is characteristic of liberal Christianity, not conservative or evangelical Protestantism. Liberal theologies presume that religion and science are given separate but complementary roles in human life, dividing the intellectual territory in such a way that science cannot conflict with faith; "the accounts of language, in extreme cases, even make dialogue between science and theology impossible. . . . The situation is entirely different for conservatives. Here scientific and religious language are of exactly the same type—commensurate."[27]

The liberal two-language theory separating science and theology is a modern one. It ought not to be confused with premodern concept of the two books. In medieval times, revelation regarding God could be read from two books, the *book of nature* and the *book of scripture*. Both science and theology could speak of things divine. Both natural revelation and special revelation pointed us in one direction: toward God.[28] The two-language theory, in contrast, points us in two different directions: either toward God or toward the world.

I have a problem with the two-language theory. It gains peace through separation, by establishing a demilitarized zone that prevents communication. In the event that a scientist might desire to speak about divine matters or that a theologian might desire to speak about the actual world created by God, the two would have to speak past one another on the assumption that shared understanding is impossible. Why begin with such an assumption? The method of hypothetical consonance makes just the opposite assumption, namely, there is but one reality and sooner or later scientists and theologians should be able to find some areas of shared understanding.

Hypothetical Consonance

This is the name I give to the frontier that seems to be emerging beyond the two language policy. The term 'consonance', coming from the work of Ernan McMullin, indicates that we are looking for those areas where there is a correspondence between what can be said scientifically about the natural world and what the theologian understands to be God's creation.[29] "Consonance" in the strong sense means accord, harmony. Accord or harmony might be a treasure we hope to find, but we have not found it yet. Where we find ourselves now is working with consonance in a weak sense—that is, by identifying common domains of question-asking. The advances in physics, especially thermodynamics and quantum theory in relation to Big Bang cosmology, have in their own way raised questions about transcendent reality. The God question can be honestly asked from within scientific reasoning. Theologians and scientists now share a common subject matter, and the idea of hypothetical consonance encourages further cooperation.

The consonance school also asks theologians to view their discipline somewhat differently. Rather than beginning from a rigid position of inviolable truth, the term "hypothetical" asks theologians to subject their own assertions to further investigation and possible confirmation or disconfirmation. An openness to learning something new on the part of theologians and scientists alike is essential for hypothetical consonance to move us forward.

The hypothetical dimension of consonance dovetails with an important theme in the work of John Marks Templeton, namely, humility. Templeton, along with his colleague Robert L. Herrmann, seek humility in the face of new knowledge for both domains, for both religion and science. "It is difficult not to see the strong element of pride and self-centeredness in both the atheistic scientist and the religious separatist. Both have excluded the possibility of other valid sources of truth. An attitude of humility would open their minds and hearts, freeing them to greater understanding. . . . We forecast tremendous advances in human understanding and development when humble scientists and theologians meet together in joint interdisciplinary research, in a kind of experimental theology."[30]

The complement to humility and hypothetical thinking is bridge building. This is the aggressive dimension of consonance, the press on the part of both scientists and theologians to construct connections. Mark Richardson and Wesley Wildman acknowledge that the metaphor of bridge building "expresses the fact that there is a breach evident at the surface between theology and the sciences in our present cultural context. There will be no intellectual traffic without *construction*."[31] Bridge building between science and theology is the task of consonance-minded scholars.

Ethical Overlap

This refers to the recognized need on the part of theologians to speak to the questions of human meaning created by our industrial and technological society and, even more urgently, to the ethical challenges posed by the environmental crisis and the need to plan for the long-range future of the planet. The ecological challenge arises from the criss-crossing forces of population overgrowth, increased industrial and agricultural production that depletes nonrenewable natural resources while polluting air and soil and water, the widening split between the haves and the have-nots around the world, and the loss of a sense of responsibility for the welfare of future generations. Modern technology is largely responsible for this ecological crisis, and theologians along with secular moralists are struggling to gain ethical control over technological and economic forces that, if left to themselves, will drive us toward destruction.

Even though I am an advocate of hypothetical consonance, I belong also to the ethical overlap camp and I believe that, at root, the ecological crisis poses a spiritual issue, namely, the crying need of world civilization for an ethical vision. An ethical vision—a vision of a just and sustainable society that lives in harmony with its environment and at peace with itself—is essential for future planning and motivating the peoples of the world to fruitful action. Ecological thinking is future thinking. Its logic takes the following form: *understanding-decision-control*. Prescinding from the scientific model, we implicitly assume that to solve the ecocrisis we need to understand the forces of destruction; then we need to make the decisions and take the actions that will put us in control of our future and establish a human economy that is in harmony with earth's natural ecology.

In order to bring theological resources to bear on the ecological challenge, most theologians have tried to mine the doctrine of creation for its wealth of ethical resources. It is my judgment that we need more than creation; we also need to appeal to eschatological redemption—that is, new creation. God's redeeming work is equally important when we begin with a creation that has somehow gone awry.

The promise of eschatological renewal can provide a sense of direction, a vision of the coming just and sustainable society, and a motivating power that speaks relevantly to the understanding-decision-control formula. We need to combine creation with new creation. Theologians can make a genuine contribution to the public discussion if, on the basis of eschatological resources, we can project a vision of the coming new world order—that is, announce the promised kingdom of God and work from that vision backward to our present circumstance. This vision should picture our world in terms of (a) a single, worldwide planetary society; (b) united in devotion to the will of God; (c) sustainable within the biological carrying capacity of the planet and harmonized with the principles of the ecosphere; (d) organized politically so as to preserve the just rights and voluntary contributions of all individuals; (e) organized economically so as to guarantee the basic survival needs of each person; (f) organized socially so that dignity and freedom are respected and protected in every quarter; and (g) dedicated to advancing the quality of life in behalf of future generations.[32]

In principle, ethical overlap between science and religion could take place at a number of junctures, most obviously the common commitment to pursue the truth. Yet, the current situation finds most shared activity in ecology. Both scientists and religious leaders are reacting with a sense of urgency to the portents of planetary deterioration. Should we want to extend the warfare metaphor we might say that a common enemy—in this case, the threat of ecocide—is making allies out of former enemies. Should we want to extend the two-language model, we might say that the language of fact needs to be complemented with the language of value if the human race is to muster the resolve and the resources to meet the planetary challenge. Consonance or convergence or such closer kinships are not required to foster this ethical partnership.

New Age Spirituality

New Age spirituality, like "hypothetical consonance" and "ethical overlap," seeks to build a bridge over the gulf between science and religion. The key to New Age thinking is holism—that is, the attempt to overcome modern dualisms such as the split between science and spirit, ideas and feelings, male and female, rich and poor, humanity and nature. New Age artillery is loaded with three explosive sets of ideas: (1) discoveries in twentieth-century physics, especially quantum theory; (2) acknowledgement of the important role played by imagination in human knowing; and (3) a recognition of the ethical exigency of preserving our planet from ecological destruction.

Fritjof Capra and David Bohm, who combine Hindu mysticism with physical theory, are among the favorite New Age physicists. Bohm, for example, argues that the explicate order of things that we accept as the natural world and that is studied in laboratories is not the fundamental reality; there is under and behind it an implicate order, a realm of undivided wholeness. This wholeness, like a hologram, is fully present in each of the explicate parts. Reality, according to Bohm, is ultimately "undivided wholeness in flowing movement."[33] When we focus on either objective knowing or subjective feeling we temporarily forget the unity that binds them. New Age spirituality seeks to cultivate awareness of this underlying and continually changing unity.

By combining evolutionary theory with physics and especially with Big Bang cosmology, New Age theorists find themselves constructing a grand story—a myth—regarding the history and future of the cosmos of which we human beings are an integral and conscious part. On the basis of this grand myth, New Age ethics tries to proffer a vision of the future that will guide and motivate action appropriate to solving the ecological problem. Science here provides the background not only for ethical overlap but also for a fundamental religious revelation. Brian Swimme and Thomas Berry put it this way: "Our new sense of the universe is itself a type of revelatory experience. Presently we are moving beyond any religious expression so far known to the human into a meta-religious age, that seems to be a new comprehensive context for all religions. . . . The natural world itself is the primary economic reality, the primary educator, the primary governance, the primary technologist, the primary healer, the primary presence of the sacred, the primary moral value."[34]

Now, I happen to find the ethical vision of the New Age inspiring. But I cannot in good conscience endorse its meta-religious naturalism. I find it contrived and uncompelling. Nearly the same ecological ethic with an even stronger emphasis on social justice can be derived from Christian eschatology.

Returning to the more theoretical tie between science and theology, I earlier recommended hypothetical consonance as the most viable option for the near future. Hypothetical consonance takes us beyond the limits of the two-language theory without initially violating the integrity of either natural science or Christian theology. Where the leading scholars find themselves, to my interpretation, is with one foot in the two-language theory and the other stretched for a stride to go beyond. In what follows we will look first at the methodological rapprochement between science and theology regarding epistemology; and then we will look briefly at some of the scholars in England and America who are taking this new bold step.

Can We Find Consonance in Faith and Reason?

Is there anything in common between the reasoning process of faith and that of science? First on the agenda of those scholars who either strive for consonance or are at least in partial sympathy with consonance is the attempt to demonstrate overlap between scientific and theological reasoning. Two insights guide the discussion. First, scientific reasoning depends in part on a faith component, on foundational yet unprovable assumptions. Second, theological reasoning should be recast so as to take on a hypothetical character that is subject to testing. What is a matter of some dispute, however, is whether or not theological assertions refer—that is, is theology a form of realism? Do theological statements merely give expression to the faith of a religious community or do they refer to a reality beyond themselves such as God? Theologians are asking to what extent *critical realism* in the philosophy of science should be incorporated into theological methodology.

Science, every bit as much as theology, rests upon faith. Science must appeal to some foundational assumptions regarding the nature of reality and our apprehension of it, assumptions which themselves cannot be proved within the scope of scientific reasoning. In its own disguised fashion, science is religious, mythical. "The activity of knowing," writes Langdon Gilkey, "points beyond itself to a ground of ultimacy which its own forms of discourse cannot usefully thematize, and for which religious symbolization is alone adequate."[35] Scientific reasoning depends upon the deeply held conviction—the passion of the scientist—that the world is rational and knowable and that truth is worth pursuing. "This is not 'faith' in the strictly religious and certainly not in the Christian sense," Gilkey observes, "But it is a *commitment* in the sense that it is a personal act of acceptance and affirmation of an ultimate in one's life."[36]

Scientist Paul Davies agrees. With Gilkey he acknowledges the faith dimension to science in terms of assumptions regarding rationality. Presumed here is a gnostic-style connection between the rational structure of the universe and the corresponding spark of rationality in the human mind. That human reasoning is generally reliable constitutes his "optimistic view."[37] Yet, he acknowledges that the pursuit of scientific knowledge will not eliminate all mystery, because every chain of reasoning will eventually hit its limit and force on us the meta-scientific question of transcendence. "Sooner or later we all have to accept something as given," he writes, "whether it is God, or logic, or a set of laws, or some other foundation of existence. Thus 'ultimate' questions will always lie beyond the scope of empirical science."[38]

That faith can function at the level of assumption, theologians and scientists—at least philosophers of science—agree. This raises a second related issue: does theology, like science, seek to explain? If so, then theology cannot restrict itself to individual subjectivity or even communal subjectivity let alone to authoritarian methods of justification that isolates it from common human reasoning. This is what Philip Clayton argues: "Theology cannot avoid an appeal to broader canons of rational argumentation and explanatory adequacy."[39] Clayton proceeds to argue for inter-subjective criticizability and to view theology as engaged in transcommunal explanation.

If theology seeks to explain, does it also refer? This is the question of critical realism to which we now turn.

Is There Consonance in Realism and Reference?

Princeton professor of theology and science Wentzel van Huyssteen argues that theological statements about God refer to God. He advocates "critical-theological realism" and a method for justifying theories in systematic theology that parallels what we find in natural science. Justification occurs through progressive illumination offered by a theological theory, not as traditionally done by appeal to ecclesiastical or some other indisputable authority. Van Huyssteen recognizes the relativistic, contextual and metaphorical dimensions of human speech that floods all discourse, theological and scientific alike. Progress toward truth requires constructive thought, the building up of metaphors and models so as to emit growing insight.[40] And, most significantly, theological assertions refer. They refer to God. They are realistic. "Theology," he writes, "given both the ultimate religious commitment of the theologian and the metaphoric nature of our religious language, is scientifically committed to a realist point of view. . . . Our theological theories do indeed refer to a Reality beyond and greater than ours."[41]

We should, on the one hand, contrast critical realism with nonliteralist methods such as positivism and instrumentalism, because it recognizes that theories represent the real world. On the other hand, we should contrast critical realism also with "naive realism," which invokes the correspondence theory of truth to presume a literal correspondence between one's mental picture and the object to which this picture refers. Critical realism, in contrast, is nonliteral while still referential. The indirectness comes from the conscious use of metaphors, models, and theories. Ian Barbour notes that "models and theories are abstract symbol systems, which inadequately and selectively represent particular aspects of the world for specific purposes. This view preserves the scientist's realistic intent while recognizing that models and theories are imaginative human constructs. Models, on this reading, are to be taken seriously but not literally."[42] Urging the adoption of critical realism by theologians, Arthur Peacocke maintains that "critical realism in theology would maintain that theological concepts and models should be regarded as partial and inadequate, but necessary and, indeed, the only ways of referring to the reality that is named as 'God' and to God's relation with humanity."[43]

The critical realist agenda is not taken up by every scholar sympathetic to consonance. Nancey C. Murphy recommends that theologians avoid critical realism on the grounds that it remains modern just when we need to move toward postmodern reasoning. Critical realism remains caught in three restrictive elements of the modern mind: (1) epistemological foundationalism which attempts to provide an indubitable ground for believing; (2) representational thinking with its correspondence theory of truth; and (3) excessive individualism and inadequate attention to the community. The postmodern elements she lifts up for the theological agenda are (1) a nonfoundationalist epistemological holism and (2) meaning as use in language philosophy.[44] What counts for Murphy is the progressive nature of a research programme; and this is a sufficient criterion for evaluating theological research regardless of its referentiality.

Pannenberg on Theological Assertions as Hypotheses

Do the tasks of explanation and reference make theology itself scientific? Yes, answers Munich systematic theologian Wolfhart Pannenberg. Describing theology as the science of God, he contends that each theological assertion has the logical structure of a hypothesis.[45] This makes it subject to verification against the relevant state of affairs it seeks to explain. But how can we confirm or disconfirm an assertion about God? A theologian cannot follow a method of direct verification because the existence of its object, God, is itself in dispute and because God—defined by Pannenberg as the all-determining reality—is not a reproducible finite entity. An indirect method of verification is available, however. Building in part on Karl Popper's procedures for critical verification and falsification, Pannenberg submits that we can test assertions by their implications. Assertions about a divine life and divine actions can be tested by their implications for understanding the whole of finite reality, a wholeness which is implicitly anticipated in the ordinary experience of meaning.

Because of the temporal process in which the finite world is ever changing, the whole, which is an essential framework for any item of experience to have a determinate meaning, does not exist yet as a totality. If there is a whole at all, then it must be future. So, it can only be imagined, anticipated. As anticipation, the very positing of a temporal whole involves an element of hypothesis. Even the reality of God fits into this class. The reality of God is present to us now only in subjective anticipation of the totality of finite reality, in a conceptual model of the whole of meaning that we presuppose in all particular experience. Christians think of the whole temporally and eschatologically. The theological idea of the eschatological kingdom of God that arises from our historic religious tradition is subject to future confirmation or refutation by what happens. It is this openness to confirmation that makes theological assertions hypothetical and, hence, scientific.

The key that makes Pannenberg's method work is the anticipation of wholeness of meaning within common human experience. We anticipate a wholeness of meaning that is not yet fully present, a wholeness which we hypothesize will come in the future as the gift of an eschatological act of the one God. The *direct confirmation* of this hypothesis is dependent upon the actual coming of that eschatological wholeness. In the meantime, while we await the eschatological fulfillment, our faith in the future takes the form of a hypothesis that can gain *indirect confirmation* by the increased intelligibility it offers to our understanding of our experience of finite reality. If in fact God is the all-determining reality, then everything else we study, including the natural world, must eventually be shown to be determined by this reality. The very raising of the hypothesis of God as the all-determining one can be evaluated positively if it increases the intelligibility of the natural world we study through scientific disciplines.[46] This overall task of increasing the intelligibility of the natural world by considering it in relation to God leads Pannenberg to engage in dialogue with scientists and to construct a theology of nature.

Torrance on "Science and Religion" vs. "Science and Theology"

We have just seen that Pannenberg believes theology can be scientific if it makes hypotheses and seeks to confirm them. In complementary contrast, Thomas Forsyth Torrance, who taught Christian Dogmatics at the University of Edinburgh from 1952 to 1979, argues that it is the objectivity of theology that makes it scientific.

The first and salient legacy of the Torrance approach is a basic distinction: "Science and Religion" vs. "Science and Theology." These two are not the same. Religion has to do with human consciousness and human behavior. Theology has to do with God. "Whenever religion is substituted in the place of God, the fact that in religion we are concerned with the behavior of *religious people*, sooner or later means the substitution of humanity in the place of religion. . . . "[47] Torrance clearly prefers to take up the distinctively theological task, defining theology as a science. He describes theology (or a philosophy of theology) as a "meta-science of our direct cognitive relation with God. Science and meta-science are required not because God is a problem but because we are. . . . It is because *our* relations with God have become problematic that we must have a scientific theology."[48] One can see clearly here the influence of Karl Barth in getting beyond religious consciousness as the object of theology and allowing our consciousness to be shaped by the true object of theology, God. "Scientific theology is active engagement in that cognitive relation to God in obedience to the demands of His reality and self-giving."[49]

Authentic inquiry is what Torrance stresses, both scientific inquiry and theological inquiry. He advocates that we attend to what is, to what is actual, to what is real; and this means that we should guard against superimposing upon reality an *a priori* or idealistic scheme. To this end we allow our inquiry to be guided by its object, by the reality of the object under study. The transition from the Newtonian worldview to the Einstein revolution could take place only when science was authentic, only when it let nature tell us what nature is like.

With this point Torrance elegantly moves natural theology from its previous position of prolegomena into positive theology proper. This move parallels Einstein's treatment of geometry. The Euclidian geometry inherited with Newtonian physics provided a context for inquiry that presupposed absolute mathematical space and time with bodies in motion. For Einstein, this constituted an idealized presupposition detached from nature as he was studying it. Einstein's revolution in the theory of relativity consisted of placing geometry into the material content of physics. Rather than treating geometry as an idealized framework, Einstein brought it into the midst of physics where it became a natural science indissolubly united to physics.

Torrance wants to learn from Einstein's example. Torrance puts natural theology where Einstein had put geometry. "So it is with natural theology: brought within the embrace of positive theology and developed as a complex of rational structures arising in our actual knowledge of God it becomes 'natural' in a new way, natural to its proper object, God in self-revealing interaction with us in space and time. Natural theology then constitutes the epistemological geometry, as it were, within the fabric of revealed theology."[50] By making this post-Barthian move, Torrance denies natural theology any independent status while making it serve as an instrument for unfolding and expressing the knowledge content of Christian theology.

Authentic theology, then, attends to its object, God. It listens to what the Word of God tells us. This form of objectivity—listening to the object of inquiry—makes science scientific and theology scientific.

> Theology is the unique science devoted to knowledge of God, differing from other sciences by the uniqueness of its object [God] which can be apprehended only on its own terms and from within the actual situation it has created in our existence in making itself known. . . . Yet as a science theology is only a human endeavour in quest of the truth, in which we seek to apprehend God as far as

> we may, to understand what we apprehend, and to speak clearly and carefully about what we understand. It takes place only within the environment of the special sciences and only within the bounds of human learning and reasoning where critical judgment and rigorous testing are required, but where in faithfulness to its ultimate term of reference beyond itself to God it cannot attempt to justify itself on the grounds occupied by the other sciences or within their frames of interpretation.[51]

Torrance recognizes the finite and perspectival limits of human knowing as it operates in theology and the other sciences; and it is just this perspectival limit that mandates that authentic inquiry attend to its object and learn from its object.

Torrance argues that theology should engage the natural sciences in conversation. This represents somewhat of a departure from his theological mentor, Karl Barth, for whom theology could be methodologically isolated from other disciplines. This engagement of the natural sciences by the theologian marks Torrance's move away from the two-language approach of Barthianism toward consonance.

The doctrine of creation requires this cross-disciplinary conversation. Torrance affirms *creatio ex nihilo*, noting that the divine transcendence implied here renders the created world contingent. The contingency of the world requires that we study the world directly to unlock its secrets. No idealistic shortcuts or revelations about God can substitute for empirical research. This functions as a sort of theological blessing upon the scientific enterprise.

Torrance wants the theologian to broaden the scope of attention, to get beyond anthropology to include nature around and in us. Theology has been suffering from tunnel vision, he complains, the tunnel vision wherein we have limited theology to the relationship between God and the human race. Theology cannot be restricted to the relationship of God to humanity. "Theology has to do with the unlimited reality of God in his relations with the universe of all time and space."[52] Hence, the sciences broaden our knowledge of God's creation and provide an understanding of the arena within which incarnation and resurrection take place.

This enlargement of the scope of theology to include all space and time provides the framework for specifying just how God can be an object of inquiry and how knowledge of God can be objective. Torrance is a trinitarian theologian, and the finite objectivity of God incarnate grounds the objectivity of theology.[53]

> The framework of objective meaning which concerns the theologian here is bound up with the incarnation of the Son of God to be one with us in our physical human existence within the world of space and time in such a way that through his vicarious life and passion he might redeem human being and creatively reground it in the very life of God himself, and therefore it is also

> bound up with the resurrection of Jesus Christ in body, or the physical reality of his human existence among us, for it is in the resurrection that God's incarnate and redeeming purpose for us is brought to its triumphant fulfillment.[54]

One of the difficulties any Barthian theologian—or any two-language theologian, for that matter—confronts when engaging in dialogue with the natural sciences is the apparent self-referentiality of the theological circle. The existence of the object of theological inquiry, God, is just what is in dispute in the modern world. To presuppose its truth and then contend that this produces knowledge seems to beg the question. Torrance is aware of the difficulty. He defends his method with a *tu quoque* argument, noting that all theories are circular, striving to establish themselves through coherence because they cannot be derived or justified on any grounds other than what they themselves constitute. In this regard, theology is no worse off than any other discipline.[55]

Peacocke's Scientized Systematic Theology

It is my observation that within the subfields of theology, one group, the systematic theologians, have taken the lead in developing a working relationship with the natural sciences. Biblical studies has long employed the investigative techniques of archaeology, to be sure; and Historical Theology and Ethics are coming to rely more and more on methods developed by the social sciences. But it has been the systematic theologians who have examined carefully scientific methods, adopted some into theological methodology, and then proceeded in certain cases to incorporate knowledge gained from natural science into the formulation of doctrinal beliefs.

The work of Arthur Peacocke is significant here. A biochemist turned theologian, Peacocke is former Dean of Clare College at Cambridge, retired from directing the Ian Ramsey Center at Oxford, and is Warden Emeritus of the Society of Ordained Scientists. "Theology needs to be consonant and coherent with, though far from being derived from, scientific perspectives on the world," he asserts.[56] The task for theology is clear: to rethink religious conceptualizations in light of the perspective on the world afforded by the sciences.

Rethinking the world in light of science leads to questions about God. God is mysterious, affirms Peacocke. Natural theology paints a picture of an ineffable and transcendent God beyond human comprehension. The special revelation of God experienced in the person of Jesus Christ only enhances the mystery of the divine. Yet mystery is by no means confined to theology. Twentieth century science is characterized by a new appreciation of the mystery of existence. Quantum physics with such things as indeterminacy and vacuum fluctuations have increased our knowledge while at the same time they have humbled our previous *hubris* for assuming causal explanations would be right around the corner. The foundation of physical reality is more elusive than once thought. "So the mystery-of-existence question becomes even more pressing in the light of the cosmic panorama disclosed by the natural sciences."[57] Also mysterious is human personhood, arising as it does from the biological sphere to that of consciousness and then becoming itself a top-down cause. Peacocke believes that "this recognition of an ultimate ineffability in the nature of the divine parallels that of our ultimate inability to say what even things and persons are in themselves."[58]

Peacocke's rethinking of theological conceptions in light of natural science is leading him to assert certain things about God: beyond the eternity of the divine *being* God is engaged in temporal *becoming*; beyond *creatio ex nihilo* God is engaged in *creatio continua*; God creates and dynamically "lets be;" God is the ultimate source and ground of both necessity and chance; God has a self-limited omnipotence and omniscience, thereby permitting necessity and chance in the history of nature; the divine act of self-limitation for the good of the creation warrants our saying that *God is love*. These reconceptualizations lead finally to a theopaschism: "God suffers in, with and under the creative processes of the world."[59]

Some interpreters of Peacocke assign the label "temporal critical realism" to Peacocke's work. Perhaps this is appropriate, for Peacocke writes, "In giving being to entities, structures and processes *in* time, God cannot have a *static* relation to that time which is created with them. Hence we have to speak of a dynamic divine 'becoming' as well as of the divine 'being'."[60]

Polkinghorne's Bottoms Up Systematics

Peacocke is a hybrid—that is, he is trained in both science and theology. Another hybrid is mathematician-physicist turned theologian John Polkinghorne, now president of Queens College, Cambridge. Polkinghorne pursues systematic theology with what he calls a "bottom-up" method. The *bottoms* with which he begins are scientific data regarding the natural world, historical data regarding the biography of Jesus, the church's threefold encounter with the economic Trinity, and such. The *up* with which he concludes is a high degree of confidence regarding the fundamental commitments of the Christian faith, commitments that are completely compatible with the truths pursued in the field of science.[61]

With the motto, "epistemology models ontology," Polkinghorne begins methodologically with faith and reason. Faith is not merely a polite expression for unsubstantiated assertion, not an excuse for believing in God as an irrational act. Rather, faith and reason belong together. Both reflect the quest for truth. Truth-seeking is something shared by scientists and theologians alike. "Although faith goes beyond what is logically demonstrable," he writes, "yet it is capable of rational motivation. Christians do not have to close their minds, nor are they faced with the dilemma of having to choose between ancient faith and modern knowledge. They can hold both together."[62]

Polkinghorne is committed to *consonance*—that is, theological reflection on creation must be consonant with what science says about Big Bang and evolution. This by no means requires that theological assertions be reducible to scientific assertions. The scientific worldview is itself subject to interrogation and expansion, and this is pursued through metaphysics.

None of us can do without metaphysics, he observes, and then admonishes us to do metaphysics deliberately. Rejecting Cartesian dualism in favor of what he calls "dual-aspect monism" Polkinghorne opens biology to the existence of supra-physical consciousness or spirit; and he opens physics to a reality that transcends the world of the Big Bang and the evolution of conscious life.[63] At this point extrapolation and speculation from a scientific basis ceases. Polkinghorne then turns to orthodox Christian commitments—such as a theistic understanding of God and *creatio ex nihilo*—and simply defends them against competing positions.

As an example, he distinguishes his position from the deism opposed by Stephen Hawking and other physicists when discussing the onset of the Big Bang with its possible edge of time at the beginning, the implication of which is that creation becomes limited to a single act at the beginning. From then on God is presumed to let nature take its evolutionary course. But Polkinghorne is a theist who believes in an active God, so he combines *creatio ex nihilo* with *creatio continua* to emphasize God's continuing involvement in nature. Polkinghorne's active God is omnipotent, but is by no means a tyrant. God's power has been withheld to make room for freedom within nature. God still acts in nature without obviating this freedom. "One is trying to steer a path between the unrelaxing grip of a Cosmic Tyrant and the impotence or indifference of a Deistic Spectator."[64]

Polkinghorne, looking in the other direction, then distinguishes his position from the panentheism of process theology, because the latter fails to provide sufficient grounds for hope. The Whiteheadian God can very well share our suffering, but there is no eschatological guarantee here that evil will be overcome. Being remembered by the consequent nature of God is unsatisfying to Polkinghorne. "I do not want to be just a fly in the amber of divine remembrance," he writes, "I look forward to a destiny and a continuing life beyond death. To put it bluntly, the God of process theology does not seem to be the God who raised Jesus from the dead."[65]

I wonder: does this defense of theism, as clear and forceful as it is, actually need the discussion of science? It seems to me that this classic debate between deists, theists, and panentheists is only occasioned by issues rising out of Big Bang physics. The physics itself does not actually influence the direction let alone determine the destination of the debate as we find it in Polkinghorne.

Polkinghorne rightly defines his position sharply against panentheistic colleagues in the field such as Arthur Peacocke and Ian Barbour. The strength of Peacocke and Barbour is perhaps that they wrestle more thoroughly with the actual scientific ideas and seek a fuller integration with theological ideas. The strength of Polkinghorne is his confidence that the Christian faith, when subjected to the same rational scrutiny that science exacts upon its data and theories, exhibits an honest pursuit of truth accompanied by a confidence in its rational motivation.

Russell's Understanding of Divine Action

A hybrid physicist-theologian on the American side of the Atlantic, Robert John Russell, founded a program in 1981: The Center for Theology and the Natural Sciences at the Graduate Theological Union in Berkeley. Methodologically, Russell belongs to the consonance school but in his own way he emphasizes a dialectic between consonance and dissonance. Science and theology can at points take different trajectories, and dissonance must be acknowledged. Like Polkinghorne, Russell is clear that scientific prognostications regarding the future of the cosmos do not square with Christian eschatology. A projected heat death due to entropy does not square with the promise of resurrection and new creation. Here is dissonance that needs to be acknowledged. Inspired by the work of his former student, Nancey Murphy, who employs the philosophy of Imre Lakatos for theological purposes, Russell seeks to embed the consonance/dissonance dialectic more tightly into a theological method that sees itself as a progressive research programme.[66]

In careful conversation with physical cosmologists and with theologians such as Ian Barbour and Wim Drees, Russell has pressed for consonance on understandings of the origin of the universe found in Big Bang cosmology and the Christian concept of creation.[67] The orienting question is this: is the Christian doctrine of *creatio ex nihilo* consonant with the Big Bang? Many answers have been given, all unsatisfying to Russell. The two-language answer is no, because this school believes in principle that no scientific picture of the universe's origin has any conceptual relevance for theology. It precludes looking for consonance at the outset. An alternative answer, a semi-literalist answer, would be: yes, they are consonant because the scientific discovery of a beginning to the universe corroborates the Christian view that the creation had a beginning boundary, before which there was nothing. Two things make this unsatisfying as well. First, current conversations regarding quantum theory make it premature to say that the scientific consensus is that the universe—at least the original singularity—

had an absolute beginning. Second, the force of the *creatio ex nihilo* idea is that the world is ontologically dependent upon God, and this could be the case even if there were no beginning boundary.

Russell feels the need to find his own answer. Following the Lakatos-Murphy distinction between the inner core commitment and the outer belt of auxiliary hypotheses in a research programme, he posits the following as core: *creatio ex nihilo* means ontological dependence. Then he adumbrates three auxiliary hypotheses: (1) ontological dependence entails finitude; (2) finitude includes temporal finitude; and (3) temporal finitude entails past finitude—that is, going backwards in finite time must take us to a beginning, a t = 0 point. This fits with what we know from Big Bang cosmology in which the data of astrophysics, the theory of general relativity, and other factors point us to an initial singularity, t = 0. That this singularity may have a quantum life of its own, does not stop Russell from tendering a modest conclusion: the empirical origination described by t = 0 in Big Bang cosmology tends to confirm what is entailed in this theory's core, namely, *creatio ex nihilo* means ontological dependence. This is not a proof, but it is a partial confirmation.[68]

Russell's contribution to the internal theological debate is the distinction he draws between finitude and boundedness. Traditionally theologians have identified the two. But they are not identical. Ontological dependence upon God requires that the world be finite but not necessarily bounded. The initial singularity may have had a quantum life of its own and, hence, no temporal boundaries; yet we can still say that the world has a beginning and that it is finite in time. Big Bang cosmology, even in its quantum form, becomes a character witness, even if not an eye witness, to the creation of the world.

Hefner's Created Co-Creator

Philip Hefner, like Russell, picks up on the Lakatos-Murphy methodology with its core-auxiliary distinction. He puts God in the hard core, "that to which all terrestrial and cosmic data are related."[69] He adds seven auxiliary hypotheses which I will not enumerate here. He believes that the test of theology is its explanatory adequacy, that it is subject to falsification by experience, and that its relative success should be measured by its fruitfulness. "What is at stake in the falsification of theological theories is not whether they can prove the existence of God," he writes, "but rather whether, with the help of auxiliary hypotheses, they lead to interpretations of the world and of our experience in the world that are empirically credible and fruitful—that is, productive of new insights and research."[70]

Hefner teaches systematic theology at the Lutheran School of Theology at Chicago, edits the journal *Zygon*, and directs the Chicago Center for Science and Religion. His career work in the field has been devoted less to physical cosmology and more to rapprochement between theology and the life sciences, especially evolutionary theory. He has sought to develop an anthropology and even a Christology in what he calls a bio-cultural evolutionary scheme. His is a grand vision, and at the focal center of this vision is the concept of the human being as the *created co-creator*. A basic element embedded within the core rather than located in an outer auxiliary hypothesis, the concept of the created co-creator is Hefner's central contribution to the Theology and Natural Science enterprise. He writes, "Human beings are God's created co-creators whose purpose is to be the agency, acting in freedom, to birth the future that is most wholesome for the nature that has birthed us—the nature that is not only our own genetic heritage, but also the entire human community and the evolutionary and ecological reality in which and to which we belong. Exercising this agency is said to be God's will for humans."[71]

Hefner has been criticized for advocating human *hubris*, for placing humanity on a level with the divine and overestimating the human potential for creativity. Such a criticism might apply to New Age thought, but not to Hefner. Hefner is clear that we human beings are creatures, brought here by God the creator even if God employed evolution to create us. This is what he means by *created* co-creator. Nevertheless, when explicating the biblical concept of the *imago Dei*, Hefner wants to include creativity in the divine image and exhort us ethically to take responsibility for creating a future that is more human, more just, and more loving.

Can We See Cosmos as Creation?

Those of us in the Christian tradition are used to speaking glibly of the natural world as God's creation. On what basis do we do this? It is not immediately obvious from observing the natural realm that it is the product of a divine hand or the object of divine care. Since the Enlightenment we in the modern scientific world have been assuming that no footprints of the divine can be discerned in the sands of the natural world. Western science assumes that if we study natural processes with the intention of learning the laws by which nature operates, what we will end up with is just a handful of natural laws. If we study natural processes with the intention of wondering about the magnificent mysteries that surround us, we will end up where we started, namely, with an imagination full of spectacular puzzles. If we study nature for her beauty, we will see beauty. If we study nature to see her violence, we will see her as did Tennyson, blood "red in tooth and claw." Nature, we have been assuming for a century or so now, does not seem to take the initiative to disclose her ultimate foundation or even her existential meaning. What natural revelation reveals is simply nature, not God. If we want to know more, we have to ask more questions. And we have to go beyond our natural relationship with nature to find the answers.

When we Christian theologians see the limits to natural revelation in a modern world replete with naturalism, we find we need to go back to the historical events of the death and resurrection of Jesus Christ, the events that stand at the heart and center of God's special revelation. Good Friday and Easter do not reveal that God is the world's creator for the first time, of course. But these events do confirm what had already been suspected in ancient Israel, namely, that the creation of the world was the necessary first act in God's continuing drama of salvation. The world in which we live is not merely a conglomeration of natural laws or puzzles; it is not merely the realm of beauty or violence. The cosmos exists because it plays a part in the divine scenario of redemption. It is on the basis of what we know about the God who raised Jesus from the dead that St. Paul can perceive how creation has been "subjected to futility," that it "has been groaning in travail," and that God has furthermore "subjected it in hope" because it "will be set free from its bondage to decay and obtain the glorious liberty of the children of God" (Rom.8:18–25).

General knowledge of nature is insufficient. What we need are special experiences of God that reveal special knowledge. We need to know—or at least need to hypothesize—that there is a God with divine intentions before we can see clearly that the world around and in us is in fact a creation. It is primarily on the strength of Israel's experience with the liberating God of the Exodus that the Old Testament writers could depict the world as God's creative handiwork. It is on the strength of our experience with the incarnate Lord that Christians in today's world can say that "God so loved the world . . . " (John 3:16). The New Testament promise of an eschatological new creation tells us something essential about the present creation. Theologically, it is God's promised kingdom that determines creation, and creation is the promise of the kingdom. Whether we interpret nature through the symbol of the Exodus, the incarnation, the kingdom or some other similar religious symbol, we find that we are dependent upon some form of revelation of God's purposes if we are to put nature into proper theological perspective—that is, if we are to think of nature as a creation.

Where does this lead? Curiously enough, we might consider the possibility of a reversal in natural theology. Traditionally the aim of natural theology has been to ask what our study of nature can contribute to our knowledge of God. But might it work in reverse? Might we ask what our knowledge of God can contribute to our knowledge of nature? To know that God is the creator is to know that the world in which we live and move and have our being is creation.

Finally, we may not have to choose between the two methods. We could begin with nature and then ask about God; or we could begin with what we think we know about God and then ask how this influences what we think about nature. Or, we could do both. Both should be on the agenda of those working in the field of Theology and Natural Science.

Notes

1. Edmund L. Andrews, "Religious Leaders Prepare to Fight Patents on Genes," *New York Times* (May 13, 1995) 1. I say misdirected here because leaders allegedly from 80 religions and denominations signed an ambiguous and embarrassingly misinformed statement regarding the patenting of human embryos, body parts, animals, and cell lines. This debacle may be the result of an odd working alliance between the Washington based Foundation on Economic Trends led by Jeremy Rifkin and the General Board of Church and Society of the United Methodist Church.

2. A. D. White, *A History of the Warfare of Science with Theology*, 2 volumes (New York: Dover, 1896; 1960).

3. Margaret Wertheim, *Pythagoras' Trousers: God, Physics, and the Gender Wars* (New York: Random House, Times Books, 1995) 7.

4. The typology developed here is updated and revised from previous publications, particularly "Theology and Science: Where Are We?" *Dialog*, 34:4 (Fall 1995) 117–132; *Zygon*, 31:2 (June 1996) 323–343; and "Theology and the Natural Sciences" in *The Modern Theologians*, ed. by David F. Ford (Oxford: Basil Blackwell, rev. ed., 1997) 649–688.

5. The lineup of alternative views I offer here is revised from that sketched previously in my Preface to *Cosmos as Creation* (Louisville: Westminster/John Knox, 1989) 13–17. It is also a more nuanced lineup compared to the one offered by Ian Barbour in his Gifford Lectures, *Religion in an Age of Science* (San Francisco: Harper, 1990) 3–30, wherein he identifies four ways: conflict, independence, dialogue, and integration. My categories of scientism and church authoritarianism fit his conflict category; and the two-language theory is a model of independence in both schemes. Yet Barbour's notions of dialogue and integration lack the nuance that I believe is operative under the notion of consonance. Consonance involves dialogue, to be sure, but it acknowledges that integration may be only a hope and not an achievement. Also, Barbour thinks of scientific creationism in terms of "biblical literalism" and thereby places it in the conflict category, overlooking the fact that the creationists think of themselves as sharing a common domain with science; they see themselves in conflict with scientism but not with science itself. John Haught offers up an alliterative four-unit typology: conflict, contrast, contact, and confirmation in his book, *Science and Religion* (New York: Paulist, 1995). Mark Richardson offers us a three-part typology: (1) integration typified by the work of Lionel Thornton, William Temple, Austin Farrar, Arthur Peacocke, and John Polkinghorne; (2) romantic typified by poets Whitman or Wordsworth and by contemporary New Age figures such as Briane Swimme, Thomas Berry, and Matthew Fox; and (3) scientific constraint, wherein one speaks univocally about the natural and transcendent worlds, typified by Paul Davies, Freeman Dyson, Stephen Hawking, and Frank Tipler. See: Mark Richardson, "Research Fellows Report," *CTNS Bulletin*, 14:3 (Summer 1994) 24–25. Philip Hefner cuts the pie six ways: (1) modern option of translating religious wisdom into scientific con-

cepts; (2) post-modern/new age option of constructing new science based myths; (3) critical post-Enlightenment option of expressing truth at the obscure margin of science; (4) post-modern constructivist option of fashioning a new metaphysics for scientific knowledge; (5) constructivist traditional option of interpreting science in dynamic traditional concepts; and (6) Christian evangelical option of reaffirming the rationality of traditional belief. Unpublished to date.

6. Langdon Gilkey, *Nature, Reality, and the Sacred: The Nexus of Science and Religion* (Minneapolis: Fortress, 1993) 14.

7. Fred Hoyle, *The Nature of the Universe* (New York: Mentor, 1950) 125.

8. Jacques Monod, *Chance and Necessity* (New York: Alfred A. Knopf, 1971) 169.

9. Stephen Hawking, *A Brief History of Time* (New York: Bantam, 1988) 136; see: Carl Sagan, *Cosmos* (New York: Random House, 1980). Even though Sagan rails against religion because it dogmatizes and allegedly refuses to allow the existence of God to be a hypothesis, he also seeks an alliance with good theology in his openly declared war against pseudo-science. *The Demon-Haunted World* (New York: Random House, 1996) 20, 34. Co-discoverer of the double helix structure of DNA Francis Crick reduces what religious people used to believe to be the disembodied soul to "nothing but a pack of neurons." All of our joys and sorrows, our memories and ambitions, our sense of personal identity and free will, "are in fact no more than the behavior of a vast assembly of nerve cells and their associated molecules." *The Astonishing Hypothesis: The Scientific Search for the Soul* (New York: Charles Scribner's Sons, 1994) 3. For aggressive anti-religious secular humanism see Paul Kurtz, *The Transcendental Temptation* (Buffalo: Prometheus, 1985) and the journal published by the Committee for the Scientific Investigation of Claims of the Paranormal, *The Skeptical Inquirer.*

10. Paul Davies, *God and the New Physics* (New York: Simon and Schuster, Touchstone, 1983) ix.

11. Frank Tipler, *The Physics of Immortality* (New York: Doubleday, 1994) ix, 10, 17, 247. Tipler borrows some eschatological theology from Wolfhart Pannenberg and places it within the scientific eschatology of physicist Freeman Dyson, *Infinite in All Directions* (New York: Harper, 1988).

12. Wertheim, *Pythagoras' Trousers*, 219.

13. Wertheim, *Pythagoras' Trousers*, 218.

14. Edward O. Wilson, *On Human Nature* (New York: Bantam, 1978) 230.

15. Wilson, *Human Nature*, 200.

16. Richard Dawkins, *The Selfish Gene* (Oxford and New York: Oxford University Press, 1976).

17. Robert Wright, *The Moral Animal* (New York: Pantheon, 1994) 146,147.

18. Michael Ruse and Edward O. Wilson, "The Evolution of Ethics," *New Scientist* 108:1478 (17 October 1985) 50, 52.

19. *John Paul II On Science and Religion: Reflections on the New View from Rome*, ed. by Robert John Russell, William R. Stoeger, and George V. Coyne (Notre Dame: University of Notre Dame Press, and Vatican City State: Vatican Observatory Publications, 1990). In October 1992 the pope completed a thirteen-year study of the Galileo affair, proclaiming that the church erred on condemning the astronomer for disobeying orders regarding the teaching of Copernicus' heliocentric theory of the universe. John Paul II described Galileo as "a sincere believer" who

was "more perceptive [in the interpretation of Scripture] than the theologians who opposed him." Because in the myths of scientism Galileo is touted as a martyr for truth over against the narrow-mindedness of theology, Owen Gingerich took the occasion to write to clear up the facts. One noteworthy fact is that Galileo was never condemned for heresy, only disobedience. "How Galileo Changed the Rules of Science," *Sky and Telescope*, 85:3 (March 1993) 32–26.

20. See: Duane T. Gish, *Evolution: The Fossils Say No!* (San Diego: Creation-Life Publishers, 1973) and Roger E. Timm, "Scientific Creationism and Biblical Theology," in Peters, *Cosmos as Creation*, 247–264.

21. Stephen Jay Gould, *Hens' Teeth and Horses' Toes: Reflections on Natural History* (New York: Norton, 1983) 254.

22. One could describe the war as a battle between atheistic science and theistic science. Langdon Gilkey suggests that scientism (what he calls scientific positivism) goes beyond the limits of science to propound an atheistic cosmology, and this initiates the reaction that results in scientific creationism. See: Gilkey, *Nature, Reality, and the Sacred*, 55.

23. Phillip E. Johnson, *Darwin on Trial* (Downers Grove IL: InterVarsity Press, 1991) 153.

24. Stephen Jay Gould, "Nonoverlapping Magisteria," *Natural History*, March 1997, p. 18.

25. Langdon Gilkey, *Creationism on Trial* (San Francisco: Harper, 1985) 49–52; 108–113.

26. In his more recent works, Gilkey has pressed for a closer relationship—a mutual interdependence—between science and religion. Gilkey attacks scientism (what he calls naturalism or scientific positivism) when it depicts nature as valueless, determined, and void of the sacred, on the grounds that these are supra-scientific or philosophical judgments that go beyond science itself. Science, therefore, must be supplemented by philosophy and religion if we are to understand reality fully. *Nature, Reality, and the Sacred*, 3; 11; 75; 111; 129.

27. Nancey Murphy, *Beyond Liberalism and Fundamentalism: How Modern and Postmodern Philosophy Set the Agenda* (Valley Forge PA: Trinity, 1996) 58.

28. The "two books" approach is embraced today by the organization, Reasons to Believe, a publishing house that "examines how the facts of nature and the truths of the Bible give each of us a reason to believe." Reasons to Believe, P.O. Box 5978, Pasadena CA 91117, fax 818/852–0178.

29. Ernan McMullin, "How Should Cosmology Relate to Theology," in *The Sciences and Theology in the Twentieth Century*, ed. Arthur Peacocke (Notre Dame: University of Notre Dame Press, 1981) 39. See: Peters, *Cosmos as Creation*, 13–17.

30. John Marks Templeton and Robert L. Hermann, *Is God the Only Reality? Science Points to a Deeper Meaning of the Universe* (New York: Continuum, 1994) 168.

31. W. Mark Richardson and Wesley J. Wildman, *Religion and Science* (New York and London: Routledge, 1996) xii.

32. See: Ted Peters, *GOD—the World's Future: Systematic Theology for a Postmodern Era* (Minneapolis: Fortress, 1992) chapter 12, and *Futures—Human and Divine* (Atlanta: John Knox Press, 1978).

33. David Bohm, *Wholeness and the Implicate Order* (London: Routledge and Kegan Paul, 1980) 11. See: Fritjof Capra, *The Tao of Physics* (New York: Bantam,

1977). See: Ted Peters, *The Cosmic Self: A Penetrating Look at Today's New Age Movements* (San Francisco: Harper, 1991) chapter four.

34. Brian Swimme and Thomas Berry, *The Universe Story* (San Francisco: Harper, 1992) 255. A variant would be the team work of physicist Joel R. Primack and musician Nancy Ellen Abrams who are trying to construct a myth out of Big Bang inflationary cosmology and medieval Jewish Kabbalah, not because the myth would be true but because our culture needs a value orienting cosmology. "In the Beginning . . . Quantum Cosmology and Kabbalah," *Tikkun*, 10:1 (January-February 1995) 66–73.

35. Langdon Gilkey, *Religion and the Scientific Future* (San Francisco: Harper, 1970) 41.

36. Gilkey, *Religion and the Scientific Future*, 50.

37. Paul Davies, *The Mind of God* (New York: Simon and Schuster, 1992) 24; see: 232.

38. Davies, *Mind of God*, 15. See: Paul Davies, *Are We Alone?* (London and New York: Harper Collins, Basic Books, 1995).

39. Philip Clayton, *Explanation from Physics to Theology* (New Haven and London: Yale, 1989) 13; see: Peters, *GOD—The World's Future*, 74–76.

40. The criterion for evaluating the progressive strength of a theory is fertility, and this constitutes the chief argument in behalf of critical realism for Ernan McMullin, "A Case for Scientific Realism," in Jarret Leplin, *Scientific Realism* (Berkeley: University of California, 1984) 26. See: Arthur D. Peacocke, *Intimations of Reality: Critical Realism in Science and Religion* (Notre Dame: University of Notre Dame, 1984).

41. Wentzel van Huyssteen, *Theology and the Justification of Faith* (Grand Rapids: Eerdmans, 1989) 162–163. "I advocate a critical realism," writes Ian Barbour, "holding that both communities [scientific and religious communities] make cognitive claims about realities beyond the human world." *Religion in an Age of Science*, 16.

42. Barbour, *Religion in an Age of Science*, 43; see: Ian Barbour, *Myths, Models, and Paradigms* (San Francisco: Harper, 1974) 38; and Sallie McFague, *Metaphorical Theology* (Minneapolis: Fortress, 1982) 133–134.

43. Arthur D. Peacocke, *Theology for a Scientific Age* (Oxford: Basil Blackwell, 1990, and Minneapolis: Fortress, enlarged ed., 1993) 14.

44. Nancey C. Murphy, "Relating Theology and Science in a Postmodern Age," *CTNS Bulletin*, 7:4 (Autumn 1987) 1–10; see her Templeton Book Prize-winning work: *Theology in an Age of Scientific Reasoning* (Ithaca: Cornell, 1990); *On the Moral Nature of the Universe*, co-authored with George F.R. Ellis (Minneapolis: Fortress, 1996); as well as *Beyond Liberalism and Fundamentalism* cited earlier.

45. Wolfhart Pannenberg, *Theology and the Philosophy of Science* (Louisville: Westminster/John Knox 1976) and *Systematic Theology*, 3 Volumes (Grand Rapids: Eerdmans, 1991–1996).

46. See: Wolfhart Pannenberg, *Toward a Theology of Nature*, ed. Ted Peters (Louisville: Westminster/John Knox, 1993) chapter one. Similarly, John Haught expands on consonance with two nuanced categories, contact and confirmation. As a gesture of confirmation he contends that the theologian can contribute to the scientific apprehension of natural reality. "The theological notion that the world was created—and is therefore neither necessary nor eternal—gives a stature to empirical science that other ways of looking at the world do not." *Science and Religion*, 63.

47. Thomas F. Torrance, *Theological Science* (Oxford: Oxford University Press, 1969) iv–v.

48. Torrance, *Theological Science*, v.

49. Torrance, *Theological Science*, v.

50. Thomas F. Torrance, *Reality and Scientific Theology* (Edinburgh: Scottish Academic Press, 1985) 39. Karl Barth is reported to have granted full agreement to this new place for natural theology. See: Thomas F. Torrance, *Space, Time and Resurrection* (Grand Rapids: Eerdmans, 1976) ix–xiii.

51. Torrance, *Theological Science*, 281–282.

52. Torrance, *Reality and Scientific Theology*, 67.

53. Thomas F. Torrance, *Space, Time and Incarnation* (Oxford: Oxford University Press, 1969).

54. Torrance, *Space, Time and Resurrection*, 13.

55. Torrance, *Space, Time and Resurrection*, 15. Wolfhart Pannenberg would fear that such a *tu quoque* ("you also" says Brutus to Caesar) might become a rational excuse for an irrational commitment. *Theology and the Philosophy of Science*, 45.

56. Peacocke, *Theology for a Scientific Age*, x.

57. Peacocke, *Theology for a Scientific Age*, 101.

58. Peacocke, *Theology for a Scientific Age*, 102.

59. Peacocke, *Theology for a Scientific Age*, 126.

60. Peacocke, *Theology for a Scientific Age*, 184. Peacocke's early masterwork of 1979, *Creation and the World of Science* (Oxford: Clarendon, 1979) is organized somewhat like a systematic theology. Yet there the scientific agenda drove the project. More recently, in *Theology for a Scientific Age*, the theological agenda has taken the driver's seat. Distinctively theological commitments are being rethought in light of scientific apprehensions of nature.

61. John Polkinghorne, *The Faith of a Physicist* (Princeton: Princeton University Press, 1994) 193.

62. Polkinghorne, *Faith of a Physicist*, 5.

63. Polkinghorne, *Faith of a Physicist*, 21.

64. Polkinghorne, *Faith of a Physicist*, 80.

65. Polkinghorne, *Faith of a Physicist*, 68.

66. See: Imre Lakatos, *The Methodology of Scientific Research Programmes: Philosophical Papers*, Vol. 1, edited by John Warrall and Gregory Currie (Cambridge: Cambridge University Press, 1978).

67. See: Barbour, *Religion in an Age of Science*; and Willem B. Drees, *Beyond the Big Bang: Quantum Cosmologies and God* (LaSalle IL: Open Court, 1990).

68. See his work in Robert John Russell, William R. Stoeger, and George V. Coyne, editors *Physics, Philosophy, and Theology* (Vatican City State: Vatican Observatory; and Notre Dame: University of Notre Dame, 1988) and Robert John Russell, Nancey C. Murphy, and C. J. Isham, editors, *Quantum Cosmology and the Laws of Nature* (Vatican City State: Vatican Observatory; and Notre Dame: University of Notre Dame, 1993).

69. Philip Hefner, *The Human Factor* (Minneapolis: Fortress, 1993) 260. This book won the 1993 Templeton Book Prize in the field of theology and natural science.

70. Hefner, *The Human Factor*, 261.

71. Hefner, *The Human Factor*, 264; see: 32.

Part One

Physics and Faith

Chapter Two

Logic and Uncertainties in Science and Religion

CHARLES H. TOWNES

Science and religion represent two different aspects of human understanding and different instincts which often seem *quite* different, yet can be closely related. Science, with its experiments and logic, tries to understand the order or structure of the universe. Religion, with its theological inspiration and reflection, tries to understand the purpose or meaning of the universe. These two are cross-related. Purpose implies structure, and structure ought somehow to be interpretable in terms of purpose.

At least this is the way I see it. I am a physicist. I also consider myself a Christian. As I try to understand the nature of our universe in these two modes of thinking, I see many commonalities and crossovers between science and religion. It seems logical that in the long run the two will even converge.

Can We Really Separate Science and Religion?

For most of Western history science and religion were closely tied to one another. Theologians were intellectuals of their communities, and although science was more limited in scope it tended to be integrated with philosophy and theology. With the advent of experimental science during the Enlightenment, the practice of empirical research grew very rapidly and very successfully. Skirmishes between science and the church signaled a change. Copernicus's heliocentric universe was condemned by the Roman Catholic Church in 1616 and Galileo was forbidden to defend it; Galileo's exoneration awaited Pope John Paul II just in recent times. By the nineteenth century open clashes between science and religion had become common, notably with the battle between the theory of evolution and the seven day creation account in Genesis.

In our time it has become difficult for many to understand how one can put the scientific world view and the scientific method together with religion. Louis Pasteur, who was a very devout person, was asked the question: How can you be both a scientist and a person of faith? His answer went something like this: "Well, I do science in my laboratory. My home and my religion are separate." That was all he could say.

What Pasteur represents is a sort of two-language approach: Whereas science provides the language of laboratory understanding, religion provides a private language of faith which is needed in our relation to other humans. Such an attempted separation is not uncommon today. I would put Pope John Paul II in the two-language camp. While he honors science and recognizes its importance, he seems to adhere to the view that these are separate tracks of thought which should not tell each other what to think. Science and theology should cooperate with each other in the common pursuit of the welfare of humanity; but, the pope believes, in the final analysis they cannot teach each other very much.

On this the pontiff seems to be in tune with our wider culture—what some call our *two cultures*—wherein we split apart the humanities and the sciences. Our cultural sensibilities separate religion and other humanistic affections from science like we separate warm from cold, the poem from the microscope, the living from the dead. We sometimes even separate nature from science, assuming that nature is warm and that this warmth can be apprehended only by the poet. The scientist, in contrast, allegedly invokes cold-hearted methods that are as deadening to nature as they are to the human spirit. Take William Wordsworth, for example:

> Sweet is the lore which nature brings;
> Our meddling intellect
> Misshapes the beauteous forms of things
> We murder to dissect[1]

Or, John Keats:

> Do not all charms fly
> At the mere touch of cold philosophy?[2]

Or, Edgar Allen Poe:

> Science, true daughter of Old Time thou art
> Who alterest all things with pondering eyes
> Why preyest thou thus upon the poet's heart
> Vulture, whose wings are dull realities.[3]

What these poets assume is a split between the aesthetic and the empirical, a rift between human affections and disciplined research. But a closer look will show that aesthetic affections are alive and well in the scientist. The vastness of the apparently limitless reaches of outer space combined with the intriguing complexities of the smallest miscroscopic things elicit an aesthetic response in the human soul. Nature communicates meaning; and science can actually facilitate this communication. Alexander Pope puts it this way:

> He who through vast immensity can pierce,
> See worlds on worlds compose one universe,
> Observe how system into system runs,
> What other planets circle other suns,
> What varied beings people every star,
> May tell why heav'n has made us as we are.[4]

Whether through the latest telescope, the microscope, or the landscape around us, we can see beauty in nature; and this beauty communicates meaning. Scientist Henri Poincaré testified to the aesthetic attractiveness of the twin facts of simplicity and immensity in nature. We seek out, he observed, the vast expanses of space and the microscopic particles of matter, in part because we take delight in them. Our aesthetic sensibilities are drawn to the vast and to the simple, the tiny and the remote.

Although science and religion are frequently separated and contrasted, I believe they can provide overlapping ways in which we apprehend the one universe of which we are a part. Nature gives voice to beauty, and beauty to meaning and purpose. The language of science may appear lifeless or deadening to some poets; but the scientist himself or herself is often sensitive to the beauty of nature, immensity of space, and the complexity of the material world.

Let's look at this again from a slightly different angle. The beauty of nature elicits a response from both our scientific and our poetic modes of understanding. Our aesthetic sensibility is triggered by our experience with nature's beauty, and it comes to voice in both scientific and religious languages.

Note how beauty and truth seem to converge for both the poet John Keats and the physicist Werner Heisenberg. Keats said it this way: "Beauty is truth, and truth beauty."[5] Heisenberg argued that when nature leads us, by way of scientific analysis, to simple and beautiful mathematical forms, we are irresistibly impressed by the feeling that these forms must be "true"; that they must in fact reveal an actual feature of the natural world. We scientists, seeing a simple relationship that seems beautiful, intuitively think it likely to be true. Both scientists and theologians give themselves to the truth that transcends and invites us.

Similarities in Logic and Uncertainty

My own view is that science and religion are remarkably similar in spite of the great differences assigned them by our culture. They are remarkably similar, very simply because of who we are as people. It is people who author both science and religion. It is we who ask how to think about things and how to learn about things. We can expect similarities in approach to both science and religion because both emerge from the same human mind.

Science and religion not only share a common logic; they also share something else, namely, uncertainty. We must recognize that we do not know things for sure. Knowledge, even scientific knowledge, is less than absolute. As research proceeds we pick out a set of postulates which seem reasonable to us. We test those postulates with our experience or with experiments. We test to see what fits. Yet the postulates remain postulates. Some level of uncertainty regarding the validity of the postulates remains.

The mathematician Gödel proved that uncertainty is inherent even in the nature of our logic. Mathematics proceeds by employing a working set of assumptions and from these, using the rules of logic, proving something particular. Gödel proved that we can never be sure that the assumptions with which we started are even self-consistent, let alone true. The only way we may show that they are self-consistent is to appeal to a new set of assumptions, and from these try to prove the original set. But of course, this new set of assumptions is subject to the same uncertainty regarding self-consistency, and so on. Thus there will always be things which we assume to be true but which cannot be proved. Logic and uncertainty come together in a single package. And to take them seriously, there must be faith.

Reason Builds on Faith, Even in Science

Religion, with its theological reflection, builds on faith. Science too builds on faith. How? For successful science of the type we know, we must have faith that the universe is governed by reliable laws and, further, that these laws can be discovered by human inquiry. The logic of human inquiry is trustworthy only if nature is itself logical. Science operates with the faith that human logic can in the long run understand nature's laws and that they are dependable. This is the faith of reason.

Why would a scientist work day and night for a long period of time on a problem that is difficult to solve? For such motivation, he or she must have faith that the problem is solvable, and that there is an inherent logic in nature which his or her mind is capable of reading. Prior to solving a problem, the scientist works with faith in the as yet unseen reasonableness of nature.

Albert Einstein was such an example. For the final twenty years of his life he worked on a Unified Field Theory. As he worked, he reasoned that there had to be some form of a unified account of the laws of nature which warranted his effort to discover them, even though in the long run he did not achieve this goal. We scientists work on the basis of a fundamental assumption regarding reason in nature and reason in the human mind, an assumption that is held as a cardinal principle of faith. Yet this faith is so automatically and generally accepted that we hardly recognize it as an essential basis for science.

Revelatory Experiences

One might think that religion and its theology have a patent on revelatory experiences. One might also think that scientific discovery consists merely in reasoning based upon existing knowledge. But revelations of new knowledge can also happen in the process of scientific discovery.

One famous case of revelation was the discovery of the benzene ring structure. The German chemist Kékulé had puzzled for some time over how carbon could form benzene and similar molecules. The story is that one evening, partly dozing in front of his fireplace, he dreamt of a snake which curled around and took its tail in its mouth. He woke up. That's it—carbon atoms form a ring!

I have had such a revelatory experience. At the time I was working on what would become the maser and the laser, I had been researching ways of producing short waves for four or five years, but nothing I tried was producing the results I was looking for. And I was chairperson of a committee organized to consider what research was needed to produce short waves. Early in the morning just before a meeting of this committee in Washington, I walked out to a park to enjoy the fresh air. I sat on a bench looking at the azaleas freshly opened. And I asked myself: "Why can't we do this?" I went through the reasoning one more time, but this would not yield an answer. We ought to be able to use atoms or molecules, I thought. They are built in a way which produces short waves. But no, I'd been through that before. The problem was limits posed by the second law of thermodynamics: you can't get more than a certain amount of power. . . . Wait a minute! Wait a minute! The second law of thermodynamics doesn't have to apply if there is no definable temperature. I sat there for a few minutes. A revelation of sorts had occurred. I could see it in my mind. I took out a piece of paper and pencil and wrote down the numbers. Sure enough, the numbers made sense. One could build a practical short wave oscillator using molecules mostly in excited energy states and hence not describable by an ordinary temperature.

If we emphasize its setting, this story can even be endowed with a certain mystique. I had stayed overnight in a hotel with A. L. Schawlow. When I had awakened, he was still asleep. To avoid waking him I had slipped out. He was to become coinventor of the laser with me. The building looking out over the park was where Alexander Graham Bell had worked intensively but unsuccessfully on using light for communications, for which the laser has played one of its major roles. At the time, I didn't even know about the closeness of Bell's former laboratory, but that was in fact the setting for this revelation.

Theologians might say that revelation both prompts faith and reflects on faith. As a research scientist, my faith came first and kept me inspired to work until a revelation occurred, one which confirmed my faith in the scientific endeavor.

Quantum Mechanics and Uncertainty

Despite our faith in the logic and reliability of nature, at the subatomic level we find counter-intuitive phenomena, generally understood by the discovery of quantum mechanics. Some of these phenomena must be thought of in terms of uncertainty, or to put it more strongly, of indeterminism.

Let us start with a question which has arisen frequently: Does light consist of particles or waves? Newton thought light was made of particles, but in the early part of the 19th century Thomas Young did interferometric experiments which convinced scientists that light is really made of waves. With the birth of quantum mechanics in the early part of this century, light took on aspects of both particles and waves. This duality is contrary to normal human intuition, and continues to be challenging. When we shine light on a glass window, some of it is reflected back while the rest passes through. Yet we should and can ask: How does an individual particle of light, a photon, decide whether to bounce back or to pass through? Attempting to answer such a question leads to the Heisenberg uncertainty principle. According to this, we can never know for certain which particular photon will pass through the glass or be reflected. A fundamental uncertainty pervades the full extent of our knowledge of the physical world. The best we can do is predict the odds—the probability—that a given thing will happen, or that a given photon pass through or be reflected.

Causal determinism no longer applies. This is the conclusion derived from quantum mechanics, or from Heisenberg's uncertainty principle. Causal determinism seems to make sense at the level of day to day observation of anything much larger than the atomic scale; but at the atomic level our science implies a heavy dose of chance operative in nature. Some scientists—for example Einstein—still convinced by their faith in the rationality of nature understood in terms of causal determinism, persisted in seeking to overcome uncertainty by positing the concept of hidden variables. This approach postulated hidden variables to represent as yet undiscovered forces which produce the quantum phenomena we observe. To these scientists the world of nature simply had to be deterministic, so such a force was assumed.

Bell's Theorem in the 1960s suggested a way in which the postulated existence of hidden variables could be tested. John Clauser at the University of California, Berkeley, first put the theory to experimental test, and revealed that no such hidden variables could be present. This has since been confirmed by many experiments. To his credit Clauser acknowledged that, even contrary to his own firm expectation, nature had spoken through an experiment announcing that no hidden variables exist.

With the advent of quantum mechanics, some religiously-oriented scientists such as Arthur Compton immediately claimed that God acts at the quantum level, and, together with nature, can make quantum events occur the way they do. But there is a basic problem with this approach. Granting Heisenberg's uncertainty principle, along with the rejection of hidden variables, science leaves no room for God to interfere. To insert God as a determining cause makes little sense when what is observed scientifically is that no causal determinant can be at work here.

Can We Do Experiments in Religion?

Is it possible to perform experiments about religious questions? The key to success in scientific research is that an experiment performed by one scientist is in principle repeatable by another scientist and, if valid, will produce a confirming result. Experiments can be repeated. Is such a thing possible with religious subject matter? My answer is a mixed one.

On the one hand, experiments and experience go together. Experiments are organized experience, so to speak. We have to recognize, of course, that certain areas of human experience are not repeatable and therefore not subject to what is ordinarily called experimentation. Each day we see things and do things that affect the actions of other people; we read history and learn about the sequence of events that brought us to where we are today. Daily activities and historical understanding represent experience which is in many ways very much like experimental observations, but it is normally experience of unique and unrepeatable events. Religious experience typically belongs in this category, as does some of social science. Theology, which among other things reflects on human experience, relies heavily on the history of unrepeatable events. But we evaluate these, applying whatever logic we can muster, perhaps subconsciously, along with intuition, to form our religious views.

Some dimensions of religious life may well be confirmable. Doubting Thomas for example, following the Easter resurrection of the crucified Jesus, wanted proof. He wanted to touch the wounds of the corpse now living in order to overcome his doubt regarding the truth of the resurrection claim (John 20:26–29). It is not unusual for a person of faith to want the same confirmation of belief that a scientist wants to find in the results of an experiment. We might think of Thomas as the first empirical Christian.

Prayer may provide us with another example of religious experience subject to experimental investigation. A recent study by Dr. Herbert Benson at Harvard undertook experiments to determine if prayer for the sick or injured has any influence on their recovery. The results of this statistical study confirmed that, yes, prayer does in fact have a positive effect on the health of patients. The experiment was done with patients who knew they were being prayed for; an experiment without the patients knowing this still needs to be done.

Now, how should we think about such an experiment? Suppose we were to draw a strict line of separation between science and religion, what would we conclude? Prior to the experiment, prayer would have been considered strictly a religious phenomenon. Now that a successful experiment has been performed, it might then enter the domain of science. Yet prayer is prayer, regardless of the experiment. This is another reason why I do not agree with those who maintain a high wall of separation between science and religion. Instead, I would rather admit that science and religion are not discretely separated domains. Rather, they constitute two complementary modes of human understanding; and at least in some areas they share a common domain of knowing. In fact, I hesitate to put boundaries on either one, and expect that as we understand each more fully, they will more fully overlap.

Creation and the Anthropic Principle

One of the most significant points of shared interest between science and theological reflection is concern for the origin of the universe. What do we now know from science about the origin and history of the universe that may touch on what theologians believe about God's creating us and our world with a purpose? First, we now know that there was a unique time in the history of the universe. About 15 billion years ago it exploded with the "Big Bang" from a minuscular size to its present enormous extent. Afterwards, the sun and the earth came together, and life began. This is contrary to the intuitive beliefs of many scientists of the past that the universe has always been more or less the same; that there can be nothing unique about us nor in the history of our universe. What lies behind this beginning is the source of much scientific thought and speculation. The theologian can say that it was God's creation, and avoid the question of what then was God's origin. Scientists try to probe beyond this beginning, but we cannot avoid confronting the concept of a "beginning."

We have also learned from science that very special circumstances were necessary for us to be here. The early kinetic energy of the Big Bang explosion had to match the mass of material more closely than one part in a million million in order for the universe to both be long-lived as it is and also to develop galaxies and stars. The nuclear and electronic forces in atoms had to have just the right ratio for this universe to have the rich variety of chemicals needed for our life. The gravitational force and nuclear reaction properties had to be very well matched to allow formation of long-lived stars. Two energy levels characteristic of oxygen and carbon nuclei had to be remarkably well matched for both carbon and oxygen to be abundant, as we need them to be. These and other remarkable "coincidences" have led to articulations of the "anthropic principle"—that the natural laws must conform to what is needed for human life. But this is only a tautology since of course we are here. What is interesting is the apparently very special conditions required by human life.

Also of particular interest is the close tie between life and the nature of our planet earth. Many planets are likely circling other stars; and so life may not be rare. In principle we must suppose that life may have developed in many locations. Yet, when we look at all the planets within our solar system, our Earth looks unique. Jupiter, Saturn, and the other large planets are too cold, too gassy, and inhospitable for anything like our kind of life. Mercury is too close to the sun and hot. Mars and Venus seem at first glance to be similar to Earth. Although life may have existed in the past on Mars, today it is cold and without an appropriate atmosphere.

Earth's sister planet Venus, earlier thought to be a promising planet for life, we now know is covered with a heavy atmosphere of carbon dioxide and the surface is hot enough to melt lead. Actually, the atmospheres of both Venus and Earth are thought to have begun similarly, with carbon dioxide being emitted from their inner material and accumulating in the atmospheres of each. Yet, life started at just the right point in Earth's history, just before the greenhouse effect became overwhelming and the planet became too hot. Life on Earth started about a billion years after planet formation, at just the right point where it could change carbon dioxide into free oxygen. It continued to keep the carbon dioxide under control, preventing Earth from becoming overheated like Venus. Now how does one evaluate this? I hesitate to draw hard and fast conclusions. Yet these observations are impressive. Freeman Dyson faces the situation with the following statement:

> I conclude from the existence of these accidents of physics and astronomy that the universe is an unexpectedly hospitable place for our living creatures to make their home in. Being a scientist, trained in the habits of thought and language of the twentieth century rather than the eighteenth, I do not claim that the architecture of the universe proves the existence of God. I claim only that the architecture of the universe is consistent with the hypothesis that mind plays an essential role in its functioning.[6]

Regardless of what one may think this can say about God, what is striking here is that scientific evidence leads to a feeling and hypothesis that the course of natural history is guided at least in part by an intelligence and a purpose.[7]

Physicists have been brought much closer to questions of interest to theologians as they succeed in delving more fundamentally into the origins of our universe and the nature of physical laws. Relativity and quantum mechanics have also changed our basic concepts since the last century. Strict causal determinism, for example, has gone. And while as a result of developments such as relativity and quantum mechanics we now understand much more than we did in the nineteenth century, I believe physical scientists have become more modest about how completely we really understand our universe.

It is particularly striking that as our experiments and thoughts have penetrated new realms—high velocities and high gravitational fields in the case of relativity, tiny particles of atomic size in the case of quantum mechanics—our basic concepts have been altered, but without changing the validity of most of our previous physical laws under the circumstances where they were previously tested. For macroscopic objects we still teach, use, and intuitively think in terms of Newtonian mechanics, even though our views of its meaning have radically changed. For ordinary velocities and ordinary gravitational fields, we still use and think intuitively in terms of a simple three dimensional space and an independent time, even though general relativity provides a rather different basic view. This may lead to the conclusion that time-tested ideas, either in science or in religion, are likely to continue to have some kind of validity even if in the distant future we understand enough to revolutionize our thinking in either area.

Chance in Biology

The biologists may at first seem fortunate because they have not run into brick walls such as physicists hit in finding quantum or relativistic phenomena that are so strange and different. But this may be because biologists have not yet penetrated far enough towards the really difficult problems where radical changes of viewpoints may be essential. In any case, biology is now in a stage where no basically new phenomena are obviously needed for its progress, and current work can be interpreted in terms of known laws of chemistry and statistics. We do not really know just how the first forms of organized life started nor whether initiation of life was very likely, even given favorable circumstances on Earth. We do not even know the details of under just what circumstances on Earth it began. Yet to many scientists, life seems a natural and almost automatic event given that the physical laws and nature of our planet turned out the way they did. Jacques Monod puts it strongly: "Chance alone is at the source of every innovation, of all creations in the biosphere."[8] Stephen Jay Gould says, "We are the accidental results of an unplanned process."[9] But some, like the evolutionist Ernest Mayer, are nevertheless impressed. He writes: "Virtually all biologists are religious in the deepest sense of this word. . . . The unknown, and maybe the unknowable, instills in us a sense of humility and awe."[10]

I believe biology may yet encounter problems which may fundamentally change our views, and wish I could watch its development over the next century to learn whether this becomes true. For example, really understanding the human brain seems an awesome task. Clearly we can understand much more than we do at present. We can, for example, imagine "intelligent" computers designed to do many of the things our brains do. But can they have anything like the sense of consciousness or the sense of free will that humans possess? The brain is immensely complex. It contains ten billion neurons, each of which has about ten thousand synapses. This represents about a million gigabits of information, interacting in complex modes. The human brain can understand many complex devices. But we can wonder whether any device can ever really understand itself, or only other devices which are somewhat simpler than that which understands them. Can the brain really understand itself?

Free Will

What do we really know about free will? I suspect that every scientist, like most humans, assumes that free will exists. It is part of our everyday reality as human beings. With quantum mechanics the world is no longer deterministic. But present science says that the chance directions in which quantum mechanics allows it to develop cannot be influenced either by a divine force or by anything like the usual concept of free will. Yet although the usual concept of free will is not consistent with our present understanding of science, we almost all assume we have some free will and live accordingly.

How can we understand our sense of free will as consistent with today's science? It is possible that free will as we experience it is a delusion. Perhaps it does not actually exist. Perhaps it can be explained simply as a delusion that has proven to have great survival value in the process of evolution. Religion, like free will, might also be explained as a delusion contributing to our evolutionary advantage, increasing the survival potential of human society. So perhaps we are just kidding ourselves when we think we observe ourselves making free choices or responding to God's will.

In spite of uncertainties, like so many others I have a fundamental sense that free will is there. It exists. I feel that I have free will and act according to it. I look around and make judgments about things. I make decisions. I take actions. I also have a sense of divine presence in the universe and in my own life and try to act out of the sense of freedom concomitant with this presence. Our sense of free will needs to be explained, or perhaps accepted rather than explained away. The same is true, I believe, of our sense of the divine. As we pursue scientific and religious understanding, how will our views of such matters develop?

Conclusion

Once the necessities of life are available, questions about its orientation, value, and meaning, which are the emphasis of religion, are more pressing and critical than those about the structure of our universe, the emphasis of science. This may be why human societies have developed and codified religious ideas much sooner than scientific ones. But in the last few centuries science has, by contrast with religion, made remarkable progress, and this has put emphasis on its methods and validity. Yet our understanding of both science and religion are dependent on human reasoning, on evidence, and on faith. And both involve profound uncertainties.

As humans, we face life. Decisions cannot be avoided; we need to choose our orientation, actions, and directions even if we understand imperfectly. Each of us decides in our own way. Yet we all make these decisions based on our experience, what our parents have told us, observations of the people and society around us, our understanding of human history, the evidence we have, and whatever logic and intuition we can muster. While assumptions and decision about our lives cannot be avoided, we also need to be open to change, listening for revelations and looking for new understandings of reality. Relativity and quantum mechanics have revolutionized science. We must be prepared for revolutions in our thinking, both in science and religion. But we can at the same time expect that our past reasoning and beliefs have important, even if imperfect, validity.

Notes

1. "The Tables Turned" in *William Wordsworth: Selected Poetry*, ed. Mark van Doren (New York: The Modern Library, 1950), 83.

2. "Sonnet to Science," in *John Keats: Poems*, ed. Gerald Bullett (London: J. M. Dent and Sons, 1974), 163.

3. *The Complete Poems and Stories of Edgar Allen Poe*, texts established by Edward H. O'Neill (New York: Alfred A. Knopf, 1967), vol. 1, 28.

4. Alexander Pope, "An Essay on Man," in *Alexander Pope's Opus Magnum, 1729–1744*, ed. Miriam Leranbaum (Oxford: Clarendon Press, 1977), 51.

5. "Ode on a Grecian Urn," in *John Keats: Poems*, ed. Gerald Bullett (London: J. M. Dent and Sons, 1974), 192.

6. Freeman Dyson, *Disturbing the Universe* (New York: Harper and Row, 1979), 251.

7. Elsewhere Freeman Dyson writes: "The universe as a whole is hospitable to the growth of mind. The argument here is merely an extension of the Anthropic Principle up to a universal scale . . . the argument from design still has some merit as a philosophical principle. I propose that we allow the argument from design the same status as the Anthropic Principle, expelled from science but tolerated in metascience. The argument from design is a theological and not a scientific argument." *Infinite in All Directions* (New York: Harper, 1988), 297.

8. Jacques Monod, *Chance and Necessity* (New York: Random House, 1972), 112.

9. Stephen Jay Gould, "Extemporaneous Comments on Evolutionary Hope and Realities," in *Darwin's Legacy,* Charles L. Hamrum, ed., Nobel Conference XVIII (San Francisco: Harper and Row, 1983), 102.

10. Ernest Mayer, *The Growth of Biological Thought* (Cambridge: Harvard University Press, 1982), 81.

Chapter Three

From Physicist to Priest

JOHN POLKINGHORNE

I grew up in the country and in a Christian home. My parents were regular worshippers at our local Anglican parish church and, since I was a well-behaved child, I accompanied them willingly from an early age. No particular provisions were made for children but we had a vicar who was a skillful preacher, able to make biblical passages come alive, and I used to enjoy listening to him. I absorbed Christianity through my pores. Religion was obviously important to mother and father but they were people who did not naturally talk much about it and I received little in the way of formal religious instruction at home. When I was about eight an aunt of mine let me have a little book of private prayers that I had found lying around in her home and I used these regularly and somewhat secretly.

I am, therefore, a cradle Christian. I cannot remember a time when I was not in some way a member of the worshipping and believing community of the church. The figure of Jesus has always been central for me and no view of reality would begin to be adequate which did not fully take the phenomenon of Christ into account. I have not been given the gift of an untroubled faith—I sometimes think that Christianity might be too good to be true—but when that mood is on me I say to myself "Well, then, deny it" and I know that I could never do that. Christ's side is one on which I have to take my stand.

When I was fourteen we moved from Somerset to Ely and I went to school in nearby Cambridge. The Perse School, which I attended, was small and very academic and for the first time I encountered clever boys who did not believe in God. We used to argue, but my faith survived that and a subsequent spell of national service in the Army before coming up to Cambridge in October 1949 to study mathematics at Trinity College.

Evangelical and Catholic, Anglican Style

In my first week as an undergraduate I was taken to a Freshers' Sermon preached on behalf of the Christian Union. The preacher used the story of Zacchaeus's meeting with Jesus as he passed through Jericho on his way to his death at Jerusalem, as the basis of a challenge to respond to Christ right now, to take this unique opportunity. I was strongly moved and went forward at the end among a crowd of those who wished to make a decision for Christ. For some years afterwards I would have spoken of this as my "conversion," but I now understand it as a moment of deeper Christian commitment along a pilgrimage path that I was already treading.

There followed a number of years of close involvement with the Christian Union. I have mixed feelings about that time. The conservative evangelical Christianity which I embraced so wholeheartedly gave me certain gifts which I continue to value and seek to retain: the importance of a personal commitment to Christ and a love of scripture. Yet it also promoted a narrow view, both of the varieties of Christian experience and of the relevance of general culture. There was a kind of defensiveness, even fearfulness, in the face of sources of truth not guaranteed as "sound." Nowhere was this more apparent than in its treatment of the Bible. I have found it immensely enhancing for my own use of scripture to be able to recognize its human and cultural character, whilst still discerning its inspired and normative status. The Church of England is such a broad comprehensive church that its members are always being invited to identify themselves as adherents of one particular party or another. Today I find it difficult to choose a label for myself, but "catholic" would certainly be part of it. I value greatly the sacramental life and the accumulated insights of the Christian tradition. I feel most spiritually at home on the occasional visits I am able to make to a small community of Anglican nuns (the Society of the Sacred Cross) living a Benedictine life in the Welsh countryside.

Mathematical Physics at Cambridge

My undergraduate studies at Cambridge were in mathematics. I had chosen the subject because I was good at it and liked getting things right, and also because my mathematical imagination had been kindled at school by an outstanding master who taught me. At the university I got interested in how one could use mathematics to understand the deep structure of the physical world, so that when I embarked on a Ph.D. in 1952 it was in the area of theoretical elementary particle physics. This was the beginning of a long career as a physicist which lasted till 1979. It was an exceptionally interesting period in the development of my subject since it spanned the long struggle, by means of experimental discovery and theoretical insight, which eventually uncovered the quark level in the structure of matter. My own work was very much on the mathematical side of this great collaborative enterprise and I attained a modest degree of professional success, becoming Professor of Mathematical Physics at Cambridge University in 1968 and being elected a Fellow of the Royal Society in 1974.

Nevertheless, I had long thought that I would not remain in particle physics all my life. The subject was always changing in response to new ideas and new discoveries. When one was young this state of intellectual flux was exciting; it became somewhat more tiring as one grew older. In mathematical thinking, most of us lose in middle age the flexibility of mind that is a characteristic of youth. We can still do the old tricks but it becomes harder to learn or to invent new ones. I had seen many senior colleagues get somewhat miserable as the subject moved away from them. I resolved I would leave physics before physics left me. I felt I owed this, not only to myself, but also to the young workers in the large research group I was privileged to lead. As my fiftieth birthday approached, and as a particular era in particle physics came to a close with the establishment of what is called the Standard Model, I realised the time had come for me to go. I was not leaving physics because I had in any way become disillusioned with it, but I had done my little bit for the subject and now it was time to do something else.

From Professor to Seminarian

I like being with people. I value the eucharistic life. I had some experience of being a Lay Reader (an unordained local preacher). These considerations encouraged in my mind the idea of a possible vocation to the Anglican priesthood. Fortunately, my wife, Ruth, concurred—it was necessarily a joint decision. The next step was to have my vocation tested and considered by a selection committee, a collection of wise and experienced people appointed by the church for that purpose. They too concurred, and I was subsequently grateful, not only for that decision but also for the care with which I felt it had been taken.

So October 1979, just before my forty-ninth birthday, saw me a beginning student at Westcott House, a small Anglican seminary in Cambridge in the liberal catholic tradition. I was the oldest person in the House, older than the Principal even! It was very odd becoming a student again—I found out how much more difficult it is to listen to a lecture for an hour than to give one—but I had a lot to learn during my two-year course. Perhaps the most important lesson of all I learned was to value the Daily Office, the round of morning and evening prayer and praise, psalmody and scripture, which it is the obligation of an Anglican priest to recite faithfully. It provides the spiritual framework for my life today.

Just before I went to Westcott, a theologically knowledgeable friend of mine suggested to me that I should read Jürgen Moltmann's *The Crucified God*.[1] I had done a little desultory theological reading on and off over the years, but this was perhaps the first substantial theological work which I read with serious attention. I was deeply affected by it and Moltmann has been one of the major theological influences on me ever since. I can understand the criticisms which some make of the occasionally rather uncontrolled exuberance of his writing, but for me he is a person of exciting theological ideas which span the two horizons of the biblical witness and the demands of the century of the Holocaust.

A Scientist with Serious Theological Interests

I cared for physics, and I continue to do so, but I have come to realise that theology grips me much more profoundly than science ever did. Yet the personal paradox is that I shall never be able to become a professional theologian. I do not have the time or opportunity to recapitulate that long apprenticeship and involvement with a world-wide academic community which is the indispensable requirement of becoming a fully-fledged practitioner. I do not think this means that I have nothing to contribute to theological thinking, but I am aware of my limitations. I cannot claim to be more than a scientist with serious theological interests. I have to say that I wish I met a few more theologians who have serious scientific interests. The interdisciplinary field of encounter between the scientific and theological world-views, which has been my predominant intellectual interest over the last fifteen or so years, calls from all its participants for a certain acceptance of risk and a certain charity towards the efforts of others with different backgrounds.

On ordination, an Anglican clergyman spends three years in apprenticeship to the parochial ministry. It is called serving one's title, and I did mine in perfectly ordinary parishes in Cambridge and Bristol. Once licensed to go solo, I became Vicar in charge of a large village parish outside Canterbury. All in all, I did five years in this kind of work. In addition to preaching and taking services, it involved a good deal of wandering around, knocking on doors and drinking cups of tea with people who were in some sort of trouble, such as illness or bereavement. The Church of England is a national church with a responsibility to the whole community. Only a minority of those I visited were in any way active participants in worship.

Return to Cambridge

I enjoyed this life very much, but of course there were intellectual aspects of me which were not greatly exercised in the course of it. I had thought originally that I had left the academic world for good, but I gradually came to recognize that thinking and writing about science and religion was part of my vocation, the particular way in which I might serve the Christian community. When an unsought opportunity came in 1986 to return to Cambridge as the Dean of Trinity Hall (a job equivalent to being the parish priest of that academic "village") I decided, after some thought, to accept it. Three years later I received an equally unexpected invitation to become the President of Queens' College, Cambridge (the Head of the College, but not its Chief Executive, rather a kind of eighteenth-century constitutional monarch in its society). This essentially secular job was possible for me because Queens', like all the ancient colleges at Cambridge, has a religious basis as part of its foundation. I continue to exercise a degree of priestly ministry as I share with our Dean in celebrating the Eucharist and preaching in the College Chapel.

Writing About the Way the World Is

My main intellectual activity is writing. I love the task of composition, the search for as clear a way as possible to convey what I want to say. The late Bishop John Robinson of *Honest to God* fame (who ordained me priest) once said to me that he could not think without a pen in his hand. I knew at once what he meant. As one reads and thinks, ideas buzz around in one's mind. It is the act of writing which causes this flux of thought to condense into some coherent thread of argument. I write all my manuscripts in scribbled longhand because, when the structure really begins to form, I cannot type fast enough to keep up with myself.

My first book in the science and religion area arose out of my experiences on leaving physics. I could not quit right away, for I had obligations to my graduate students which had to be fulfilled through an orderly withdrawal. In the eighteen months it took me to wind up my scientific affairs, I had quite a few conversations with colleagues over a cup of coffee in some laboratory canteen as they asked me what on earth I was up to? Mostly, they were probing my reasons for Christian belief. In half an hour or so I could no more do justice to that theme than I could have conveyed to an arts friend, on a similar timescale, my reasons for belief in quarks. I decided I would put down on paper what I would have said if I had had a few hours at my disposal. The result was a small book with a grandiose title: *The Way the World Is*.[2] There isn't a great deal of explicit science in the book (the first publisher I approached rejected it on those grounds) but it exemplifies in a simple way a conviction that runs through much of my writing: that religious insight, like scientific insight, depends upon the search for motivated belief. The title was intended to convey that idea of rationally grounded understanding, rather than constituting a ridiculous claim to total metaphysical adequacy!

I did not have time for writing when I was a curate learning the trade but as I wandered round the streets of my working class parish in Bristol, I used to think about the similarities and differences of science and religion and what they had to say to each other about the one world of human experience. When I came to Kent as a vicar, part of the arrangement was that I should have a chance to write and this enabled my thoughts to crystallise into *One World*,[3] a survey of the scene which has proved a fairly steady seller.

I have never been able to see more than a book ahead and I did not then envisage writing a trilogy of little volumes on the topic of science and religion. Nevertheless the other two offerings followed in fairly quick succession. *Science and Creation*[4] is mainly concerned with two themes. One is the revival, as I see it, of natural theology in the modest mode of proffered insight based on the very structure of the laws of nature themselves which seem, in their deep rational beauty and intelligibility and in their "finely-tuned" anthropic fruitfulness, to point beyond science to a more profound Reality. This is an insight that is particularly appealing to someone whose scientific experience has been in fundamental physics. Biologists see a more messy and ambiguous picture of the process of the world and the second theme I tried to address was that of an evolutionary world "making itself" in an unfolding act of continual creation, necessarily precarious and costly in its character. Here I was helped by the thoughts of my seniors, Ian Barbour and Arthur Peacocke, and by W. H. Vanstone's wonderfully insightful *Love's Endeavour, Love's Expense*,[5] another book which I had read early in my theological studies and which has remained an abiding influence.

Epistemology Models Ontology

In chapter five of *Science and Creation*, I began the tentative exploration of a theme which has recurred in much of my subsequent writing: that we should seek to understand the relationship of mind and matter as being that of complementary poles of a single "world stuff" in flexible and open organisation. The task of a proper understanding of this metaphysical issue is far beyond my modest capacity (or that of anyone today, I believe) but I have come to think that the insights of so-called chaos theory may offer a clue to a useful direction in which to wave our hands in cautious speculation.

I propose that the undoubted unpredictabilities of these exquisitely sensitive physical systems should be treated, not as unfortunate signs of epistemic ignorance, but as sources of ontological opportunity. Coining the phrase "Epistemology models Ontology" as a slogan of scientific realism, I suggest that the ontology of deterministic equations aligns poorly with the epistemology of intrinsic unpredictabilities and that it should be replaced (as almost everyone does in the case of quantum uncertainties) by a more subtle and supple ontological account. This leads eventually to the notion of an enhanced range of causal principles in which the "bottom-up," bits and pieces, energetic causality of physics is supplemented by the operation of "top-down" causality of a non-energetic, pattern-forming, kind that might be called "active information." I suggest that this is how we act in the world and that it is consistent to suppose that God interacts with creation in this mode also.

My first sustained attempt to discuss divine action was in the third book of the trilogy, *Science and Providence*.[6] Here I also took up a theme to which I have returned in later writing, the consideration of how God relates to time. Although contemporary science affords no satisfactory account of the basic human experience of the present moment, my view is, "so much the worse for science!" I reject a block universe account[7] and assert the true temporality of the world. Since God knows things as they really are, I believe that this implies that God knows creation in its temporality. In my view, there must be a temporal pole to the divine nature in addition to an eternal pole (an idea which I accept from the process theologians whilst rejecting a number of their other proposals), and that even God does not yet know the unformed future.

My writing has been characterised by a succession of short books. I think and read about a topic and then reach a stage at which I have to try to set down what I think about it. This seems to result in a series of volumes of just over a hundred pages. I try to write with all the intellectual seriousness and scrupulosity I can muster but I do not write in an overtly academic style. This is a deliberate choice; I decided early on that my target audience should be two-fold: the educated unbeliever whom I am wishing to persuade of the rationally motivated credibility of Christianity and the educated believer whom I am wishing to persuade to take science seriously and to enhance Christian understanding by so doing. I do not think these aims are inconsistent with also seeking to offer some intellectual input into the interaction between science and theology.

After the trilogy, I found I wanted to return to some themes I had touched on earlier and discuss them in greater detail. This resulted in *Reason and Reality*,[8] whose chapters seek to consolidate the consideration of how scientific and theological thinking relate to each other, the role of natural theology, and a number of other issues including more discussion of how to interpret chaos theory.

Gifford Lectures

The invitation to give the Gifford Lectures in Edinburgh in 1993 encouraged me to write what is my longest book to date. Rather exasperatingly, it has different titles on the different sides of the Atlantic: *Science and Christian Belief/The Faith of a Physicist*,[9] but at least it has the same subtitle:

"Theological Reflections of a Bottom-up Thinker." The idea was to weave a discussion of Christian belief around phrases selected from the Nicene Creed, using arguments based on a bottom-up movement from experience to interpretation. Scientists know that the world is strange and exciting, beyond our prior powers of anticipation, and they are open to unexpected insights provided they are based on evidence to show that this is indeed the case. The lectures are an exercise in that search for motivated belief which is so central to my own thinking. In a sense they are a much more developed account of the programme I attempted with *The Way the World Is*. The final chapter discusses a theological problem which is much in my mind, of how we are truly to understand the interrelationships of the world's great faith traditions, so obviously concerned with a common spiritual realm but so obviously making clashing cognitive claims about its nature. This unresolved diversity contrasts perplexingly with the universality of scientific understanding which has spread so readily across the globe.

After the Giffords I needed a holiday, but I love to write so I dashed off a chatty book about science and religion which I called *Quarks, Chaos and Christianity*.[10] It is rather a favourite of mine.

Scientists as Theologians

My latest offering is called *Scientists as Theologians*.[11] My valued colleagues, Ian Barbour and Arthur Peacocke, have also recently given Gifford Lectures,[12] and comparison of the three sets reveals both many common themes but also some interesting divergences of method and conclusion, mostly relating to the question of how great a degree of conceptual autonomy has to be claimed by theology and to what extent it can harmonise its thinking with scientific patterns of understanding. In attempting the delicate task of a comparison between the three of us, I have concluded that there is a spectrum, which I characterise as running from consonance to assimilation, in which I am near the conceptual autonomy (consonance) end, Barbour is near the integrationist (assimilation) end, and Peacocke is somewhere in between us.

I think that the science-and-theology debate is currently in an interesting phase in which the action has to some extent moved away from the obvious border areas of natural theology and the doctrine of creation into a closer engagement with central Christian questions such as Christology and eschatology. The bottom-up thinking that characterises scientific thought has something to offer here, not as a uniquely effective method of doing theology but as a possible source of insight, comparable with the particular insights offered, in their very different ways, by black or feminist theology.

I do a fair amount of public speaking about science and religion. I quite often end a talk by saying that I am both a physicist and a priest and that I believe that I can hold these two aspects of me together, not only without compartmentalisation or dishonesty, but also with a significant degree of mutual enhancement. It is to that task that I seek to devote my current endeavours.

Notes

1. Jürgen Moltmann, *The Crucified God* (London: SCM, 1974).
2. John Polkinghorne, *The Way the World Is* (London: Triangle; Grand Rapids: Eerdmans, 1983).
3. John Polkinghorne, *One World* (London: SPCK; Princeton: Princeton University, 1986).
4. John Polkinghorne, *Science and Creation* (London: SPCK; Boston: Shambhala, 1988).
5. William Vanstone, *Love's Endeavour, Love's Expense* (London: Darton, Longman and Todd, 1977).
6. John Polkinghorne, *Science and Providence* (London: SPCK; Boston: Shambhala, 1989).
7. Cf. Christopher Isham and John Polkinghorne, "The Debate over the Block Universe," *Quantum Cosmology and the Laws of Nature*, ed. Robert Russell, Nancey Murphy and Christopher Isham (Rome: Vatican Observatory, 1993) 135–44.
8. John Polkinghorne, *Reason and Reality* (London: SPCK; Philadelphia: Trinity Press International, 1991).
9. John Polkinghorne, *Science and Christian Belief:* Theological Reflections of a Bottom-up Thinker (London: SPCK, 1994)/*The Faith of a Physicist* (Princeton: Princeton University, 1994).
10. John Polkinghorne, *Quarks, Chaos and Christianity* (London: Triangle, 1994; New York: Crossroads, 1995).
11. John Polkinghorne, *Scientists as Theologians* (London: SPCK, 1996).
12. Ian Barbour, *Religion in an Age of Science* (London: SCM, 1990); Arthur Peacocke, *Theology for a Scientific Age* (London: SCM, enlarged edition, 1993).

Chapter Four

Is the Universe Absurd?

PAUL DAVIES

When I was sixteen and studying theoretical physics, an arts student once expressed astonishment that I was able to use mathematical equations to work out facts about the natural world. "How can equations tell you what is happening in nature?" she asked. I have been wondering how ever since.

Science Works

Science works. In fact, it works spectacularly well. You don't have to accept Stephen Hawking's claim[1] that the end of theoretical physics is in sight to agree that vast areas of nature, from subatomic particles to galaxies, have been satisfactorily brought within the scope of science. Galileo proclaimed that the great book of the universe was written in the language of mathematics. Since Galileo's own work on the nature of motion, mathematical equations have been used to describe all aspects of fundamental physics, to the extent that a theory is generally considered credible only when it has a comprehensive mathematical basis.

It would be too simplistic to say that mathematics is the ultimate truth, but ever since ancient Greece mathematics has enjoyed a curious status in human thought. Plato envisaged mathematical and geometrical objects located in an invisible, timeless, abstract realm of their own. The Pythagoreans believed that the physical universe was a direct manifestation of number, geometry and harmony. Mathematics was therefore rooted in an otherworldly domain, a domain of the intellectual and spiritual. By contrast, physics was recognized as dealing with the physical world of matter—of tangible things that impinge directly on our senses. Viewed in this way, mathematical physics provides a bridge between the abstract, transcendent and spiritual on the one hand, and the physical and corporeal on the other. It is an image that is deeply appealing; it led the British astronomer Sir James Jeans to proclaim that God is a pure mathematician.

How credible is such a view of mathematical physics today? Can we really glimpse something of the divine in the subtle workings of nature?

Having trained as a theoretical physicist, I began by taking for granted the fact that science in general, and physics in particular, works. But as my career progressed I returned again and again to that question asked of me in my teens: Why can we do this wonderful thing called science?

Science is founded on a number of tacit assumptions about the nature of the physical world that are rarely questioned:

The universe is ordered in a rational and lawlike manner. The job of the physicist is to uncover the details of the lawlike order in nature at its most fundamental level, to discover the laws that apply to this order and, in practice, to cast them in mathematical language. A crucial point is that the order in nature is regarded as *real.* It is sometimes claimed that scientists merely impose their mental constructs on nature—that is, they read their own preconceived notions of order *into* nature, and not out of it. This claim appeals to cultural relativists who assert that science is just another collection of myths about the world, to be placed alongside ancient folklore, magic, New Age mysticism, and so forth, as valid descriptions of reality. This is insidious nonsense. The sun's gravitational field that determines the motion of the planets *really does* obey an inverse square law. That is not a human invention. It is a fact about the world in the same way that the Earth being round is a fact about the world. Human beings do not determine the shape of the Earth to suit their culture, nor do we select the law of gravitation.

The universe could have been otherwise. Einstein once remarked that what really interested him was whether God had any choice in the nature of his creation. There is no evidence for the claim that is sometimes made that the laws of physics have to be what they are from logical necessity. Most scientists agree that the particular lawlike order we observe in nature isn't the only possible order. The laws could have been different, or there might have been no laws—or even no universe—at all. One job of the theoretical physicist is to construct idealized and simplified imaginary universes (e.g., a two-dimensional universe with a single self-interacting quantum field) to clarify certain theoretical concepts. These mathematical models are logically possible candidate realities. The real universe is not very much like them, but it could have been. The purpose of experiment and observation in science is precisely to determine which out of the (probably infinite) set of possible universes our actual universe happens to be. In a nutshell, nature is contingent.

Nature is intelligible. It would be impossible to be a scientist without believing that the world can be understood, at least in part, by human thought. Why bother to do science otherwise? But the fact that we humble *Homo sapiens*, with our mental abilities reflecting evolutionary happenstance, can nevertheless unravel the mysteries of nature, is astonishing. Why can we do this? It is easy to imagine a world which is both rational and ordered, but arranged in a way that is either far too subtle or far too complicated for human beings to understand. It is also easy to imagine a world (a rather boring one) in which the lawfulness of nature is blindingly obvious at a glance. The order found in the real world, however, is generally hidden from us, and can be discerned only by arcane procedures of experimentation and mathematical processing. In summary, the order in nature is characterized by *contingent intelligibility*. Scientists take this contingent intelligibility for granted. I believe it represents powerful evidence for something deeper going on in nature. At the very least it demonstrates that there is an intellectual as well as a physical component to nature.

Let me develop a little further this notion of hidden abstract order. When physicists study natural phenomena, the lawlike order is usually not immediately apparent. It manifests itself only under special conditions. A good example concerns the law of falling bodies investigated by Galileo. Drop two everyday objects together, such as a cup and a tissue, and it is likely that they will strike the ground at different times. But drop them in a vacuum and they will fall at the same rate. The laws of gravitation and motion that this experiment illustrates apply to much more than objects dropped to the ground, however. The same laws connect the motion of the cup and the tissue to the motion of the moon. This deep linkage is typical of physical laws: They have universal applicability.

One way to express this is to say that physics reveals a hidden subtext in nature. The process of physics does not stop with the actual phenomena studied; those phenomena conceal a "message," in mathematical code, that is much more profound, and in a very real sense much more fundamental, than the specific phenomena to which it refers. The late Heinz Pagels, an avowed atheist, nevertheless waxed lyrical about "the cosmic code" represented by this hidden subtext in nature.[2]

Let me give another example. The laws of electromagnetism are very obscure. We are certainly familiar with basic electrical and magnetic phenomena in daily life, but the subtle way in which these forces are intertwined was revealed only after a long and painstaking series of experiments in the early-to-mid nineteenth century. These experiments consisted of doing things with wires and magnets that no ordinary person would consider, in arrangements and circumstances that would never occur naturally. And even after all this it took the amazing intellectual leap of James Clerk Maxwell, who on largely aesthetic grounds appended an extra mathematical term in the equations of electromagnetism for which there was at the time no experimental evidence, to expose a hidden link between electromagnetism and optics. This connection, when probed with further mathematical analysis, revealed another link—between space and time—that led to the theory of relativity. My point is that doing such things—doing science in the manner to which we have become accustomed, with its curious laboratory procedures and mathematical manipulations—is a strange, even bizarre, activity. Had it not been for historical circumstances we might never have stumbled on this mode of enquiry, and might never have guessed that we were able to dig beneath the surface of phenomenal reality to discern the hidden subtext of nature.

The lawfulness of the universe is completely dependable. The laws of physics are taken to be absolute, universal and unfailing. Miracles are not allowed. Because scientists reject the idea of an interventionist, miracle-working God—a God of the gaps—they must instead have faith that the laws of the universe will not falter.

Many of these philosophical underpinnings of science are shared with the monotheistic religions. Judaism, Islam and Christianity are also founded on the belief that the universe does not have to be as it is: God is free to order it differently, to leave it chaotic, or to refrain from creating any universe at all. The actual order is therefore contingent on God, who is a rational and intelligent Creator and orders his creation in a dependable, lawlike manner. This *consonance* between science and monotheistic theology is no surprise. Science took root in Western Europe under the twin influences of Greek philosophy, with its emphasis on rational reasoning, and the monotheistic religions, which stressed the contingency of nature. The early scientists such as Galileo, Kepler and Newton were deeply religious. They believed that in doing their science they were uncovering God's rational plan for the world. The laws of nature were widely regarded as thoughts in the mind of God, and the mathematical order that those laws express was God's cryptic code. So alongside the scriptures, with their mystical revelations of God, lay "natural theology"—the chance of glimpsing God at work in the order and harmony of the cosmos.

Today, most scientists profess to be atheists, and the theological dimension of their work has been jettisoned. Scientists think it their rightful business to elucidate the laws of nature—to crack the cosmic code if you like—but they are suspicious of metaphysical topics, even when cast in non-theological language. Questions such as: Where did the laws of physics "come from"? and Why those laws? cause physicists to shift uneasily. They no longer regard the laws as thoughts in the mind of God. The laws have been cut loose from their theological moorings, and left to float freely. Ask why these free-floating laws exist at all, or why they have the form they do, and most physicists will regard it as none of their business. While I agree that such questions, strictly speaking, lie beyond the domain of science as a discipline, it is natural for us to ask them, and it is understandable that we look to science for pointers to the answers.

Big Bang Physics Does Not Need a God of the Gaps

Before addressing the question of where the laws of physics "come from," I should clear away a very common misconception, which is that somehow the laws of physics were "there" before the universe existed, so that in asking for an explanation of the laws we should reflect on what happened before the Big Bang that marked the origin of the physical universe. The Big Bang is perhaps the last refuge of the God of the gaps. Even people who reject the idea of an interventionist God will often claim: "Something must have caused the Big Bang in the first place!" They conjecture that a preexisting God made the laws at some moment in time before the universe began, or perhaps at the moment of creation.

Unfortunately this betrays a complete misunderstanding of the nature of time and causation as understood in modern physics and cosmology. The usual concept of a cause requires the existence of time. The idea of a Creator who exists within time for all eternity, and then suddenly makes a universe at some arbitrary moment, was rejected long ago by St. Augustine of Hippo.[3] He insisted that "the world was made with time and not in time." In other words, time itself is part of creation.

Augustine's suggestion meshes well with modern physics. Einstein showed that time is part of the physical universe, and closely interwoven with space and matter. So any scientific explanation for how the universe as a whole originated has to explain how time came into existence. The Big Bang theory attempts to do this by providing a physical mechanism to enable space, time and matter to originate from nothing.[4] Although the theory exists only in outline, it already demonstrates well enough that the universe could have come into existence spontaneously without violating the laws of physics. There is no need for a divine act, or suspension of the laws, to explain the Big Bang. However, it would be wrong to say that the laws of physics to which one appeals to explain the Big Bang came into existence *with* the universe (or for that matter after it), for one could not then appeal to those laws to *explain* the origin of the universe.

Also, it is a category mistake to compare abstract mathematical laws with the physical universe itself. These are not two "things" that must both originate in time somehow. The laws are *descriptions* of physical things, not objects to be created at some moment. The laws transcend space and time; they have an abstract timeless existence, and are in some sense more fundamental than the universe they seek to describe, as indeed they must be if they are to account for how the universe originated from nothing in the first place.

Science has therefore shown that questions such as What happened before the Big Bang? or What caused the Big Bang? are in fact meaningless. Stephen Hawking has remarked that it is a bit like asking what lies to the north of the north pole.[5] The answer is, nothing, not because there is some mysterious Land of Nothing there, but because the place in question simply does not and cannot exist, by definition. By the same token, the time before the Big Bang did not exist. There was no "before."

The lesson seems to be clear. The concept of God as a cosmic magician, pre-existing within time, creating a universe at some moment, then watching it unfold largely unassisted, but prodding it fitfully on rare occasions, is both scientifically and theologically repugnant. Given the laws of physics, the universe can look after itself, including its own origination in a Big Bang. Augustine sought to place God outside of time altogether, regarding him as the sustainer and guarantor of physical existence of the universe at all times. This became the dominant view among Christian theologians, some of whom preferred to treat God not so much as *a* being, but rather as being-itself. Contrary to popular belief, the Christian notion of "creation" is not about God's manipulative role in the origin of the universe, but refers to the existence of the universe being grounded in God at all times.

This brings me back to the problem of the laws of physics and their provenance. A good way to approach such metaphysical issues is to ask, Given that the laws could have been otherwise, is there anything special or remarkable or felicitous about the actual (as opposed to the many possible alternative) laws? The answer, most definitely, is yes, in several respects.

Nature Includes Chance, Indeterminism, Creativity, and Life

The biologist Jacques Monod has stressed that nature is an amalgam of chance and necessity.[6] If nature were all chance there would be total chaos and the world would not be rational and coherent (as it is). If it were all necessity (that is, determined in its every detail by fixed laws) then there would be no genuinely new physical systems and processes, no freedom or complexity. The actual laws of the universe permit an exquisite mix of chance and necessity. There is enough lawfulness to produce a unitary, coherent, organized whole—that which we call "the universe"—without rigidly fixing everything in advance. The result is a richness and diversity that may in some sense be the best of all possible worlds.[7] It permits human freedom and creativity as part of a wider freedom and creativity in nature. Stuart Kauffman has argued that complex systems have a tendency to evolve at "the edge of chaos," with enough law to guard against descent into cosmic anarchy, and enough chance (or chaos) to provide opportunities for novelty to evolve.[8] Laws that permit both determinism and indeterminism in such a felicitous mix are likely to be very special in their form. Any old ragbag of laws won't do.

Indeterminism occurs at the subatomic level in the form of quantum uncertainty. This has the most crucial implication for the science/theology discussion because it is to quantum physics that cosmologists appeal to explain the spontaneous origin of the universe. As I mentioned above, there exists the outline of a theory that permits the universe to come into being from nothing, entirely naturally. The sudden origination of a physical entity where none existed before may be counterintuitive, but it is familiar to physicists. Laboratory experiments often produce particles of matter where none existed before, via quantum processes. An extrapolation of this quantum principle (albeit a huge one!) leads to the possibility of space and time also originating in this manner. However, laws of physics that permit a universe to come into existence spontaneously are very remarkable in form, depending crucially on that exquisite mix of chance and necessity I referred to above. Again, any old laws won't do.

Creation amounted to much more than a Big Bang! In a sense, the universe that "got created" was actually rather bland: just a uniform soup of subatomic particles, or possibly even expanding empty space and little else. All the richness and diversity of physical forms and systems that characterise the universe today have emerged since the beginning in an extended chronology of self-organizing processes. So nature has never ceased to be creative.[9]

The creativity of nature depends on a number of special properties of matter and energy that are only recently being elucidated. A new science—the science of complexity—is revealing the way in which many physical systems have an innate tendency to leap spontaneously into new more complex and/or more organized states. A simple example is the so-called Benard instability.[10] Heat a pan of water from below, and its initially featureless and uniform state will suddenly give rise to an orderly pattern of convective flow. If the experiment is done carefully, the convection currents form into a systematic pattern of hexagons. Similar self-organizing and self-complexifying phenomena are observed in chemistry, astronomy, biology and even economics. So the laws of physics not only bring the universe into existence from nothing, they permit it to self-organize and self-complexify to the point where something truly remarkable happens.

At a sufficient level of organization and complexity, a new phenomenon emerges in the universe: life. Scientists are still ignorant of how or where life originated. Most likely some form of chemical self-assembly occurred in a broth of chemicals somewhere—possibly deep beneath the Earth's crust.[11] Opinions differ sharply about how probable were the chemical steps leading up to life. A majority of biologists supposes that random molecular shuffling was responsible. If so, then the odds against life forming were super-astronomical.[12] Even if a molecular soup covered every planet in the observable universe there is negligible likelihood that life would happen twice in the age of the universe by crude chance. If this conventional view is correct, we would be forced to concur with Jacques Monod that we finally know conclusively that we are alone in "the universe's unfeeling immensity."[13]

An alternative view is that life is the result of an extended process of self-organization and self-complexification, that hugely shortened the odds.[14] In chemistry and physics, self-organization can cause a featureless system to leap spontaneously, with remarkable facility, into an apparently very unusual state of organized complexity. It is conceivable that a chain of chemical self-organizing processes can channel matter in the direction of life, fast-tracking it to states of ever greater organizational complexity until Darwinian processes could start to assist. In this way, life would be seen not as a chemical freak—a stupendously improbable accident that just happened to occur in an insignificant corner of the cosmos—but as part of the natural outworking of the basic laws of the universe. It would imply that life is a *fundamental*, and not an *incidental*, aspect of nature.[15] If, as I contend, the universe is *about* something—that is, if there is something like a cosmic "purpose"—then the question of whether life is merely a chemical freak or, by contrast, whether it is in some sense "expected," is crucial. A purposeful universe that generates life "naturally" is one in which life (and by extension *Homo sapiens*) can be regarded as part of that "purpose." A test of this position is, therefore, whether life exists elsewhere in the universe, or whether it is confined to our local region.

"Yes" to Extraterrestrial Life and Cosmic Purpose

In regard to extraterrestrial life, the recent excitement about the possibility of life on Mars is, most unfortunately, likely to be a red herring. The same cosmic impact mechanism that brought the Mars rock, with its putative fossil microorganisms, to Earth could also convey live organisms from Mars to Earth and Earth to Mars.[16] Life probably existed on Earth 3.8 billion years ago, when the planets were still suffering intense bombardment by asteroids and planetesimals. Huge quantities of rocky debris would have been ejected into space, much of it eventually being swept up by other planets. We know that microbes can thrive deep inside rock, so it seems inevitable that planetary cross-contamination occurred. Thus the existence of life on Mars could not be used to argue that life has happened twice in the solar system, unless martian and terrestrial life were radically different biochemically. In spite of this, it is possible that we may one day obtain evidence for microbial life that has arisen independently of life on Earth. This would dramatically confirm the existence of bio-friendly laws of nature and confirm the claim that life is a fundamental cosmic phenomenon. Again, any old laws won't do to make the universe bio-friendly. Only laws of a very special form will canalize and encourage matter to self-organize in the highly specific way needed for life to emerge. (One aspect of this specialness has been much commented upon under the topic of the so-called anthropic principle.[17]) To establish that the universe is teeming with life would be a strong pointer to a meaningful universe, but only so long as panspermia[18] can generally be ruled out.

After several billion years of evolution, life has given rise to consciousness and intelligence and beings like ourselves who have come to make sense of the world through science and reasoning; beings who have developed mathematics—the key to the universe. In this way, the most complex system we know (the human brain) supports mental activity that meshes with the most basic aspect of the universe—its mathematical laws. The laws have given rise to a system that can comprehend the same laws that produced it. Again however, the significance of this amazing consonance depends crucially on whether evolution on Earth is totally blind, or in some sense preordained. If intelligence and consciousness are simply evolutionary freaks, like eyebrows or jawbones, we might well argue that our mental powers are purely incidental and our ability to comprehend the universe through science and mathematics is purely coincidental. But if the emergence of intelligence and consciousness are an inevitable outcome of a law-like evolutionary trend—a continuation of the canalization of matter towards greater organizational complexity implied by the theory of self-organization—then once again we could view ourselves as products of a universe that is not only bio-friendly, but mind-friendly too. Intelligent life would then have a truly cosmic significance.

Biologists are strongly aligned behind the former position: evolution is totally blind, there are no preordained goals, teleology is anathema.[19] Darwinian random mutation and natural selection is the only mechanism responsible for evolutionary change. Self-organization, which biologists concede might play a role in the prebiotic phase, is supposed to obligingly vanish as soon as Darwinian processes get going. Wipe out life on Earth and rerun the movie, and intelligence/consciousness would almost certainly never happen the next time around, they say. Similarly, we should have no serious expectation that intelligent life exists anywhere else in the universe. So again, the search for extraterrestrial life takes on a new significance. If we were to discover, perhaps through the Search for Extraterrestrial Intelligence (SETI) program, that we are after all *not* alone,[20] then it would provide powerful circumstantial evidence for a purposeful universe, and that the emergence of life and consciousness were part of a trend towards complexity that is written into the laws of the universe in a basic way. Those commentators and scientists who carelessly assume that the universe must teem with intelligent life forms are seriously misjudging how unlikely ET is according to conventional Darwinian evolutionary theory, and how profoundly teleological and anti-Darwinian the discovery of such intelligent life forms would be. Such a discovery would therefore change our world view more drastically than the findings of Copernicus, Darwin and Einstein put together. It would shatter the oft-repeated claim about the pointlessness of physical existence.[21]

Atheists Wriggle at Absurdity

I hope I have convinced the reader that we do not live in any old universe, but one that is ruled by a set of remarkably ingenious and felicitous laws, and one in which human beings might well turn out to be a fundamental part. We are not at the center of the universe or at the pinnacle of God's creation, but neither are we insignificant: We are the product of very special laws.

How do atheists respond to these arguments? How do they answer the question of where the ingenious and felicitous lawlike order in nature comes from? In my experience most atheists wriggle uncomfortably at this point. Having insisted that everything in the world can be explained in terms of natural laws, when it comes to the origin of the laws themselves a mental backflip is performed: the system of laws must simply be accepted as a brute fact, they say. The laws exist reasonlessly. At rock bottom, the universe is absurd.

The glaring contradiction in this argument is that it attempts to ground a logical and rational world in cosmic absurdity. To escape this trap, some atheists resort to the cosmic selection theory, according to which our universe is merely one among an infinity of different universes.[22] Only in a tiny fraction of these parallel realities will the laws and conditions favor biology and conscious beings. It is then no surprise that we live in such an ordered universe: we could not survive in most of the others.

The trouble with the cosmic selection theory is that it requires an infinity of unseen universes just to explain the one we do see. In this respect it is scarcely an improvement on theism, with its hypothesis of an unseen God. Moreover, the theory may explain why we observe the laws we do, but it does not explain why there are universes and laws of some sort in the first place.

Perhaps the most telling argument against the many universes theory is that the degree of lawfulness we observe in our universe is far more stringent than is necessary for life. The extraordinary regularities observed in the subatomic realm, for example, have no obvious connection with biology. To take an example, the law of conservation of electric charge is a basic law of physics. If it were grossly violated, so that—for instance—electrons had wildly fluctuating charges, then stable atoms (and hence chemistry as we know it) would be impossible. Life would be most unlikely in such a universe. So a gross violation of the law of electric charge would certainly be life-threatening. However, a small violation wouldn't matter as far as life is concerned. In fact, we know from experiment that the charge on the electron is constant to better than one part in a billion. This is far more stringent than life requires; fluctuations of that order would be largely insignificant at the level of chemistry. So it cannot be the existence of life that selects such a stringent law. As the cosmic selection theory is based on randomness, simple statistics make a stark prediction: the observed order in nature is overwhelmingly likely to be the minimum amount required for life to exist. The fact that there is a far *greater* degree of order observed in nature shows that there must be additional principles of order over and above any crude random bio-selection principle.

Theists Need to Ask: Who Made God?

However, if the atheist is struggling when it comes to ultimate questions, the theist is no better off. Simply declaring that God made the world and selected a judicious set of laws offers no real explanation at all. It also invites the question of who, or what, made God. Unless one can say why God exists, and how God goes about imposing an order on nature, the explanation is vacuous. Since one corollary of the Christian tenet of *creatio ex nihilo* is that God could have made a different universe, the problem of why God made *this* universe is acute. If the choice is arbitrary, we are back with cosmic absurdity. On the other hand, if the choice is determined by God's personal nature, then what decides that nature? Might God have been different too?

If God is unique, then God's nature is necessarily as it is, and therefore God's creation is inevitable. But if the universe is inevitable, why do we need God at all? Thus both atheistic and theistic arguments collapse in a bewildering melee of contradictions once we attempt to go beyond the natural world and ask what lies behind physical existence. The problem always occurs when linear reasoning is applied to explanation. Any chain of reasoning has to start somewhere, with certain facts accepted as given, be it God, the universe, the laws of physics, or some logical principle.

Is the Universe Absurd or Purposeful?

In my opinion the key issue is not which abstract metaphysical argument—theism or atheism—is the more cogent, but whether the universe as revealed by science has a place for meaning and purpose (I am aware that these are loaded words that need a careful discussion, which for reasons of space I cannot give here). That is the crux of the matter. Do we live in a universe that arose for no reason, which consists of nothing more than a collection of mindless particles moved by blind and purposeless forces towards a meaningless final state? Or is there more to it than that—something deeper, something significant? In short, is the universe ultimately an absurdity, or is it *about* something? I know of no better way of addressing these questions than through pursuing our scientific investigations in a spirit of humility and openness.

Notes

1. Stephen Hawking, *Is the End in Sight for Theoretical Physics?* Lucasian Chair Inaugural Address (Cambridge: Cambridge University Press, 1980).
2. Heinz Pagels, *The Cosmic Code* (New York: Bantam, 1983).
3. St. Augustine of Hippo, *Confessions*, Book 12, Ch. 7.
4. Paul Davies, *The Mind of God* (New York: Simon & Schuster, 1992); Stephen Hawking, *A Brief History of Time* (New York: Bantam, 1988).
5. Hawking, *Brief History*.
6. Jacques Monod, *Chance and Necessity* (New York: Knopf, 1971).
7. Paul Davies, *The Mind of God* (New York: Simon & Schuster, 1992), Ch. 7.
8. Stuart Kauffman, *At Home in the Universe* (Oxford: Oxford University Press, 1995).
9. Paul Davies, *The Cosmic Blueprint* (New York: Simon & Schuster, 1987).
10. Ilya Prigogine and Isabelle Stengers, *Order out of Chaos* (London: Heinemann, 1984), Ch. 5.
11. Paul Davies, *The Fifth Miracle* (New York: Simon & Schuster, forthcoming).
12. Bernd-Olaf Kuppers, *Information and the Origin of Life* (Cambridge, Mass.: MIT Press, 1990), Ch. 6.
13. Monod, *Chance and Necessity*.
14. Kauffman, *At Home in the Universe*.
15. Paul Davies, *Are We Alone?* (New York: Basic Books, 1995).
16. Paul Davies, "The Transfer of Viable Microorganisms Between Planets," in *Evolution of Hydrothermal Ecosystems on Earth (And Mars?)*, Ciba Foundation Symposium 202 (New York: Wiley, 1996), pp. 304–317.
17. John Barrow and Frank Tipler, *The Anthropic Cosmological Principle* (Oxford: Clarendon Press, 1986).
18. Svante Arrhenius, *Worlds in the Making* (London: Harper, 1908), Ch. 8; Fred Hoyle and Chandra Wickramasinghe, *Our Place in the Cosmos* (London: Dent, 1993).
19. Richard Dawkins, *The Blind Watchmaker* (New York: Norton, 1987).
20. Davies, *Are We Alone?*
21. Steven Weinberg, *The First Three Minutes* (London: Andre Deutsch, 1977), p. 149.
22. Lee Smolin, *The Life of the Cosmos* (London: Orion Books 1997).

Chapter Five

Does the "God Who Acts" Really Act in Nature?

ROBERT JOHN RUSSELL

> *The "mighty acts" (Ps. 145:4), the "wondrous deeds" (Ps. 40:5), the "wonderful works" (Ps. 107:21) of God are the fundamental subject matter of biblical history, and the object of biblical faith is clearly the One who has acted repeatedly and with power in the past and may be expected to do so in the future.*
>
> —**Gordon D. Kaufman**[1]

> *[T]he Bible is a book descriptive not of the acts of God but of Hebrew religion. . . . [It] is a book of the acts Hebrews believed God might have done and the words he* [sic] *might have said had he done and said them—but of course we recognize he did not.*
>
> —**Langdon Gilkey**[2]

At the core of Christian faith and praxis lies the prayer Jesus taught his disciples, centered around these supplications: "Thy kingdom come, thy will be done on earth as it is in heaven." These requests were intelligible in the New Testament era, even if they were extraordinarily challenging to personal faith because of the sacrifices demanded by discipleship. But we live in the twentieth century, where their challenges are amplified almost beyond bearing. What could these supplications mean—how could they possibly make sense, let alone be central to the truth of Christian faith—given our context, which is shaped by at least five features?

1. scientific cosmology, with its fifteen billion-year-old universe whose vastness challenges our imagination and whose uniform secularity

makes any differentiated conception of creation ("heaven and earth") almost inconceivable;

2. the reductionist, materialist and determinist philosophy of nature which held sway during the massive theological developments of the eighteenth and nineteenth centuries and which, by portraying nature in terms of a closed causal web, undercut an integrated understanding of human or divine action in nature;
3. the real and striking divergences in truth claims of the world religions, which seem to undercut any normative epistemology for each of them, including Christianity's language about a universal reign of God on earth;
4. the pervasive presence and destructive consequences of patriarchical conceptions of divine (and human) power in the biblical and theological tradition associated with "kingdom" language, demanding of us a renewed emphasis on divine immanence and the inclusion of feminist language about God's actions in and through the world;
5. the immeasurable cost of human evil and natural peril plaguing the world this century, where the immensity and depravity of human wickedness empowered by almost unimaginable technological power has wreaked desolation and genocide and threatened nuclear nightmare, where the ecosystem is threatened with massive extinctions due to human greed, where the extent of "natural evil" looms ever larger as we recognize the billion year old history of evolutionary nature "red in tooth and claw?" The challenges to the intelligibility of the Christian faith are truly fundamental today, especially for those for whom there is little solace in a Kantian, an existentialist, or a neoorthodox solution, or in the reduction of faith to personal or social praxis/liberation, all of which relegates theology to a cultural ghetto removed from mainstream intellectual life.

The very modest task of this chapter is to point to one part of this overall picture, that of the intelligibility of divine action in light of the natural sciences and non-reductive epistemology. It now seems that contemporary physics, cosmology, evolutionary biology, and the psychological and neurosciences, together with recent moves in post-modern, holist philosophy, actually provide new modes of reflection on nature which allow Christians to talk coherently about God's action not only in human life but in the "immense journey" of evolution, as Loren Eisley so beautifully put it, stretching back over three billion years on earth, back even to the beginning of the universe in the Big Bang. Moreover, God's action can be understood in a non-interventionist way if the case can be made that nature is intrinsically open and that "top-down" and "whole-part" as well as "bottom-up" causality are at work in complex biological systems like us. I find recent efforts in this direction promising and deserving of further pursuit and broader recognition.

These efforts presuppose that theology and science are entering into a new relationship of mutual creative modification. Like any good partnership, which honors asymmetries and boundaries but recognizes underlying internalized relationships, each side will learn from the interaction, finding value added to their own research programs and a common orientation to the human community. Rather than remaining locked in two separate worlds, or draining public credibility in unseemly and unnecessary conflict, a new, more consonant relationship between theology and science is essential to both sides.

For the past two to three centuries, we were given a choice between two understandings of special providence: (1) as the objective acts of God in nature and history to which we respond—but these acts can only be understood as divine *interventions* into the natural and historical world, or (2) as our subjective response to God's acts—but these acts must be understood as *uniformly the same* in all events. My thesis is that this assumption no longer holds and we now have a third option. The old choice was based on classical physics and modern, reductionist philosophy. Today, because of changes in the natural sciences, including quantum physics, genetics, evolution, and the mind/brain problem, and because of changes in philosophy, including the move from reductionism to holism and the legitimacy of including whole/part and top/down analysis, *we can now understand special providence as the objective acts of God in nature and history and we can understand these acts in a non-interventionist manner consistent with science.* Whether God did, or does, act in specific instances remains an open question, of course, but it can no longer be ruled out automatically by the charge of interventionism. In short we can begin to do what we thought was impossible for over one hundred years: Believe credibly that God may really have done some of the "mighty acts" to which the Bible testifies. Gordon Kaufman may be right in the passage quoted above, and the defeat Langdon Gilkey reports may be replaced by a new theological paradigm! The "strange world of the Bible" might, in a surprising way, be the real world after all!

In what follows, I will survey a variety of research proposals being pursued actively today. These include the works of individual scholars as well as a very promising collaborative project. I will conclude with a recommendation on which are the most promising and deserving of continued programmatic and financial support. Take this chapter as a report from the frontiers of the problem, where pitfalls abound, blind alleys loom, but progress is actually being made, in giving credible support to the kerygma of faith that God acts as creator and redeemer in the world God so loves.

Historical Perspectives

We pick up the story of how divine action is conceptualized in general, and special providence in particular, at the midpoint of the twentieth century.[3] The scene is the deep chasm running through both Protestant and Roman Catholic theologies between what can broadly be referred to as liberal and conservative voices. Does God really do anything new in the world, or is it all just our response to God's uniform action? The importance of the question should not be underestimated, nor the difficulty of answering it convincingly.

The notion of God's acting in the world is central to the biblical witness. From the call of Abraham and the exodus from Egypt to the birth, ministry, death and raising of Jesus and the founding of the church at Pentecost, God is represented as making new things happen.[4] Through these "mighty acts," God creates and saves.

Belief in divine providence continued relatively intact, though deployed (not unproblematically[5]) in many and varied forms, throughout the Patristic period, the Middle Ages, and well into the Protestant Reformation. Questions about human freedom and the reality of evil were seen more as problems requiring serious theological attention than as reasons for abandoning belief in God's universal agency.

The rise of modern science in the seventeenth century and Enlightenment philosophy in the eighteenth, however, led many to reject the traditional view of providence. Newtonian mechanics depicted a causally closed universe with little, if any, room for God's *special* action in specific events—and then only by intervention. A century later, Pierre Simon Laplace combined the determinism of Newton's equations with epistemological and metaphysical reductionism to portray all of nature as an impersonal mechanism. David Hume challenged the arguments for God as first cause and as designer. In response, Immanuel Kant constructed a "critical philosophy" in which religion lies not in our knowing (the activity of pure reason) but in our sense of moral obligation (the activity of practical reason). The effect was to separate the domains of science and religion into "two worlds," a move which was to have an immeasurable effect on Christian theology.

Theology in the nineteenth century underwent a fundamental questioning not only of its contents and structure, but even of its method. Arguably the century's most influential figure, Friedrich Schleiermacher responded to Kant by relocating religion in personal piety, the feeling of absolute dependence. Schleiermacher understood God's relation to the world in terms of universal divine immanence; the result was to collapse the distinction between creation and providence. As for miracle, this is ". . . simply the religious name for event. Every event, even the most natural and usual, becomes a miracle, as soon as the religious view of it can be the dominant."[6]

In the late nineteenth century, debates over Darwinism added to the theological doubt concerning providence, causing many to abandon any notion of divine action in nature.[7]

Protestant theology in the first half of the twentieth century was largely shaped by Karl Barth and thematized around the God who is "wholly other." Recognizing that a religion founded in the subjective can lead to the critiques of a Feuerbach or a Freud, Barth and his followers held fast to the objective action of God in creating and redeeming the world.[8] The "God who acts" continued as a hallmark of the ensuing "biblical theology" movement in the 1940s and 1950s.[9]

But do Barthian neoorthodoxy and the biblical theology movement succeed in producing a credible account of divine action? In his well-known 1961 article quoted at the head of this chapter, Langdon Gilkey forcefully argued that they do not. According to Gilkey, neoorthodoxy is an unhappy composite of biblical/orthodox language and liberal/modern cosmology. It attempts to distance itself from liberal theology by retaining biblical language about God acting through wondrous events and by viewing revelation as including an objective act. Yet, like liberalism, it accepts the modern premise that nature is a closed causal system, as depicted by classical physics. The result is that, whereas orthodoxy used language univocally, neoorthodoxy uses language at best analogically, at worst, equivocally.[10]

With the failure of neoorthodoxy to account satisfactorily for divine action, we find ourselves at the heart of the problem which this chapter seeks to redress: the deep chasm between liberals and conservatives over the problem of divine action. Given the scientific account of a closed, mechanical universe and modern reductionist philosophy which says that the parts determine the whole, it seems as though there are but two options: Either God intervenes objectively in special events by breaking or suspending the laws of nature (the "conservative" approach), or God acts uniformly in all events, though subjectively we respond in different ways to some than to others (the "liberal" approach.)[11] Is any other option possible?

The Center of the Doctrine of Providence

Let us sharpen the problem theologically by briefly clarifying its context: The problem of divine action lies at the heart of the doctrine of providence.[12] The *doctrine of providence* presupposes a doctrine of creation, but adds significantly to it.[13] (This point is not shared with process theology, but I intend to include process theology in the typology; I shall defer further remarks to the section below that deals with process thinkers.) If creation stresses that God is the cause of the existence of all that is, providence stresses that God is the cause of the meaning and purpose of all that is. God not only creates but guides and directs the universe towards the fulfilling of God's purposes.

These purposes are mostly hidden to us, though they may be partially seen in the course of natural and historical events. The way God achieves them is also hidden. Only in the eschatological future will God's action throughout the history of the universe be fully revealed (1 Cor. 13:12).

General providence refers to God's universal action in guiding all events; *special providence* refers to God's specific action in particular events. The traditional warrant for the distinction lies in the fact that convictions about providence tend to arise in the context of particular salvific moments in personal life and history, and are thus most readily understood in terms of special providence.

Should special providence be understood primarily in *subjective terms* as our response to God's uniform and undifferentiated action, or in *objective terms* as our response to God's particular action in special events? As we saw above, this question divided liberal (and existentialist) theologies from conservative theologies over the past century. Rudolf Bultmann, Gordon Kaufman and Maurice Wiles are important representatives of the subjectivist interpretation.[14] Charles Hodge, Donald Bloesch, and Millard Erickson take the objectivist view.[15]

The question then is whether or not we are right to call these events "special" because we are actually responding to God's distinctive action in, together with and through them: Is subjective response based on objective divine action? This point can be made even more sharply: Is it the case that, had God not acted in a special way in a particular event, that event would not have occurred precisely the way it did occur? To quote once again the inimitable Gilkey, "for those of faith [the act of God] must be objectively or ontologically different from other events. Otherwise, there is no mighty act, but only our belief in it. . . . Only an ontology of events specifying what God's relation to ordinary events is like, and thus what his relation to special events might be, could fill the now empty analogy of mighty acts. . . . "[16]

To summarize, the essence of the debate over the meaning of special providence is the question whether God acts differently in these occasions than in those falling under the rubric of general providence. For those who take a subjective view, special providence tends to be absorbed into general providence and the latter is usually blended in with creation to give a single undifferentiated view of divine action. For those who hold for objective special providence, our response to specific events or experiences is based on God's special action in these events and experiences.

Objective Special Providence and Intervention

Since the Enlightenment, the idea of objective special providence has seemed to entail belief in divine intervention: for God to act in particular events, God must intervene in nature, violating or at least suspending the laws of nature. It cannot be stressed too strongly that the cause of this perceived linkage between objective special providence and intervention was the combination of mechanistic physics and reductionistic philosophy. If the physical world is a causally-closed, deterministic system, and if the behavior of the world as a whole is ultimately reducible to that of its physical parts, the action of a free agent—whether human or divine—must entail a violation of natural processes.[17] Thus, though disagreeing on practically everything else, most liberals, existentialists, neoorthodox and conservatives took for granted the link between objective special providence and intervention.[18] Thus by and large the choice has been either to affirm objective special providence at the cost of an interventionist and, in some extreme cases, an anti-scientific theology, or abandon objective special providence at the cost of a scientifically irrelevant and, in many cases, a privatized theology. In this light, a third option is crucial.

While twentieth century theology wrestled with the inheritance of mechanistic science, science itself was undergoing a revolution of tremendous consequences. By the close of the nineteenth century, classical physics was increasingly challenged by new fundamental discoveries. During the first decades of the twentieth century, classical physics was replaced by two new theories which were to drastically alter our understanding of space, time, matter and causality: special relativity and quantum mechanics. In that same period, the infinite and static cosmology of Newton was replaced by the expanding Big Bang universe of Einstein, while the study of classical systems by thermodynamics and chaos theory was shedding new light on the spontaneous emergence of order out of disorder.[19] A case can now be made that nature, at least as understood by quantum physics and perhaps in other areas of the natural sciences, is not the closed causal mechanism of Newtonian science. Instead, it is more like an open, temporal process with the ontology of "Swiss cheese"—one in which the genuine, material effects of human and even divine agency are at least conceivable.

At the same time, the philosophical climate has been undergoing its own enormous shift. Although the term "postmodern" carries a stunning variety of meanings, in most cases it includes a rejection of the reductionist epistemology of the modern period and its replacement with a holist philosophy. As we shall see, this will includes such categories as "supervenience," "top-down" and "whole-part" causality along with "bottom-up" causality. It is the combined moves in philosophy and in the natural sciences that set up the possibility for what I am calling "noninterventionist objective special providence."

Nevertheless, what still seems astonishing is that, while an exponential increase and radical transformation of our scientific knowledge was happening worldwide, the theological community of the twentieth century doggedly pursued strategies designed to cope with a mechanistic physics now long abandoned, and in the process it failed by and large (Teilhard and process theology being notable exceptions) to recognize these changes, let alone their significance. As we shall see, the apex of the theological debate over divine action—can God act objectively in special events without intervening in nature?—is precisely the point where these changes in science are most promising, and it is only now, near the end of this astonishing century, that these connections are being made by theologians.

Noninterventionist Objective Special Divine Action

In light of contemporary, post-Newtonian science and postmodern philosophy, I believe we can construct a new view of special providence which holds both that God acts in the world objectively, and yet that such action is not by intervening in or suspending the laws of nature.[20] I call this idea "noninterventionist objective special divine action." Much of the current discussion in the field of theology and science regarding divine action now turns on this possibility.

In the following pages, we turn first to a philosophical justification of this position in terms of postmodern holism. In principle, we would want to consider both top-down and whole-part arguments as well as bottom-up arguments in hopes of eventually constructing a complete, bottom-up and top-down account of agency. For the sake of brevity, however, we will focus strictly on our primary concerns: quantum physics, bottom-up causality, and the realization of the intentions of free agents in nature. We suggest a specific example in the domain of genetics and evolution, ending with some challenges to the proposal and some responses to them.[21]

Postmodern Holism

According to Nancey Murphy, we stand at the end of the modern period in philosophy, and "the good news is that all of the philosophical positions that have so limited theological options have themselves run into insurmountable obstacles and new positions have been proposed in their place."[22] She draws specifically on Karl Popper, W. V. O. Quine, Imre Lakatos and Alasdair MacIntyre in support of a "historicist-holism" which promises "a softening of the distinctions between liberal and conservative theologians."[23]

How then does this affect the problem of divine action? Murphy begins with the sciences as hierarchically ordered, but from an emergent, not a reductionist, view which she calls "nonreductive physicalism." According to scientists such as Silvan Schweber, Arthur Peacocke and Neil A. Campbell, there is growing recognition within both physics and biology of top-down, as well as bottom-up, analysis. Top-down causality can be described philosophically in terms of *supervenience*, in which the context at the higher level determines the relation between a higher-level property, such as moral valence, and a lower-level property, such as physical violence.[24] We are thus "free to speculate that the totality of natural laws, comprising all levels in the natural-scientific and social-scientific hierarchy, are together incomplete. . . . [D]ivine acts may need to be recognized for a complete account of the direction of natural and human history."[25]

But is a contextual analysis sufficient to guarantee top-down *causality*? In a forthcoming book, Philip Clayton defends an even tougher form of supervenience, called "strong supervenience." Here the upper level, though emergent out of the lower, includes causal interactions that are not reducible to those of the lower level.[26] I think Clayton is moving in the necessary direction, and I would add to the argument that without indeterminism at the lower levels, it is hard to see how mental agency is physically enacted in the world.

What then of top-down or whole-part interactions? Murphy endorses the approach offered by Arthur Peacocke, who describes God's action in a strictly top-down manner on the universe as a whole. Murphy also endorses the need for bottom-up causality, and we will turn with her to quantum indeterminism as a possible basis for it.

Quantum Physics and the Indeterministic Interpretation

In the traditional Aristotelian sense, as incorporated in the natural sciences from classical physics to evolutionary biology, a chance event is the unanticipated juxtaposition of two unrelated causal trajectories, such as a car crash, the casting of dice, the motion of chromosomes in a thermal gradient, fluctuations in chaotic systems, changes in the weather, earthquakes and volcanic activity, movements of the ocean and the surf, genetic recombination when cells divide, and so on. Chance so viewed is depicted mathematically by Boltzmann statistics (the familiar "bell-curve") and pervades the natural sciences. We speak of this kind of chance when we do not know, or prefer to ignore, the underlying causal factors—while believing they are there in principle. We could in principle give a complete causal—i.e., deterministic—description of natural processes from the cells to galaxies; we chose a statistical description merely out of convenience.[27]

Instead of limiting chance to epistemology, one might argue that some natural processes are, in fact, *ontologically* indeterministic. Here the claim would be that the total set of natural conditions affecting the process, that is the total set of conditions which science can discover and describe through its equations, are *insufficient* in principle to determine the precise outcome of the process. The future is ontologically open, influenced, of course, but *under*determined by the factors of nature acting in the present.

The statistics found in our equations are *not* just a shorthand for inordinately detailed calculations of underlying causal processes. Instead they indicate that there is no exhaustive set of underlying natural causes. In, through and beyond the causal conditions we can describe scientifically, things just happen.

Is chance of this sort a characteristic of nature? If one turns to the atomic and subatomic levels where quantum physics is employed, the answer may well be "yes."[28] Classical physics was enormously successful in explaining data drawn in scales ranging from the world of our everyday experience to the immense magnitudes of our galaxy (i.e., what was then the visible universe). By the 1890s, however, areas were coming under increasing scrutiny in which classical physics began to break down: black-body radiation, specific heat of metals, the optical spectrum of hydrogen, the photoelectric effect, and so on. These problems, and a profusion of phenomena discovered in the early decades of the twentieth century through new experimental procedures and devices, led to the formulation of quantum mechanics (c. 1900–1930).[29]

In the decades since then physics has progressed beyond these early formulations, developing quantum field theory, unifying the electromagnetic, weak and strong forces, and continuing currently with the search for quantum gravity. Still, scholars in physics and the philosophy of science continue to wrestle over questions about the implications of quantum mechanics. How do we understand the probabilistic features here, which are strikingly different from those of classical physics? Do theoretical terms like the wave function in any way refer to, or "picture," reality, or are they merely mathematical symbols whose only use is to help us predict the outcome of experiments? Consequently, almost a century from its beginnings, quantum physics continues to be subject to a variety of alternative interpretations.[30] Within these debates, however, there are strong arguments for interpreting quantum chance as signaling a fundamental *ontological indeterminacy* in nature.[31] From this perspective, the use of statistics in a quantum analysis is not a mere convenience to avoid a more detailed causal description. Instead a causal description of the sequence of events in time is impossible. Quantum statistics is all we can have, for there is no underlying, fully deterministic natural process.

So to summarize, science employs two categories of chance: (1) chance in the classical domain, where "chance is epistemological," i.e., the result of our ignorance of the presumably underlying deterministic processes in physical, chemical and biological systems, and, if the presumption is correct, suggestive of an underlying metaphysical determinism in the macroscopic domain; and (2) chance in the quantum domain, where (following the approach we adopt here) "chance is ontological," i.e., an indicator of an underlying metaphysical indeterminism in the atomic and sub-atomic domain.

The story is complicated further, however. There are not really two different worlds—classical and quantum—but only one world seen through two different epistemologies. Ultimately physics would attempt to understand the classical world as a result of quantum physics. (I obviously reject a thoroughgoing reductionism, in which physics would account for the entire world of human experience. Arguments by Murphy and Clayton for epistemic holism help us avoid such interdisciplinary reductionism.) In other words, the ordinary physical properties of our world, like the solidity of rock or the colors of the sky, should eventually be explained by quantum physics. Even the statistics we use to describe the classical world, the bell-curve statistics, should arise out of the statistics of quantum physics.

It turns out that quantum statistics explain both features of the classical world: the physical properties of matter and energy, and the bell-curve statistics they obey. But quantum statistics do so in a very surprising way.[32] First of all, they come in two different forms. Particles such as protons, electrons, and neutrons, what one could call the constituents of matter, are described by Fermi-Dirac statistics. The impenetrability or hardness of matter (i.e., the fact that matter is extended in space) and its chemical properties arise directly from the form of the Fermi-Dirac statistics. Particles such as photons and gravitons are described Bose-Einstein statistics. The four fundamental interactions, such as gravity and electromagnetism, and such phenomena as superconductivity and stimulated emission (for example, the laser), are the direct result of Bose-Einstein statistics. Second, both Fermi-Dirac and Bose-Einstein statistics tend towards the bell-curve mathematically when Planck's constant can be ignored. In this sense quantum statistics (in their two distinct forms) underlie and produce the fundamental properties of the classical world. One could even say metaphorically that the classical world is an artifact of the quantum world, or more precisely, that the classical world is an anthropocentric construct, however convincing to everyday experience. Indeed, the ontological hints we get from quantum physics suggest that the world is far different from what it appears to be classically. Far from being composed of "billiard balls in motion," quantum physics suggests that matter carries an irreducibly holistic and non-local or non-separable character, challenging our traditional metaphysical categories of space, time, matter and causality.

What is truly subtle here is that the bell-curve is what we would get mathematically if we started with deterministic laws. Thus it is natural to assume that the processes of nature, if described by the bell-curve as they are classically, do indeed arise from classical, deterministic laws (e.g., Newton's laws). Now what we understand is that the bell-curve is actually a mathematical approximation to the actual quantum statistics (e.g., Fermi-Dirac and Bose-Einstein), and these, as I have already suggested, can be given an indeterministic interpretation. In short, the statistics of quantum physics produce the properties of matter and energy as we experience them, including its structure, its chemical properties, the forces of nature, and so on. But more importantly they produce the statistics of classical physics which led us to conclude—*erroneously*—that the world really is mechanistic, which, we now know, it is not. [33]

Appropriating Quantum Physics Theologically

How then should we proceed to appropriate quantum physics into a philosophy of nature and into constructive theology concerning divine action? Let us anticipate some objections and cautions in advance.

Suppose physics changes; are we not risking too close a connection with theology? Actually, it is not only possible but virtually certain that quantum physics will be replaced eventually by a new theory which will most likely contain it as a "limiting case." Will this entail a return to metaphysical determinism? Clearly any answer to this would be highly speculative, since we do not yet have the new theory in place. How should this sort of historical relativity within physics affect the philosophical and theological discussions of existing theories in physics? Indeed this is a profound question lying at the heart of any conversations about "theology and science."

One response would be to refrain from such conversations, at least with theories which are at the frontier of science and open to replacement. Instead, according to the prevailing wisdom here, we should stick with proven theories. The liability of this approach is twofold: (1) We've done that already. Though enormously diverse in other ways, the broad sweep of theology in the nineteenth and twentieth centuries has consistently operated, if even implicitly, with a view of space, time, matter, and causality which is both pre-relativistic and pre-quantum mechanical. But our interest here is in constructive theology as it engages with the changes brought about in our concept of nature by the discoveries which undercut classical science. (2) Many of these theologies have been judged to have failed precisely because of this reliance on a classical ontology, as we have already seen.

The response chosen here, then, is to engage in this conversation, but in full realization of the tentativeness of the project. Clearly we must keep in mind not only the possibility that a future theory might undercut the positions taken here, but that existing alternative interpretations of quantum physics already have the potential to do so.[34] However, most scholars now agree that *any* future theory concerned with the atomic and sub-atomic realms will have to favor either non-local realism or local anti-realism. *In short, we will never return to the metaphysics of classical physics.*

I see this project as part of theological research, and as with all research, I would stress its hypothetical character. We are not seeking to validate theology but to explore the strength of a theological doctrine, special providence, in the realm of biology by means of an appropriate philosophy of nature. Our response presupposes a methodological commitment at the deepest levels of our research. We take theology as it engages with secular inquiry to be hypothetical in character, concerned to discover whether central commitments held by faith are in fact intelligible, consistent and coherent with such inquiry. We are driven, therefore, to follow out the consequences of taking radically seriously a given vein of secular work, recognizing as well its hypothetical character, and seeking to discover what can be gained while both the theological and the secular views are given their day in court. As one or both fail the test of such inquiry, we start afresh, recalling what has been learned, leaving behind what is no longer promising. This method is thus rooted in the ancient formula *fides quaerens intellectum*, which we take to be in an implicit dialectical relation to its converse formula, *intellectum quaerens fides*.

Theological Implications of Quantum Physics

In the mid-1980s, I began to explore the implications of quantum physics, and particularly Bell's theorem, for the doctrines of creation and providence.[35] I suggested that (1)we can view God as acting, in general, at the level of quantum physics to create the general characteristics and properties of the classical world, and (2) in addition we can view God as acting in particular quantum events to produce, indirectly, a specific event at the macroscopic level, one which we call an event of special providence.

The basic argument is that God acts together with nature to bring about a quantum event. Nature provides the necessary causes, but God's action together with nature constitutes the sufficient cause of the occurrence of the event. In short, and metaphorically, what one could say is that what we normally take as "nature" is in reality the activity of "God + nature."[36] Alternatively, from this perspective we really do not know what the world would be like *without* God's action. It is as much a leap of "secular" faith to view "God + nature" as just "nature" as it is for a theistic leap of faith to view "nature" as "God + nature," although this is the working assumption of modernity (and with it science). One could say that we are presented with a choice between naturalism and theism: The same evidence from science is available, but the choice of presuppositions is crucial.[37] In my view, quantum mechanics is particularly suited for a theistic interpretation—especially a trinitarian one![38]

My proposal is not meant to entail that God's action is equivalent to a natural cause, since by hypothesis, the set of natural causes is insufficient to bring the event to realization. The point becomes clearer if we think about how a quantum event occurs. However one describes such an event, it is not the result of an additional force or "push," but more like an actualization or realization of a potential quality. Heisenberg used language like this, and John Polkinghorne uses similar language today, speaking about information rather than energy. My proposal is also not meant as an argument that God acts, which I assume for theological (not scientific!) reasons, nor is it a description of the "causal joint" but only of one domain, the subatomic, in which the effects of God's action occur. We will return to this issue in more detail below.

Quantum Physics and Creation

When scholars focus on the classical world, God's action as ongoing creator is often seen as bringing order out of chaos. With a quantum perspective, we can now claim that God creates the (classical) world not by reordering its structures ("order out of chaos") but by creating the quantum processes which produce the classical world. To be more precise, we must abandon the distinction between order and chaos and recognize that classical order is a description at a higher epistemic level of quantum chaos. Thus if (quantum) chance gives (classical) order its form and structure—the texture of wood is ultimately the statistical dance of electrons and protons—then God creates (classical) order by creating (quantum) chance.

> From a theological perspective we can add to the view that God creates the universe through chance and law the claim that the order God is creating is in some sense the order of quantum chaos. Rather than saying that God creates order in place of (i.e., out of) chaos, from a quantum perspective we could say that one way God creates order is through creating the properties of chaos.[39]

This is continuous creation indeed!

It is precisely this classical world in which God can act (without intervening) in specific events, if we recognize that the classical world is not an irreducible given but a result of the quantum world. Thus the laws which describe the classical world are approximations to the laws of quantum mechanics which describe how the classical world, with its Newtonian regularity, arises directly out of the quantum world, with its two kinds of statistics. If I adopt the interpretation that these quantum statistics reflect ontological indeterminism, then I may argue that God can act together with nature to bring about all events at the quantum level, and that these events give rise to the classical world.

What about a specific event in the classical world, one which would fall under the category of objective noninterventionist divine action? Here the response is that God acts in a particular quantum event which has the potential for a macroscopic effect within the ongoing macroscopic world. God acts in all quantum events, but in some cases the effects "matter" in the classical world more than others. It turns out that there is a tremendously important case in which this kind of understanding of noninterventionist objective special providence is of critical importance, and it is precisely where the critics of Christianity have been the most vocal: neo-Darwinian evolution!

Quantum Physics, Biological Evolution, and Special Providence

Elsewhere, I extend the argument that God may be thought of as acting in a noninterventionist way in nature by exploring the role of quantum mechanics in evolutionary biology.[40] I seek to connect (1) a theological commitment to extend special divine action to include evolutionary biology, (2) a philosophical view in which we interpret quantum physics in terms of metaphysical indeterminism, and (3) a scientific claim regarding the role of quantum mechanics in genetic mutation and thus in evolution. The purpose is to explore the claim that God might be thought of as acting to achieve specific results that otherwise would not occur in the evolution of biological complexity, though *without* intervening in or violating the laws of nature.[41]

The thesis can be stated as follows: *God shapes and guides biological evolution providentially by actions whose effects occur within the quantum mechanical processes underlying specific genetic mutations.* This action is to be considered a form of objective noninterventionist special divine action. The effect of the acts of God in specific quantum events within the DNA molecule is to realize specific genetic mutations whose presence in the germ-line, amplification by replication, and expression in the phenotype, may bequeath to progeny potential adaptive advantage. In this way, and in others, God directs evolution towards God's purposes.

If the thesis is sustained, it can turn defeat into victory. One of the key reasons for the rejection of Christianity by its highly vocal critics is the charge that genetic variation in evolution is "blind" and thus anathema to God's purposes. My argument reinterprets genetic variation as essential for a noninterventionist special divine action in nature; God acts in evolution *precisely because of* and within genetic variation. Moreover, it undermines the declared reason for scientific creationism, since there is now no reason to seek to replace "atheistic" science by what is in reality religious pseudo-science. Instead we can give a robust Christian interpretation of science, showing that it is not science *per se* but its atheistic interpretation that is the real challenge for Christians. This move would also enable us *theologically* to extend the domain of God's special providence beyond human history to include the biosphere out of whose several billion years of evolution we have emerged.[42]

Answering the Critics

A number of important challenges and criticisms arise immediately, and must be met fairly. Here I can only cite them briefly:[43]

1. The proposal is not intended an explanation of how God acts, but a claim that if one believes God acts, quantum physics provides a clue as to one location or domain where that action may have an effect on the course of nature.
2. The proposal is not intended as an interventionist argument since it relies on a claim about ontological indeterminism and not epistemological ignorance. God is thought to work together with nature to bring sufficiency, but not as a natural cause *per se* (since by hypothesis these are insufficient for the task). It is also not a gaps argument in the sense that it is based on what we know from science, not on gaps in our knowledge (see Tracy below).
3. The proposal is not meant to limit scenarios of divine action to bottom-up, but it also recognizes that in fields like cosmology and in the early stages of biological evolution, God's action at the quantum level may be the only mode possible (no "tops" available!). When top-down causality and whole-part constraints are available, as in evolved complex organism, these will play a part in a combined bottom-up/top-down causal dialectic. Here I refer the reader again to the writings of Arthur Peacocke, Sallie McFague, John Polkinghorne, and process theists such as Ian Barbour.
4. For a complete defense of God acting purposefully in biology, I would have to include a discussion of the problem of time and eternity in a trinitarian theology and its relation to the discussions over temporality *vis-a-vis* special relativity. Clearly this discussion is beyond the limits of this chapter.
5. Other key topics to consider include: the "double agency" problem (how does God act while preserving and responding to human free will?) and theodicy (if God is good and God can act, why is there evil?). The latter issue is particularly acute given the enormity of pain and suffering in evolution, the fact that life evolves out of and through death and the predator/prey cycle, the fact that most mutations do not lead to selective advantage, and the fact that so much disease has its basis in the genes where, I am arguing, God does act.[44]

Further Refinements

In her essay in the book *Chaos and Complexity*, Murphy argues that the problem of divine action will only be solved by a fully revised metaphysical theory of natural causation that is both theologically adequate and consistent with science.[45] Along with creation, sustenance, providence and continuing creation, any acceptable theory of divine action must allow for objectively special divine acts. Any such theory should "explain how God and natural causes conspire to bring about the world *as we know it*" via our scientific picture of law-like regularity and the genuine randomness of quantum events, as well as our experience of free will. The contemporary understanding of nature as a non-reducible hierarchy of increasing complexity is "absolutely crucial." Here both top-down and bottom-up causality are at work.

Quantum physics provides the latter. If we reject both an epistemic and a hidden variables interpretation, then it appears as though there is no sufficient reason in nature to determine a quantum event. Such ontological indeterminism allows for a bottom-up account of divine action wherein God has no need to overrule or intervene in natural processes. In Murphy's view, all quantum events involve a combination of natural and divine causality; they are determined, though only in part and not solely, by God. God's role is in "activating or actualizing one or another of the quantum entity's innate powers at particular instants . . . these events are not possible without God's action." Thus the charges of intervention and divine determinism are also avoided. Moreover God sustains the macro-level by means of God's action at the quantum level. " . . . [T]he laws that describe the behavior of the macro-level entities . . . are indirect though intended consequences of God's direct acts at the quantum level. . . . I am proposing that the uniformity of nature is a divine artifact."[46] Here Murphy cites an essay of mine in which I argue that most of the broad, general characteristics of the macroscopic world are a function and result of the character of quantum events and God's action as creator there.[47]

Thomas Tracy has also endorsed quantum indeterminism as a route to noninterventionist special providence. In his essay in *Chaos and Complexity*[48] he reminds us of Dietrich Bonhoeffer's rejection of the use of "gaps" in our scientific knowledge as a way to talk about God. "(It is wrong) to use God as a stop-gap for the incompleteness of our knowledge. . . . (Instead) we are to find God in what we know, not in what we don't know."[49] But suppose scientific theory convinces one of the existence of causal gaps; should this be relevant to theology? Yes, says Tracy, and it would not lead to the earlier "God of the gaps" theology since that was based on explanatory gaps. Rather, with Bonhoeffer, we would be basing our theology of divine action on what we infer as the best explanation of the world's causal structure, namely that causal gaps exist in nature.[50] In so doing, we would move beyond the position taken by much of contemporary theology. Thus ". . . if we wish to affirm not only that God enacts history . . . but also that God acts in history, then there are good reasons to think that the world God has made will have an open ('gappy') structure. Note that the motivation for this claim is entirely theological."[51]

We can put conditions on these causal gaps. First, such gaps must be part of the order of nature and not arbitrary events in it; in other words, God's special action should continuously contribute to the direction of events in nature. Moreover, these events must be such that God's action "can make a difference in the course of events which follow them." Tracy thus focuses on quantum mechanics. According to Tracy, "[c]hance will be irrelevant to history if its effects, when taken together in probabilistic patterns, disappear altogether into wider deterministic regularities."[52] Thus we come to what is so far, in my opinion, the most important condition *theology* places on the kind of causal gaps we are looking for. In Tracy's words, these events must ". . . fall within the expected probabilities [and yet] have significant macroscopic effects over and above contributing to the stable properties and lawful relations of macroscopic entities." But this is precisely what quantum physics provides; witness the infamous "Schrödinger's cat" experiment, where the occurrence of a quantum event (such as a radioactive decay) triggers a Geiger counter and leads to a "life-or-death" effect on the cat! In fact, as Tracy points out, such micro-macro amplifications may be at work throughout nature.

In sum, quantum mechanics allows us to think of special divine action without God overriding or intervening in the structures of nature. God's action will remain hidden within that structure, and it will take the form of realizing one of several potentials in the quantum system, not of manipulating subatomic particles as a quasi-physical force. Moreover, we are still free to think in terms of divine action at other levels of nature, including God's interaction with humanity and God's primary act of creating and sustaining the world. Thus, ". . . if we understand God to be the creator of all that is, and if the world God has made includes indeterministic chance in its structures, then *God is the God of the gaps as well as the God of causal connection*. It is part of the theologian's task to try to understand God's relation to the former as well as to the latter."[53] Tracy closes with a key question. Does God act to determine all quantum events or merely some? He understands Murphy to take the former position, but Tracy is cautious since it can seem to lead to universal divine determinism through the higher levels of nature.[54]

Concluding Assessment

Owen Thomas begins a 1991 essay with this rather caustic comment: "Theologians continue to talk a great deal about God's activity in the world, and there continue to be only a very few who pause to consider some of the many problems involved in such talk."[55]

According to Thomas, the question of double agency still remains "the key issue in the general problem. . . . "[56] How can we assert coherently that both divine and creaturely agents are fully active in one unified event? After evaluating the current state of the discussion, Thomas's position is that one must either follow the primary/secondary path of traditional theism or the process theology approach. He asserts that if there *is* another solution to the problem, he has not heard of it, and concludes that this question should be a major focus of future discussions.

A lot has changed since 1991. An appreciation for the importance of developing an objective noninterventionist interpretation of special providence is on the rise. Neither neo-Thomism nor process theology seems strongly equipped to meet the challenge. The former is less interested in the problem when the domain is nature, and the latter offers a metaphysical system which may be significantly outmoded by changes in physics since Whitehead's work in the 1920's. Of course insights from both can be gleaned towards a new, more tentative and ongoing metaphysical approach which will learn from the ongoing and continued interactions of scientists, theologians, and philosophers as we see taking place even at the time of this essay. Moreover, a growing consensus of scholars seems to point to the importance of both non-reductive holism, at least epistemically and perhaps ontologically, as providing the philosophical structure for the case, and twentieth-century natural science as providing the material content of the case. Quantum physics, if interpreted in terms of ontological indeterminism, offers the best basis for a bottom-up strategy. Non-linear, non-equilibrium thermodynamics, cosmology, and the neurosciences offer tantalizing possibilities for bases for a top-down and/or a whole-part approach. A shared goal is to combine these approaches. It might well be that the specific events which we refer to as special providence in nature are the indirect results of divine action at both the subatomic and the cosmological levels, and those we experience as special providence/revelation are the combined result of bottom-up and top-down action in the complex matrix of the human person as psychosomatic unity. Trinitarian theology, which emphasizes the triune presence and activity of God in the world (and not just the interaction of God with the world) offers the tantalizing promise of a proleptic view of how God's action is initiated—from the future in the past/present—and may allow us to relocate special providence not strictly within the doctrine of creation but within the doctrine of new creation (and creation there too!). We may well be coming to a new period of theological reflection when we can speak about God's special providence and our response to it in full awareness and appreciation of our best understanding of nature and human nature as provided by the discoveries and theories of contemporary natural science. If so, to ignore the sciences in the doing of theology would be a tremendous step backwards, one I hope few will recommend in the future.

Notes

1. Gordon D. Kaufman, "On the Meaning of 'Act of God,'" *Harvard Theological Review* 61:175–210 (1968). This article was reprinted in Gordon D. Kaufman, *God the Problem* (Cambridge: Harvard University Press, 1972), Ch. 6, and in

Owen C. Thomas, ed., *God's Activity in the World: The Contemporary Problem* (Chico: Scholars Press, 1983), Ch. 9.

2. Langdon B. Gilkey, "Cosmology, Ontology, and the Travail of Biblical Language," *The Journal of Religion* 41 (1961), p. 197. Reprinted in Thomas, *God's Activity*, p. 198.

3. For recent accounts of divine action, see Thomas, ed., *God's Activity*. Thomas' typology is recapitulated by Arthur Peacocke in his own detailed treatment of divine action. See *Theology for a Scientific Age: Being and Becoming—Natural and Divine* (Oxford: Basil Blackwell, 1990; and second enlarged edition, London: SCM Press, 1993 and reprinted, Minneapolis: Fortress Press, 1993), chap. 9, section f, pp. 146–148. In a more recent publication, Ian Barbour offers a lucid description and creative comparison of the problem of divine action in classical theism, process theism, and their alternatives, including several types of personal agency models. See Barbour, *Religion in an Age of Science*, The Gifford Lectures 1989–1991, vol. 1 (San Francisco: HarperSanFrancisco, 1990), chap. 9. See also Thomas F. Tracy, ed., *The God Who Acts: Philosophical and Theological Explorations* (University Park, PA: Pennsylvania State University, 1994). See also Michael J. Langford in *Providence*, p. 6, and Peacocke, *Theology for a Scientific Age*, Ch. 9 (especially p. 135). In my Introduction to *Chaos and Complexity* I expanded Thomas' typology: To clarify the similarities and differences in approaches to special divine action I provided a working typology which was developed during the CTNS/Vatican Observatory research on divine action. See also my Introduction to *Chaos and Complexity.* I am grateful for extensive interaction with Nancey Murphy in developing this typology.

4. See, for example, Gen. 45:5; Job 38:22–39:30; Ps. 148:8–10; Is. 26:12; Phil. 2:12–13; 1 Cor. 12:6; 2 Cor. 3:5.

5. For example, God could be understood as the first or primary cause of all events; all natural causes are instrumental or secondary causes through which God works. God was also thought to act immediately in the world through miracles, without using or by surpassing finite causes. This view of divine action led to such problematic issues as "double agency": Can a single event issue simultaneously from two free agents (e.g., God and human agents) if each alone is sufficient to accomplish the event? If so, how does an infinite agent (God) preserve the finite freedom of a creaturely agent when they act together? It also led to the problem of theodicy: If God acts in all events and God is good, why is there so much evil in the world?

6. Friedrich Schleiermacher, *On Religion: Speeches to its Cultured Despisers* (New York: Harper Torchbook, 1958), p. 88. See also *The Christian Faith* (Edinburgh: T&T Clark, 1968), #47.3, p. 183.

7. To others, Darwinian evolution could be accommodated into theology, since they viewed God as working immanently through the very processes of nature. See "Evolution and Theology: Détente or Evasion?" in Claude Welch, *Protestant thought in the Nineteenth Century, Volume 2, 1870–1914* (New Haven: Yale University Press, 1985), Ch. 6.

8. "The Gospel is . . . not an event, nor an experience, nor an emotion—however delicate! . . . [I]t is a communication which presumes faith in the living God, and which creates that which it presumes." Karl Barth, *The Epistle to the Romans*, 6th ed. (London: Oxford University Press, 1968), p. 28.

9. See for example G. Ernest Wright, *God Who Acts: Biblical Theology as Recital* (London: SCM Press, 1952); Bernard Anderson, *Understanding the Old Testament* (Englewood Cliffs: Prentice-Hall, 1957).

10. Langdon B. Gilkey, "Cosmology, Ontology, and the Travail of Biblical Language," *The Journal of Religion* 41 (1961): 194–205.

11. I am indebted to Nancey Murphy for illuminating this issue in her recent book, *Beyond Liberalism and Fundamentalism: How Modern and Postmodern Philosophy Set the Theological Agenda* (Valley Forge: Trinity Press International, 1996).

12. For helpful introductions to the doctrine of providence, see Michael J. Langford, *Providence* (SCM Press Ltd., 1981); Julian N. Hartt, "Creation and Providence" in Peter C. Hodgson and Robert H. King, eds., *Christian Theology: An Introduction to Its Traditions and Tasks*, Second Edition, Revised and Enlarged (Philadelphia: Fortress Press, 1985).

13. The doctrine of creation asserts that the ultimate source and absolute ground of the universe is God. Without God, the universe would not exist, nor would it exist as "universe." Creation theology has typically included three related but distinct claims: (1) the universe as God's creation had a beginning; (2) the universe as God's creation depends absolutely and at every moment of its history on God for its sheer existence; and (3) the universe is the locus of God's continuing activity as creator. These have traditionally been grouped in terms of *creatio ex nihilo* (1 and 2) and *creatio continua* (3).

14. Rudolf Bultmann, *Theology of the New Testament*, Complete in One Volume, translated by Kendrick Grobel (New York: Charles Scribner's Sons, 1951/1955); *Kerygma and Myth*, ed. by H. W. Bartsch, Vol. 1, pp. 197–199; *Jesus Christ and Mythology* (New York: Charles Scribner's Sons, 1958), particularly chapter 5; Gordon D. Kaufman, *Systematic Theology: A Historicist Perspective* (New York: Charles Scribner's Sons, 1968); also the previously-cited "On the Meaning of 'Act of God'"; reprinted in *God the Problem* (Cambridge: Harvard University Press, 1972), pp. 119–147; Maurice Wiles, *God's Action in the World: The Bampton Lectures for 1986* (SCM Press:1986); "Religious Authority and Divine Action," *Religious Studies* 7 (1971), pp. 1–12, reprinted in Owen Thomas, *God's Activity*, pp. 181–194.

15. Charles Hodge, *Systematic Theology*, 3 vols. (New York: Scribner's Sons, 1891); Donald G. Bloesch, *Holy Scripture: Revelation, Inspiration and Interpretation* (Downers Grove, IL: InterVarsity Press, 1994); Millard Erickson, *Christian Theology*, Three volumes in one (Grand Rapids: Baker, 1983). I am indebted to Nancey Murphy for these references; see *Beyond Liberalism and Fundamentalism*, chapter 3.

16. Gilkey, "Cosmology, Ontology, and the Travail of Biblical Language," p. 200.

17. See for example, Peacocke, *Theology for a Scientific Age*, pp. 139–140.

18. As suggested already, various strategies were tried to circumvent the problem, with varying degrees of success. For some, Kant offered a solution: since we can never extrapolate the causal properties of things in themselves from the apparent causal properties of phenomena, we really cannot say that nature is causally closed in itself. For others, God was thought to relate strictly to the world as a whole: God "enacts history" but does not act within history. Still others relied entirely on "two

language" methods, or restricted religion to social, political, moral or spiritual areas. The result of these moves was to make science irrelevant to theology, and in turn theology irrelevant to science—and to most of the secular world in the process. Finally some took a conflict tack: If faith in providence seemed to contradict the authority of science, so much the worse for science. This "anti-science" stance surfaced dramatically in the Scopes trial of the 1920s, and it still rages today as fundamentalists challenge evolutionary science and seek to replace it with so-called "scientific creationism."

19. The story is complicated, however, by a strange turn of events. Just as physics, the bastion of realism, was increasingly viewing nature as ephemeral, open, temporal, even leading to anti-realist strategies, biology was moving from its long flirtation of vitalism onto solid mechanistic grounds. By the mid-1950s, the last evidences of those vitalist hopes that had lingered after Darwin were to vanish with the triumph of a mechanistic and reductionistic account of variation through the discovery of the molecular structure of the gene by Watson and Crick. Given the combined movements of physics and biology towards and away from mechanism and reductionism, how are we to construct a contemporary philosophy of nature so necessary to the theological engagement with science? This may well be the most challenging of all the questions facing our present-day encounter with science, certainly explaining some of the complexity of the research being pursued in "theology and science" discussions internationally.

20. If nature is actually open to alternative possibilities, and the actual direction that takes place is not determined by nature alone, then the course taken because of divine action working with nature is a kind of "intervention," though I prefer not to use this term because of its connotations of violation or suspension of the laws of nature. The point here is that God brings something to be which would not otherwise have occurred, not by changing things and processes but by actualizing potencies and possibilities. God's acts are thus a part of creation, not manipulation (see below).

21. For important insights about top-down causality and other aspects of the overall project that have been left unattended here, see the writings of Arthur Peacocke, Sallie McFague, John Polkinghorne, the Roman Catholic theologian William R. Stoeger, and the process theist Ian Barbour:

Arthur Peacocke, *Theology for a Scientific Age: Being and Becoming—Natural, Divine, and Human*, (Minneapolis: Fortress Press, 1993); also "Chance and Law in Irreversible Thermodynamics, Theoretical Biology, and Theology," in Robert John Russell, Nancey Murphy and Arthur R. Peacocke, eds., *Chaos and Complexity: Scientific Perspectives on Divine Action* (Vatican City State: Vatican Observatory Publications, and Berkeley: The Center for Theology and the natural Sciences, 1995), pp. 123–143; and "God's Interaction" in *Chaos and Complexity.* In his earlier work he adopted an embodiment model. See *Creation and the World of Science* (Oxford: Clarendon, 1979), pp. 142ff., 207; *Intimations of Reality* (Notre Dame, IN: University of Notre Dame Press, 1984), pp. 63ff., 76.

Sallie McFague, *Models of God: Theology for an Ecological, Nuclear Age* (Philadelphia: Fortress Press, 1987), pp. 69–78; and *The Body of God: An Ecological Theology* (Minneapolis: Fortress Press, 1993). See also, "Models of God for an Ecological, Evolutionary Era: God as Mother of the Universe," in *Physics, Philosophy and Theology*, pp. 249–271.

John Polkinghorne, *Science and Creation: The Search for Understanding* (Boston: Shambhala, 1989), p. 43; *Reason and Reality: The Relationship between Science and Theology* (Philadelphia: Trinity Press International, 1991). See especially Ch. 3, pp. 39, 41; "The Laws of Nature and the Laws of Physics," in Russell, *et al., Quantum Cosmology,* pp. 437–448; *The Faith of a Physicist: Reflections of a Bottom-Up Thinker*, The Gifford Lectures for 1993–4 (Princeton: Princeton University Press, 1994).pp. 67–69, 77–82. "The Metaphysics of Divine Action," in Russell, *et al., Chaos and Complexity,* pp. 147–156; *Serious Talk: Science and Religion in Dialogue* (Valley Forge: Trinity Press International, 1995), Ch. 6, esp. pp. 81–84; *Quarks, Chaos & Christianity: Questions to Science and Religion* (New York: Crossroad, 1996), pp. 65–73; *Scientists as Theologians: A Comparison of the Writings of Ian Barbour, Arthur Peacocke and John Polkinghorne* (London: SPCK, 1996), Ch. 3.

William R. Stoeger, "Contemporary Physics and the Ontological Status of the Laws of Nature" in Russell, *et al., Quantum Cosmology and the Laws of Nature*; "Describing God's Action in the World in Light of Scientific Knowledge of Reality," in Russell, *et al., Chaos and Complexity;* "The Immanent Directionality of the Evolutionary Process and Its Relationship to Teleology," in Russell, *et al., Evolution and Molecular Biology.*

Ian G. Barbour, *Religion in an Age of Science, The Gifford Lectures, Volume One* (San Francisco: Harper & Row, 1990), Ch. 8.

22. Murphy, *Beyond Liberalism and Fundamentalism,* pp. 80–82.

23. Murphy, *Beyond Liberalism and Fundamentalism*, pp. 88–89, 95–96. She develops these arguments further in *Anglo-American Postmodernity: Philosophical Perspectives on Science, Religion and Ethics* (Westview Press, forthcoming 1997). See also "Supervenience and the Non-Reducibility of Ethics to Biology" in Russell, *et al., Evolution and Molecular Biology*; "Nonreductive Physicalism and the Soul" (forthcoming).

24. Murphy defines supervenience as "a relation between properties of different types or levels such that if something instantiates a property of the higher level id does so in virtue of (as a non-causal consequence of) its instantiating some lower-level property" (p. 141). This definition avoids both causal language and identity relations by focusing on different but related levels of analysis of a single system.

25. Murphy, *Beyond Liberalism and Fundamentalism*, p. 147.

26. Philip Clayton, *In Whom We Have Our Being: Theology of God and Nature in Light of Contemporary Science* (Edinburgh University Press and Eerdmans, forthcoming).

27. Recent studies show that chaotic dynamic systems are no exception; even here, the outcome is determined uniquely by the precise initial conditions and the governing equations, including the interactions with the environment. However, unlike non-chaotic classical systems, chaotic systems thus represent an unusual combination of epistemic unpredictability and ontological determinism typically called "chaotic randomness." Their theological importance is discussed in *Chaos and Complexity: Scientific Perspectives on Divine Action*, Robert John Russell, Nancey Murphy and Arthur Peacocke, eds. (Vatican City State: Vatican Observatory and Berkeley: The Center for Theology and the Natural Sciences, 1995).

28. For a recent introduction to quantum mechanics for science undergraduates, see P. C. W. Davies, *Quantum Mechanics* (London: Routledge & Kegan Paul,

1984). For the general reader see J. C. Polkinghorne, *The Quantum World* (Princeton: Princeton Scientific Library, 1989).

29. Let us move quickly through a few key moments in this fascinating history. A crucial first step came in 1900 when Max Planck explained the energy spectra of black-body radiation (i.e., the properties of light emitted by a glowing surface) by introducing a new fundamental constant into physics, since called Planck's constant h. At first Planck's argument was seen as strictly mathematical. It soon became clear, however, that it led to physical consequences: light, construed by classical physics as a continuous or wavelike phenomenon, is actually composed of discrete particles called photons. By 1912 Niels Bohr had produced a simple quantum model of the atom. In 1924, Louis de Broglie suggested that if light, classically considered a wave, actually had particle-like properties, then perhaps matter, classically considered as made of particles, should have wavelike properties. The wavelike aspects of atomic physics were given their definitive formulation by Irwin Schrödinger. In 1925 he produced the Schrödinger wave equation which was immediately applied with remarkable success to a vast range of atomic and subatomic processes, giving rise to what we now call wave mechanics. Within a year, Werner Heisenberg announced his famous "uncertainty principle" according to which the product of the uncertainty in position x and momentum p (in the x-direction) of any particle must be at least as large as Planck's constant. In 1927, Bohr formulated his "principle of complementarity" which brought together the wavelike properties of matter and the particlelike properties of light into a coherent theoretical framework often called "wave-particle duality" or the "Copenhagen interpretation." Moreover Bohr showed that the mathematics of wave-particle duality can provide a mathematical foundation for Heisenberg's uncertainty principle. Finally in 1930, P. A. M. Dirac combined quantum mechanics with special relativity to produce relativistic quantum mechanics.

30. Albert Einstein pressed for ontological determinism, as did David Bohm in terms of "hidden variables," though in Bohm's case the kind of ontology employed is highly non-classical (cf. his "implicate order"). Heisenberg argued for ontological indeterminism. Eugene Von Neumann proposed that the mind of the observer has to be taken into account. Everett and colleagues pressed for a "many worlds" interpretation. In the 1960s a new wave of interest in quantum interpretations was sparked by the work of J. S. Bell. Bell's theorem is often taken as implying that one must chose between a non-local realist and a local anti-realist interpretation of quantum physics. For additional reading see Jammer, *The Philosophy of Quantum Mechanics: The Interpretations of Quantum Mechanics in Historical Perspective* (New York: John Wiley & Sons, 1974); R. J. Russell, "Quantum Physics in Philosophical and Theological Perspective," in Robert J. Russell, William R. Stoeger, and George V. Coyne, eds., *Physics, Philosophy and Theology: A Common Quest for Understanding* (Vatican City State: Vatican Observatory, 1988).

31. The ontological interpretation of quantum physics has a number of current supporters. See, for example, C. J. Isham, *Lectures on Quantum Theory: Mathematical and Structural Foundations* (London: Imperial College Press, 1995), pp.131–132, and Davies, *Quantum Mechanics*, p. 4.

32. See Russell, "Quantum Physics in Philosophical and Theological Perspective," pp. 343–368.

33. This leads to a further, profound question: how both in theory and in the historical evolution of the universe did the macroscopic world, with its classical character, arise if the very early universe was governed by quantum physics? See for example, Roger Penrose, *The Emperor's New Mind: Concerning Computers, Minds, and the Laws of Physics* (New York: Oxford University Press, 1989).

34. David Bohm's quantum potential approach is a case in point. It is equivalent in predictive content with standard quantum mechanics but it suggests a deterministic view of nature. (For a recent appraisal see James T. Cushing, *Quantum Mechanics: Historical Contingency and the Copenhagen Hegemony* [Chicago: University of Chicago Press, 1994]). The determinism suggested by Bohm's approach is definitely not classical determinism, but a highly non-local view in which the whole of nature determines each part to be as it is. Thus his approach challenges both classical ontology and classical (i.e., pre-relativistic) determinism.

35. See Russell, "Quantum Physics in Philosophical and Theological Perspective," pp. 343–368.

36. The symbol "God + nature" is not meant ontologically; instead it is meant to suggest that the domain or scope of God's activity is what we normally mean by "the world" or "nature."

37. This point emerges very clearly in Clayton, *In Whom We Have Our Being*.

38. The claim that the world is "God + nature" is highly compatible with a Trinitarian doctrine of God which goes beyond an interaction model and beyond more diffuse forms of pantheism to starkly claim that God is the source, form, and energy of the world. See Moltmann's rejection of the interaction model as presupposing a "worldless God" and a "Godless world" in "Reflections on Chaos and God's Interaction with the World from a Trinitarian Perspective" in *Chaos and Complexity*, pp. 205–210.

39. Russell, "Quantum Physics in Philosophical and Theological Perspective," p. 364.

40. Robert John Russell, "Special Providence and Genetic Mutation," in Robert John Russell, Nancey Murphy and Francisco Ayala, *Evolution and Molecular Biology: Scientific Perspectives on Divine Action* (Vatican City State: Vatican Observatory Publications, and Berkeley: The Center for Theology and the Natural Sciences, forthcoming 1998).

41. Indeed it is the precise character of these laws which make such a claim possible. If the evolutionary process was in fact entirely deterministic, so that its apparently random character (i.e., the predominance of what Jacques Monod called "blind" chance) was due only to our ignorance of the underlying causal processes, it would seem impossible for God to act in specific events *except* by intervention. Thus the role of quantum mechanics in genetics and the possibility of giving quantum mechanics an indeterministic interpretation are crucial to my case.

42. The proposal being studied here draws on several sources, including Karl Heim, *The Transformation of the Scientific Worldview* (London: SCM Press, 1953); William G. Pollard, *Chance and Providence: God's Action in a World Governed by Scientific Law* (London: Faber and Faber, 1958); Mary Hesse, "On the Alleged Incompatibility between Christianity and Science," *Man and Nature*, ed. Hugh Montefiore (London: Collins, 1975), pp. 121–131.

43. For details, see Russell, "Special Providence and Genetic Mutation."

44. For a fuller treatment than I can offer here of theodicy in the case of evolution, see Thomas F. Tracy, "Evolution, Divine Action, and the Problem of Evil," in Russell, *et al., Evolution and Molecular Biology*. I also wish to point to the careful analysis of these and related issues by George F. R. Ellis, particularly his concern for divine action and for a defense of divine action against the charge of capriciousness ("Ordinary and Extraordinary Divine Action: The Nexus of Interaction," in *Chaos and Complexity*, pp. 359–395). Philip Clayton defends a similar view of divine action in his forthcoming book, *In Whom We Have Our Being*.

45. "Divine Action in the Natural Order: Buridan's Ass and Schrödinger's Cat" in Russell, *et al., Chaos and Complexity*, pp. 325–357. See also Nancey Murphy, *Theology in the Age of Scientific Reasoning* (Ithaca: Cornell University Press, 1990); "Evidence of Design in the Fine-Tuning of the Universe" in Russell, *et al., Quantum Cosmology and the Laws of Nature*, pp. 407–435; and references below.

46. Murphy, "Divine Action in the Natural Order," pp. 342, 346, 348.

47. Robert John Russell, "Quantum Physics in Philosophical and Theological Perspective," pp. 343–368.

48. Thomas F. Tracy, "Particular Providence and the God of the Gaps," in Russell, et al., *Chaos and Complexity*, pp. 289–324.

49. Dietrich Bonhoeffer, *Letters and Papers from Prison*, ed. Eberhard Bethge, enlarged ed. (New York: Macmillan, 1979), 311.

50. If there truly are causal gaps in nature, then God's action within them, however understood theologically, can not be equated with a natural cause or physical force.

51. Tracy, "Particular Providence and the God of the Gaps," p. 310.

52. Tracy, "Particular Providence and the God of the Gaps," p. 317.

53. Tracy, "Particular Providence and the God of the Gaps," p. 320.

54. In his response to the problem of theodicy and God's action in the evolutionary process, Tracy argues in detail that the evolution of free agents requires the kind of world in which there will be pain, suffering and death for physical and biological reasons, and not just for moral development. See his essay in Russell, *et al., Evolution and Molecular Biology.*

55. Owen C. Thomas, "Recent Thought on Divine Agency," in *Divine Action*, ed. Brian Hebblethwaite and Edward Henderson (Edinburgh: T&T Clark, 1990), pp. 35–50.

56. Thomas, "Recent Thought," p. 46.

Chapter Six

Theology, Cosmology, and Ethics

NANCEY MURPHY

In this article I intend to present a model for understanding the relations among the sciences, both natural and social, and for relating the sciences to both theology and ethics. To do so I shall draw upon the consequences of two very important changes in our Western intellectual world. These are recent changes, developments that have taken place only within the past twenty years. They are truly revolutionary in character; in fact, I see them as part of a shift in worldview so radical that it may mark the end of the Modern Era itself.

I proceed as follows: first, I describe three characteristics of the worldview just passing; second, I describe the two revolutionary changes in our basic intellectual assumptions; and finally, I propose a model for relating theology, ethics, and the sciences, which makes use of the revolutionary changes so described. I recommend that universities include in their course offerings *subjunctive theology*, the study of natural and social reality *as if* there exists a creating and loving God.

The Orthodoxy of the Recent Past

The three characteristics of late modern thought to which I wish to draw attention are the following: first, the reductionist thesis, that all of the sciences can and should be reduced to physics; second, the so-called "fact-value" distinction; and third, the exclusion of God from the intellectual world—the thesis that the existence of God makes no difference to intellectual pursuits. To put these theses in terms of the college curriculum: physics is the most basic discipline in the curriculum; the sciences have nothing to say about ethics; and theology doesn't belong on campus at all. Let me explain each of these.

Reductionism

The reductionist thesis was promoted most enthusiastically by the logical positivists, a group of philosophers, scientists, and others, who took their cues from the thinking of the Vienna Circle, meeting in the 1920s and '30s. One of their goals was the unification of the sciences. This goal was based on the observation that it is possible to organize the sciences hierarchically, according to the complexity of the entities or systems they study. Thus, physics is at the bottom, since it studies the smallest, simplest entities. Chemistry comes next, since it studies the tiniest systems of elementary particles, the atoms and molecules. Then biology, studying the parts of an organism, and then perhaps psychology, studying the behavior of the entire organism, and sociology studying social groups.

But the positivists wanted to do more than the hierarchical ordering. They wanted to show that each science could be reduced to the one below—that is, that the behavior of entities at a given level could be explained in terms of the operation of its parts, the entities at the next level down. And since physics is at the bottom, ultimately everything was to be understood as a consequence of the laws of physics.[1]

This was an exciting vision. I began college as a psychology major, primarily interested in the causes of mental illness, and this was an era of important discoveries regarding the role of neuro-transmitters in psychopathology—clear-cut evidence for the truth of the positivists' vision. I was convinced.

Now, there is no question that reduction was and still is an important research strategy in science: the behavior of electrons explains chemical bonding; biochemical processes affect human behavior, and so on. But the success of the strategy became a justification for a metaphysic, a theory about the nature of reality, that creates more problems than it solves. The most obvious problem relates to human freedom. If human behavior is entirely reducible to chemistry, and chemistry to physics, then is it not the case that the laws of physics ultimately determine everything we do, and human free will is an illusion?

Also, there is a crass materialism built into the reductionist orthodoxy. If the complex wholes are really nothing but the sum of their parts, then to be is, ultimately, to be material. Nothing of a non-material nature can have causal efficacy; in fact, non-material beings become nearly inconceivable. The implications for theology are clear enough.

The Fact-Value Distinction

A second aspect of the now-passing worldview that I wish to highlight has to do with ethics, and this aspect is not unrelated to the reductionist thesis.

This is a view expressed by talking about "the fact-value distinction," and in the slogan that "you cannot derive an ought from an is."

What's at issue here is the relation between judgments belonging to the realm of ethics or morality, and statements about the way the world is. The modern doctrine has been that there are two distinct spheres, and that the moral sphere is autonomous—not logically dependent on any other.

Immanuel Kant, the great Enlightenment philosopher, has done more than anyone else to formalize this dichotomy. He distinguished not only two subject matters—science and ethics— but also two reasoning faculties—pure reason and practical reason. Kant's motivation for this distinction was, in part, to protect human freedom. In order to insulate the will from the determinism of Newtonian science, it was necessary, he believed, to distinguish the sphere of "noumena," including the self, from the phenomenal world, governed by the laws of physics.

So the fact that ethics, the systematic study of morality, was *not* to be placed in the positivists' hierarchy of sciences represented a victory for Kant. However, there was a negative side to this development as well. Whereas Kant believed that ethics had a solid rational foundation of its own, which would serve as a basis for adjudicating ethical disputes, it has not turned out to be so. Its logical connections to an all-encompassing worldview sundered, ethical discourse has grown more and more fragmented. One result is the appalling moral relativism we find in our society, probably best exemplified by the views of the typical college sophomore.

The Exclusion of God

A final characteristic of late modern thought has been the exclusion of God from academia. I don't mean, of course, that there are no religion courses, or that many academics are not believers. Rather, it's that what one believes about God is supposed to be a private matter, and to make no difference to one's views in either the natural or the social sciences. As Bruno Latour puts it: "No one is truly modern who does not agree to keep God from interfering with Natural Law as well as with the laws of the Republic." This "crossed-out God" is distanced from both Nature and Society, yet kept presentable and usable nonetheless. "Spirituality was reinvented," he says:

> the all-powerful God could descend into men's heart of hearts without intervening in any way in their external affairs. A wholly individual and wholly spiritual religion made it possible to criticize both the ascendancy of science and that of society, without needing to bring God into either. The moderns could now be both secular and pious at the same time.[2]

So, in effect, the late modern world offers the scholar three sealed compartments: the sciences, the moral sphere, and the religious sphere, if indeed one countenances a religious sphere at all. A purely private God, sealed off from nature and society, is little different from no God at all.

Given this vision of reality, it's no wonder that scholars such as Robert John Russell and Ted Peters devote so much attention to the problem of divine action: how can we even conceive of a provident, active God, given the current state of scientific research?

Revolutionary Changes

In this section of my article I shall describe two recent developments in Anglo-American thought. One of these is the rejection of reductionism in favor of a view that recognizes what has come to be called "top-down causation." The second is a rapprochement between ethics and the rest of our system of knowledge. Along the way, we shall see what these two changes suggest regarding the role of God in academia.

Top-Down Causation

Top-down causation refers to the effect of the environment, or of the more complex system, on the entity in question. In other words, to understand a phenomenon, say, human behavior, one needs to take into account not only lower-level factors, such as genetic predispositions, but also higher-level factors, pertaining especially to the social environment.

Now, most psychologists and social scientists never lost sight of this fact—the positivists notwithstanding. Why else the ongoing arguments over nature versus nurture, biology versus social environment? What *is* new in the discussion is the contested, yet growing, recognition, first, that the environmental factors themselves cannot all be reduced to psychological factors. For example, birth order is an important predictor of individual achievement, but it is irreducibly social. Second, it is now increasingly recognized that top-down causation applies in the basic sciences as well. For example, biologists explain evolutionary change in terms of the interplay between mutation (a bottom-up factor) and environment (a top-down factor).

Thus, in any science there are many questions that can be answered by reference to factors at the level in question; there are many questions that can only be answered by referring to factors at a lower level; and finally, there are questions that can only be answered by reference to factors described at higher levels of analysis. These latter questions I shall call "boundary questions."

Redrawing the Hierarchy

Before proceeding to talk about ethics, I need to say more about the hierarchy of the sciences. Since the days of the logical positivists, we have invented some new sciences that need to find a place in the hierarchy—ecology, for instance.

Also, there is a distinction that, so far, I have passed over. When I have spoken of the higher levels in the hierarchy, I have not made it clear whether the higher levels pertain to more *encompassing* wholes or to more *complex* systems. These two criteria usually overlap, but not in every case. If the hierarchy is taken to be based on more encompassing wholes, then cosmology is the highest possible science in the hierarchy, since it studies the universe as a whole. However, if the hierarchy of the sciences is based on increasing complexity of the systems studied, then the question arises whether a social system is or is not more complex than the abstract account of the cosmos provided by cosmologists.

I think there is no good way to answer this question, and that it is therefore helpful to represent the relations among the sciences by means of a branching hierarchy, with the human sciences forming one branch and the natural sciences above biology forming the other. So I want you now to think of the hierarchy of the sciences as rather like a tree: physics, inorganic chemistry, biochemistry, and the various levels of biology form the trunk, but then we have one branch that completes the natural sciences with ecology, astrophysics, and cosmology, and another branch that contains the human sciences: psychology, sociology, economics, political science, and perhaps jurisprudence.[3]

God and the Hierarchy of the Sciences

Now, having made this slight correction in the original view of the hierarchy of the sciences, it's time to consider a more radical move, one that relates directly to the role of God in the academic world. I have been much influenced in my thinking about theology and science by Arthur Peacocke, an Anglican priest and biochemist. In fact, it was through Peacocke's writings that I learned for the first time about the concept of top-down causation.[4] So I owe him a debt of gratitude for having laid to rest all the worries I acquired along with the reductionist thesis when I bought into it so enthusiastically as a college student.

Peacocke's proposal is that *theology* should be seen as the science at the top of the hierarchy, since it is the study of the most encompassing system possible: God in relation to everything else that is. Now, I want to suggest some of the reasons why this proposal makes sense. Consider some boundary questions that arise in the natural sciences, especially in cosmology. For example: What happened before the Big Bang? It is not yet clear whether science can address this issue at all, Stephen Hawking notwithstanding.[5] If cosmologists do produce a scientific account of the cause of the Big Bang, then the boundary question is simply pushed back a step.

Another example: Why are the cosmological constants apparently "fine-tuned" for life? That is, why do the particular laws of nature that we find in operation in the universe, among all of the uncountably many other possibilities, happen to be among the very narrow range of those resulting in a life-supporting universe? This is surely one of the most intriguing questions to emerge from recent cosmology. Scientists such as John Leslie[6] and John Barrow and Frank Tipler[7] have written books showing, in calculation after calculation, that if the basic numbers involved in the laws of physics—the strength of the gravitational constant, the ratio between the charges of subatomic particles, and countless others—had been different, even by trivially small amounts, the evolution of the universe from the Big Bang until now would have gone quite differently. And in almost every case, the resulting universe would be unsuitable for the development of life—too short-lived, too cold, or lacking the heavier elements. In all of these countless ways things could have gone wrong, from the point of view of the requirements for life—and yet they did not. Why?

For that matter, why are there any natural laws at all? Where are they? What is their ontological status? What gives them their force?

While none of these questions strictly require a theological answer, it is clear enough to people of the Bible that our traditional conception of God and of God's purposes answers all of these questions rather easily. God is the ultimate cause of the universe, whatever that first event may have been. God designed the universe with creatures like us in mind; so of course the cosmological constants are fine-tuned to permit life. The laws of nature reflect the will of God for ordering the cosmos.[8]

Ethics in the Hierarchy of the Sciences

Now, back to ethics. Recall that the modern doctrine about the status of ethics has been the thesis of "the autonomy of morals": you cannot derive a statement about what ought to be from statements about the way things are. The second of the revolutionary changes in the very recent past, to which I wish to call your attention here, is the rejection of this thesis.

Consider the following value claim: this is a good wristwatch. I can support this value judgment by reference to a few straightforward factual statements: It keeps good time. It has continued to work for twelve years. It didn't cost very much, and so on. The reason we can make this evaluation is that we know the purpose of a wristwatch.

Philosopher Alasdair MacIntyre makes the same point about moral judgments. If we know what is the ultimate purpose or goal or *telos* of human life, then we can make straightforward judgments about what counts as a good person, or character trait, or action, based on what does or does not serve that purpose.[9]

So MacIntyre is calling into question the doctrine of the autonomy of morals. He argues that the correct form of ethical claims is something like the following conditional statement: "If you are to achieve your *telos*, then you ought to do x." It is a peculiar feature of modern Enlightenment views of ethics, he says, that their proper form has been taken to be apodictic: "You ought to do x"—period. Moderns have developed competing theories regarding the most basic moral claims: you ought to act so as to achieve the greatest good for the greatest number; versus, you ought to act so that the maxim of your action can be willed universally. But because morality is autonomous, there is no way to arbitrate between these most basic construals of the moral "ought." There is no way to go beyond these very basic and opposing moral "intuitions." This impossibility results in the interminability of moral debates in our society, such as those over abortion or economic justice. However, the interminability, says MacIntyre, should not be taken as the intrinsic nature of moral discourse, but ought rather to be seen as a sign that the entire Enlightenment project has taken a wrong turn.

The wrong turn was the attempt to free morality and ethical reasoning from religious tradition. For it is religious traditions (or metaphysical traditions) that provide the starting point for settling moral disputes. Such traditions provide the resources for answering the question: What is the greatest good for humankind? Is it happiness? Is it living in accord with the dictates of reason? Is it a just heavenly reward? Or is it more complex than any of these?

So theology or metaphysics provides an account of the purpose for human life. Ethics, then, is the discipline that works out answers to the question, how ought we to live in order to achieve the purpose for which we exist? In addition, MacIntyre argues, such theories of human flourishing can only be fully understood insofar as we know how they have been or could be socially embodied, so the social sciences are the descriptive side of a coin whose reverse, normative, side is ethics.

Thus, MacIntyre's contribution is to argue that the modern view, which insulates moral reasoning from knowledge of the nature of reality, whether theological or scientific, is an aberration. Ethics needs both theology and the social sciences.

Let me now put MacIntyre's point in the language I've been using previously. The study of ethics raises boundary questions that ethics alone cannot answer. The most important of these is the question: What is human life *for*? Theology provides ready answers to such questions. As in the cases arising from cosmology, it is not *necessary* in principle to provide a theological answer; certain non-theistic schemes will offer their own more or less adequate accounts. But it is clear that theological answers are available and adequate, even if not generally accepted as necessary.

We can now make a further step in connecting ethics with the rest of our knowledge. I shall attempt to show, briefly, that the social sciences raise boundary questions that they themselves cannot answer, and that ethics is the discipline needed to supply such answers.

It has often been argued that the social sciences can be and must be "value-free"; that is, they only describe social reality as it is, or at most provide information for making limited means-ends calculations. For example, *if* you wish to avoid shortages and surpluses, *then* you should institute a free-market economy. However, it is becoming increasingly common to recognize that there are ethical positions already incorporated into the social sciences, not only in the theories they provide but also in the methodological choices they make. If, indeed, there are such assumptions, then they need to be made explicit and criticized. And this is exactly the job of the ethicist. So the social sciences raise questions that can only be answered at the level of ethics.

Theories of the Ultimate Human Good

For an example of the role of ethical assumptions in social theory, consider modern positions on the necessity for violent coercion in society. This assumption can be traced to Thomas Hobbes's claim that the state of nature, prior to the social contract, is the war of each against all. Most social theorists since then have claimed that coercion is necessary to maintain society, and that violence is merely the ultimate form of coercion. Max Weber's classic statement on the relation between politics and violence is found in his essay "Politics as Vocation."

> Ultimately, one can define the modern state sociologically only in terms of the specific *means* peculiar to it, . . . namely, the use of physical force . . . the state is a relation of men dominating men, a relation supported by means of legitimate . . . violence.[10]

Reinhold Niebuhr has influenced a generation of policy-makers with the thesis he developed in *Moral Man and Immoral Society*:[11] The needs of an institution for its very survival require the people involved in them to do things they would not do (and would not be morally justified in doing) as individuals. Niebuhr's thesis has been dubbed with the congratulatory title of "Christian realism." In the Preface to *Moral Man* he says:

> The thesis to be elaborated in these pages is that a sharp distinction must be drawn between the moral and social behavior of individuals and of social groups, national, racial, and economic; and that this distinction justifies and necessitates political policies which a purely individualistic ethic must always find embarrassing. . . . In every human group there is less reason to guide and check impulse, less capacity for self-transcendence, less ability to comprehend the needs of others and therefore more unrestrained egoism than the individuals, who compose the group, reveal in their personal relationships. . . . When collective power, whether in the form of imperialism or class domination, exploits weakness, it can never be dislodged unless power is raised against it.[12]

More recently, Peter Berger has concurred that there is inevitably an element of coercion required in order that society not be destroyed by the disruptive forces within it. "Violence," he says, "is the ultimate foundation of any political order."[13]

Now, in what sense is this an ethical assumption? Is it not, rather, a simple statement of empirical fact; a law of human behavior? The very fact that one of the theorists I have quoted here, Reinhold Niebuhr, is known primarily as a Christian ethicist might at least make us suspicious that we are not dealing with pure social fact.

Niebuhr's views on the possibility of non-coercive, nonviolent social structures is dependent upon a prior ethical judgment, a judgment regarding the highest good for humankind. This view of the human good is in turn the consequence of a particular theological doctrine. Niebuhr wrote:

> Justice rather than unselfishness [is society's] highest moral ideal. . . . [T]his realistic social ethic needs to be contrasted with the ethics of religious idealism. . . . Society must strive for justice even if it is forced to use means, such as self-assertion, resistance, coercion and perhaps resentment, which cannot gain the moral sanction of the most sensitive moral spirit. . . . [14]

Niebuhr's judgment that justice is the highest good that can reasonably be expected in human history is in turn based upon his eschatology—that is, on his theological views regarding the end of time. He believes that salvation, the kingdom of God, the eschaton, are essentially *beyond* history. Since it is not possible to conceive of the eternal being realized in the temporal, he concludes that the kingdom of God is beyond history, and this, in turn, means that guilt and moral ambiguity must be permanent features of the interim.

Weber's justification is also overtly ethical: it is based on a distinction between an "ethic of ultimate ends" and an "ethic of responsibility." The ethic of ultimate ends is concerned with pure intent and pure means. The ethic of responsibility is concerned with the politically foreseeable results of one's actions in a political order where imperfection and evil are presupposed. The political realist is committed to achieving his ends even at the expense of morally dubious means. And as already noted, the decisive means for politics is violence.[15]

So this is one example of the way ethical theories—theories about the ultimate good for humankind—are woven right into social-scientific reasoning. A more thorough-going argument for the inescapability of ethics in social science comes from recognition that the very methods of social-scientific research involve ethical judgments. Alexander Rosenberg states that "taking sides on questions of scientific method may commit us to taking sides in fundamental matters of moral philosophy."[16] For a very simple example, consider the question whether informed consent ought to be required for all experimentation on human subjects. Kant's ethical theory is based on the categorical imperative. One of the ways Kant formulated it was to say that other people must always be treated as ends in themselves, never merely as means to an end. The consequence of this for the question about research is that no one can be *used* for research purposes without consent. But, alternatively, for utilitarians the moral criterion is the greatest good for the greatest number. Thus, it is conceivable that so long as an experiment does little or no harm to the subjects, and brings about great good for society as a whole, subjects ought to be used without informed consent if giving them information would ruin the experiment. Here we see that ethical differences contribute to significant differences in experimental design.

So, contrary to claims about the value-free character of the social sciences, it takes but a little scratching to find ethical judgments under the surface. These judgments may be taken for granted within the mainstream of the intellectual world. For instance, who could doubt that justice is the highest good at which governments aim?

But these assumptions *are* questionable; there exist alternative points of view, and we need to know whether and how such judgments are justifiable. Thus, the social sciences raise questions that they alone are not competent to answer—boundary questions, again.

So it would be useful if we could add to the top of the hierarchy of the social sciences the 'science' of ethics. This would be the science whose job it is to compare and evaluate systematic theories of the good for humankind, and assist in spelling out the consequences when such theories are embodied in social theory.

And MacIntyre has given us just what we need in order to reconceive ethics along these lines. Ethics can be defined as the systematic elaboration of the consequences for action of a theory about the ultimate good for human life. Some of these consequences will be testable—that is, subject to confirmation by observation of the effects of living one way rather than another.

The details of the overall assessment of such a theory are too complicated to go into here, but, as in any scientific theory, would involve both empirical data and other theoretical values such as coherence and consistency. (For MacIntyre's own account of the justification of a moral tradition, I refer you to his rather magnificent book, *Whose Justice? Which Rationality?*)[17]

A New Model of Enquiry

I am now in position to present a model for the relations among all of the disciplines. Recall the branching hierarchy of the sciences, with the natural sciences completed in one branch, the human sciences comprising the other. My proposal is that ethics needs to be the science that completes the human science branch, since it answers boundary questions that the social sciences raise but cannot themselves answer. But theology needs to be the science that tops off both branches since it answers boundary questions that arise from both ethics and cosmology. Notice that in each case the boundary questions call for an account of purpose. A theological view of God's purposes in creating the universe answers both the question of what it takes for a fulfilling human life, as well as the question, what is the reason for having these particular physical laws? It answers at one stroke a highly prominent boundary question from the natural-science side and the human-science side of the hierarchy of the sciences, explaining the fine-tuning at the same time as it answers the central question for ethics of the *telos* of human life.

Consequences for College Education. What does this model of enquiry suggest for the future of academia? In general, we can say that each of the disciplines I've talked about occupies its own proper and irreducible level. There are entities, systems, processes, causal relations, germane to each discipline, which can be studied with relative autonomy from the other levels. So, for instance, sociologists should not have to fight battles against psychologists who hope to show that social facts are nothing but the aggregation of facts about individual behavior, attitudes, and so forth.

Nonetheless, we know that it is often the case that a strategy of reduction or analysis allows for the explanation of regularities or processes that, prior to the reduction, are merely brute facts. For example, the Mendelian laws of heredity were brute facts until we could define genes and their behavior biochemically.

But, most important, we need now to be aware that there are also aspects of the entities and processes at each level that will remain unintelligible until we relate them to a higher level in the hierarchy of the sciences. This is the place where exciting new developments ought to be expected in the future. And perhaps there will be as great a scientific revolution produced by this new strategy as there has been in the modern era as a result of the reductionist strategy.

Supervenience. Such a revolution makes work for philosophers. At present we are still struggling even to devise and define concepts appropriate for describing these top-down relations. The development of systems theory is an important start. Much has been done in the past twenty years in the areas of cognitive theory and philosophy of mind. Two of the most important of the new concepts available for thinking about these issues are the concepts of *supervenience* and *realization*. A property (F) is said to supervene on another (G) if the properties pertain to the same entity, and the entity has F in virtue of its having G. This relation is extremely useful for talking about the relations among properties at different levels of the hierarchy. So, for instance, we may say that mental properties supervene on physical properties.

However, an important recognition within the past generation is that the same mental property can supervene on a variety of physical properties. For example, different species have differently constructed nervous systems, so the property of being in pain must supervene on a different set of physical properties in the different species. The terminology developed to describe this fact is to say that there are a variety of ways in which the mental property can be physically realized. These concepts of supervenience and multiple realizability may be the key to explaining free will.

Of course, the most startling outcome of the model I've presented here is the role it attributes to theology. Can we really say, must we, in fact, say that our scientific account of reality will be essentially incomplete without a theory about the nature and purposes of God? This is exactly the consequence of my picture of how the various disciplines relate. But if this seems outrageous, let me suggest a variety of factors that have already been pointing in this direction.

One striking fact is the extent to which natural scientists, with no prior interest in religion, have begun intentionally to dabble in theological issues. They are compelled to do so, they claim, by discoveries in their own fields. Thus, we see books by agnostics such as Paul Davies, titled *God and the New Physics*, and *The Mind of God*.[18] An epigraph at the beginning of *God and the New Physics* is a quotation from Einstein: "Religion without science is blind; science without religion is lame." (I would actually want to turn it around, and say that science without religion is blind—or at least, that it has permanent blind spots.)

In a strange way, avowed atheists such as Carl Sagan are just as helpful in making my point. What Sagan puts forward is a peculiar mix of science and what can only be called "naturalistic religion." He begins with plain old biology and cosmology but then uses concepts drawn from science to fill in what are essentially religious categories—categories, by the way, that fall into a pattern surprisingly isomorphic with the Christian conceptual scheme. He has a concept of ultimate reality: "The Universe is all that is or ever was or ever will be." He has an account of ultimate origins: Evolution with a capital E. He has an account of the origin of sin: the primitive reptilian structure in the brain, which is responsible for territoriality, sex drive, and aggression. His account of salvation is gnostic in character—that is, it assumes that salvation comes from knowledge. The knowledge in question is scientific knowledge, perhaps advanced by contact with extraterrestrial life forms who are more advanced than we.[19]

The point of this example is to suggest that if one refrains from placing a recognizable theological system at the top of the hierarchy, there is an "empty space" there that cries out to be filled by something. Sagan and others oblige by creating new scientistic religions.

Of course, I could also mention scientists who are believers: Robert John Russell in physics, Arthur Peacocke in biology, George Ellis in cosmology, and a host of others. But they are more easily dismissed by skeptics as engaging in special pleading for the religious convictions that they already hold on other grounds.

On the social-science side, there is a much talked-about book by John Milbank of the Divinity Faculty at Cambridge. *Theology and Social Theory*[20] argues that the presuppositions of modern social sciences are inherently theological. However, the theologies so embodied are either pagan, or Christian heresies. His argument raises the intriguing question of what sort of competing theories might be developed by a social science that was both intentionally theological and orthodox.

Again, the skeptic might write this off as perceptions distorted by personal interest. For this reason, I am much impressed by the recent turn in philosophical ethics. I have already described MacIntyre's argument regarding the defects of any attempt at ethics that has no place for an account of the purpose of human life, an account most readily provided by theology. What I did not mention earlier is that MacIntyre used to be one of the foremost spokesmen for philosophical atheism. I believe that his return to the Christianity of his childhood was to some extent a consequence of this conclusion regarding ethics and theology, *not* its motivation.

In addition, there is Bernard Williams, another of the great philosophical ethicists of our day, who surveys most of the approaches to ethics in Western history from Antiquity to the present, and finds most of them defective. However, he says, there is a sort of theory

> that . . . seeks to provide, in terms of the transcendental framework, something that man is *for*: if he understands properly his role in the basic scheme of things, he will see that there are some particular sorts of ends which are properly his and which he ought to realize. One archetypal form of such a view is the belief that man was created by a God who also has certain expectations of him. . . .
>
> If God existed, there might well be special, and acceptable, reasons for subscribing to morality.[21]

However, Williams, an atheist, believes that, unfortunately, the very concept of God is incoherent; that religion itself is incurably unintelligible.

I doubt that Williams' judgment regarding the unintelligibility of the notion of God is either naive or unconsidered. But a sad fact about contemporary intellectual life is that the concepts many people have of God and of other matters theological are indeed naive and unconsidered, and this is as true of believers as of atheists. If what I have said today is true—that is, about the essential role of theology in completing our understanding of reality—then we need to be as discerning and sophisticated about theological theories and methods as we are about scientific theories and methods.

Sophisticated theological theories are readily available in seminaries, but seminary professors are often isolated from the rest of academia. And the rest of academia, these days, tends to be isolated from theologians. For a variety of reasons, theology has disappeared from American universities. Many take the constitutional separation of church and state to forbid the teaching of theology in public institutions. Also, religiously-affiliated colleges are increasingly severing their denominational ties and attempting to serve a religiously plural student body. For this reason, it is considered appropriate to teach descriptive courses about religions, but not to consider the truth claims of those religions.

Subjunctive Theology. I offer a modest proposal: what I shall call *subjunctive theology*. First, to remind you of your grammar lessons: the subjunctive mood is used in conditional or hypothetical statements; for example, "If I were a great orator I would finish this lecture with a rousing conclusion."

My proposal is that in contexts where it is inappropriate to teach theology in the indicative mood, much less the imperative, it could nonetheless be studied conditionally and, of course, comparatively. I can imagine university courses focusing on what I have called the boundary questions, arising primarily from cosmology and ethics, but also from other sciences, and examining the answers various theological traditions would provide, were that tradition's theological claims true. So, for instance, there is the issue of the fine-tuning of the cosmological constants. What could we say about this if the Genesis account is true, and what differences do the various theological developments of that story in the traditions of Judaism, Christianity, and Islam make when employed for this purpose? And how do they compare to a Neoplatonic account such as John Leslie's; and do any of the Eastern religions provide their own answers to the same question, or do they fail here? Similarly, what are the consequences of these various accounts of ultimate reality for the tough ethical questions.[22]

There is a danger, of course, in promoting courses such as I envision. It may well be that through no fault of her own, the professor may find that one particular brand of theology turns out to be more useful for answering these boundary questions than the competitors, and she or he might thereafter have great difficulty feigning neutrality—as much difficulty, say, as Lavoisier would have had maintaining a facade of neutrality when discussing the merits and demerits of phlogiston theory. But perhaps this is a risk worth taking.

Notes

1. It is important to note that there was never universal agreement on the reduction of the social sciences to psychology, or on the "naturalist" thesis, the view that there is continuity between the natural and the human sciences.

2. Bruno Latour, *We Have Never Been Modern*, trans. Catherine Porter (Cambridge, MA: Harvard University Press, 1993), 33.

3. I first suggested the branching model in "Evidence of Design in the Fine-Tuning of the Universe," in Robert Russell, Nancey Murphy, and C. J. Isham, eds., *Quantum Cosmology and the Laws of Nature: Scientific Perspectives on Divine Action* (Vatican City State and Berkeley: Vatican Observatory and Center for Theology and the Natural Sciences, 1993; distributed by University of Notre Dame Press), 407–35. Further refinements can be found in my book, *On the Moral Nature of the Universe: Theology, Cosmology, and Ethics* (Minneapolis, MN: Fortress Press, 1996), co-authored with George F.R. Ellis. This lecture is largely inspired by our joint work on that volume.

4. See *Creation and the World of Science* (Oxford: Clarendon Press, 1979); and *Theology for a Scientific Age*, 2nd enlarged ed. (Minneapolis: Fortress Press, 1993).

5. See *A Brief History of Time* (Toronto and New York: Bantam, 1988).

6. See *Universes* (London and New York: Routledge, 1989).

7. See *The Anthropic Cosmological Principle* (Oxford: Oxford University Press, 1986).

8. For a discussion of this issue, see my "Evidence of Design in the Fine-Tuning of the Universe," and George F.R. Ellis, "A Theology of the Anthropic Principle," in *Quantum Cosmology and the Laws of Nature*, op cit.

9. *After Virtue* (Notre Dame: University of Notre Dame Press, 1981; second enlarged edition, 1984).

10. *Politics as a Vocation* (Fortress, 1965), 1.

11. New York: Charles Scribner's Sons, 1932.

12. Niebuhr, *xi-xii.*

13. Peter Berger, *Invitation to Sociology* (New York: Doubleday, 1963), 69.

14. Moral Man, 257–8.

15. Account found in James W. Douglass, *The Non-Violent Cross: A Theology of Revolution and Peace* (Toronto, Ontario: The Macmillan Co., 1966), 262–63.

16. *Philosophy of Social Science* (Boulder, CO: Westview Press, 1988), 177.

17. Notre Dame: University of Notre Dame Press, 1988.

18. New York: Simon and Schuster, 1983 and 1992, respectively.

19. See Thomas M. Ross, "The Implicit Theology of Carl Sagan," *Pacific Theological Review* 18 (1985) 3:24–32.

20. Oxford, Blackwell, 1990.

21. *Morality*, ninth ed., (Cambridge: Cambridge University Press, 1993), 63, 72.

22. Sir John Templeton, whose foundation helped fund this lecture series, is hoping to promote courses in science departments that will further our knowledge of God. Perhaps what I envision here would be a viable model for such a course.

Part Two

Evolution, Ethics, and Eschatology

Chapter Seven

So Human an Animal: Evolution and Ethics

FRANCISCO J. AYALA

Then God said, "Let us make humankind in our image, according to our likeness." . . . So God created humankind in his image, in the image of God he created them; male and female he created them.

—Genesis 1:26–27 (NRSV)

There is grandeur in this view of life, with its several powers, having been originally breathed into a few forms or into one; and that, whilst this planet has gone cycling on according to the fixed laws of gravity, from so simple a beginning endless forms most beautiful and most wonderful have been, and are being, evolved.

—Charles Darwin, *On the Origin of Species*[1]

The theme of this essay is set forth by the two quoted texts, from *Genesis* and from Darwin. I see human nature as continuous with the rest of the living world, through the process of biological evolution. Biologically, we are animals, but we are very distinct and unique kind of animals. We are anatomically distinct, bipedal in gait, and have enormous brains. But we are notably different also, and more importantly, in our individual and social behaviors, and in the products of those behaviors. With the advent of humankind, biological evolution transcended itself and ushered in cultural evolution, a more rapid and effective mode of evolution than the biological mode. Products of cultural evolution included complex social and political institutions; religious and ethical traditions; language, literature, and art; electronic communication; roads and cities.

Here we will explore ethics and ethical behavior as a model case to illuminate the interplay between biology and culture. I will propose that our exalted intelligence—a product of biological evolution—inclines us to form ethical judgments, that is, to evaluate actions as either good or evil. But I will further argue that the moral codes that guide our ethical behavior transcend biology in that they are not biologically determined; rather they are products of human history, including social and religious traditions.

I will conclude by advocating both that science provides necessary insights for understanding what we are and our place in the universe, and that science, by itself, is hopelessly insufficient for this purpose.

The Biological Origins of Humankind

I have quoted above the final sentence of Darwin's *Origin*: "There is grandeur in this view of life." A few pages earlier, he had made clear that among the "most beautiful and most wonderful" forms that have been evolved, he included humans. "When the views entertained in this volume on the origin of species, or when analogous views are generally admitted, we can dimly foresee that there will be a considerable revolution in natural history. . . . Light will be thrown on the origin of man and his history."[2]

Humanity is a biological species that has evolved from other species that were not human. In order to understand human nature, we must know our biological make-up and whence we come, the story of our humbler beginnings.

Our closest biological relatives are the great apes and, among them, the chimpanzees, who are more related to us than they are to the gorillas, and much more than to the orangutans. The hominid lineage diverged from the chimpanzee lineage 5–8 million years ago and it evolved exclusively in the African continent until the emergence of *Homo erectus*, somewhat before 1.8 million years ago. The first known hominid, *Ardipithecus ramidus*, lived 4.4 million years ago, but it is not certain that it was bipedal or in the direct line of descent to modern humans, *Homo sapiens*. The recently described *Australopithecus anamensis*, dated 3.9–4.2 million years ago, was bipedal and has been placed in the line of descent to *Australopithecus afarensis*, *Homo habilis*, *Homo erectus*, and *Homo sapiens*. Other hominids, not in the direct line of descent to modern humans, are *Australopithecus africanus*, *Paranthropus aethiopicus*, *P. boisei*, and *P. robustus*, who lived in Africa at various times between 3 and 1 million years ago, a period when three or four hominid species lived contemporaneously in the African continent.

Shortly after its emergence in tropical or subtropical eastern Africa, *Homo erectus* spread to other continents. Fossil remains of *Homo erectus* are known from Africa, Indonesia (Java), China, the Middle East, and Europe. *Homo erectus* fossils from Java have been dated 1.81 (plus or minus 0.04) and 1.66 (plus or minus 0.04) million years ago, and from Georgia between 1.6 and 1.8 million years ago. Anatomically distinctive *Homo erectus* fossils have been found in Spain, deposited more than 780,000 years ago, the oldest known in southern Europe.

The transition from *Homo erectus* to *Homo sapiens* occurred around 400,000 years ago, although this date is not well determined owing to uncertainty as to whether some fossils are *erectus* or "archaic" forms of *sapiens*. *Homo erectus* persisted for some time in Asia, until 250,000 years ago in China, and perhaps until 100,000 ago in Java, and thus was coetaneous with early members of its descendant species, *Homo sapiens*. The subspecies *Homo sapiens neanderthalensis* appeared in Europe around 200,000 years ago and persisted until 30,000 or 40,000 years ago. The Neanderthals were earlier thought to be ancestral to anatomically modern humans, but now we know that modern humans appeared at least 100,000 years ago, much before the disappearance of the Neanderthals. Moreover, in caves in the Middle East, fossils of modern humans have been found dated 100,000–120,000 years ago, as well as Neanderthals dated at 60,000 and 70,000 years ago, followed again by modern humans dated at 40,000 years ago. It is unclear whether the two forms repeatedly replaced one another by migration from other regions, or whether they coexisted, or indeed whether interbreeding may have occurred.

There is considerable controversy about the origin of modern humans. Some anthropologists argue that the transition from *Homo erectus* to archaic *Homo sapiens* and later to anatomically modern humans occurred consonantly in various parts of the Old World. Proponents of this "multiregional model" emphasize fossil evidence showing regional continuity in the transition from *Homo erectus* to archaic and then modern *Homo sapiens*. In order to account for the transition from one to another species (something which cannot happen independently in several places), they postulate that genetic exchange occurred from time to time between populations, so that the species evolved as a single gene pool, even though geographic differentiation occurred and persisted, just as geographically differentiated populations exist in other animal species, as well as in living humans. This explanation depends on the occurrence of persistent migrations and interbreeding between populations from different continents, of which no direct evidence exists. Moreover, it is difficult to reconcile the multiregional model with the contemporary existence of different species or forms in different regions, such as the persistence of *Homo erectus* in China and Java for more than one hundred thousand years after the emergence of *Homo sapiens*.

Other scientists argue instead that modern humans first arose in Africa or in the Middle East somewhat prior to 100,000 years ago and from there spread throughout the world, replacing elsewhere the preexisting populations of *Homo erectus* or archaic *Homo sapiens*. Some proponents of this "African replacement" model claim further that the transition from archaic to modern *Homo sapiens* was associated with a very narrow bottleneck, consisting of only two or very few individuals who are the ancestors of all modern mankind. This particular claim of a narrow bottleneck has been shown to be erroneous.[3] But the African (or Middle East) origin of modern humans is, however, supported by a wealth of recent genetic evidence and is, therefore, favored by many evolutionists.

The Uniqueness of Humankind

The most distinctive human anatomical traits are erect posture and large brain. We are the only vertebrate species with a bipedal gait and erect posture; birds are bipedal, but their backbone stands horizontal rather than vertical. Brain size is generally proportional to body size; relative to body mass, humans have the largest (and most complex) brain. The chimpanzee's brain weighs less than a pound; a gorilla's slightly more. The human male adult brain is 1,400 cubic centimeters (cc), about three pounds in weight.

Evolutionists used to raise the question whether bipedal gait or large brain came first, or whether they evolved consonantly. The issue is now resolved. Our *Australopithecus* ancestors had, since four million years ago, a bipedal gait, but a small brain, about 450 cc, a pound in weight. Brain size starts to increase notably without *Homo habilis* ancestors, about 2.5 million years ago, who had a brain of about 650 cc and also were prolific toolmakers (hence the name *habilis*). Between one and two million years afterwards, there lived *Homo erectus*, with adult brains up to 1,200 cc. Neanderthal man had a brain as large as ours. Our brain is not only much larger than that of chimpanzees or gorillas, but also much more complex. The cerebral cortex, where the higher cognitive functions are processed, is in humans disproportionally much greater than the rest of the brain when compared to apes.

Erect posture and large brain are not the only anatomical traits that distinguish us from nonhuman primates, even if they may be the most obvious. A list of our most distinctive anatomical features includes the following (of which the last five items are not detectable in fossils):

- Erect posture and bipedal gait (entail changes of the backbone, hipbone, and feet)
- Opposing thumbs and arm and hand changes (make possible precise manipulation)
- Large brain
- Reduction of jaws and remodeling of face
- Changes in skin and skin glands

- Reduction in body hair
- Slow development
- Modification of vocal tract and larynx
- Reorganization of the brain

Humans are notably different from other animals not only in anatomy, but also and no less importantly in their behavior, both as individuals and socially. A list of distinctive human behavioral traits includes the following:

- Subtle expression of emotions
- Intelligence: abstract thinking, categorizing, and reasoning
- Symbolic (creative) language
- Self-awareness and death-awareness
- Toolmaking and technology
- Science, literature, and art
- Ethics and religion
- Social organization and cooperation (division of labor)
- Legal codes and political institutions

Humans live in groups that are socially organized, and so do other primates. But primate societies do not approach the complexity of human social organization. A distinctive human social trait is culture, which may be understood as the set of nonstrictly biological human activities and creations. Culture includes social and political institutions, religious and ethical traditions, language, common sense and scientific knowledge, art and literature, technology, and in general all the creations of the human mind. The advent of culture has brought with it cultural evolution, a superorganic mode of evolution superimposed on the organic mode, and that has in the last few millennia become the dominant mode of human evolution. Cultural evolution has come about because of cultural change and inheritance, a distinctively human mode of achieving adaptation to the environment and transmitting it through the generations.

Cultural Versus Biological Heredity

There are in mankind two kinds of heredity—the biological and the cultural, which may also be called organic and superorganic, or *endosomatic* and *exosomatic* systems of heredity. Biological inheritance in humans is very much like that in any other sexually reproducing organism; it is based on the transmission of genetic information encoded in DNA from one generation to the next by means of the sex cells.[4] Cultural inheritance, on the other hand, is based on transmission of information by a teaching-learning process, which is in principle independent of biological parentage. Culture is transmitted by instruction and learning, by example and imitation, through books, newspapers and radio, television and motion pictures, through works of art, and by any other means of communication. Culture is acquired by every person from parents, relatives and neighbors, and from the whole human environment.

Cultural inheritance makes possible for people what no other organism can accomplish—the cumulative transmission of experience from generation to generation. Animals can learn from experience, but they do not transmit their experiences, their "discoveries" (at least not to any large extent) to the following generations. Animals have individual memory, but they do not have a "social memory." Humans, on the other hand, have developed a culture because they can transmit cumulatively their experiences from generation to generation.

Cultural inheritance has ushered in cultural evolution, that is, the evolution of knowledge, social structures, ethics, and all other components that make up human culture. Cultural inheritance makes possible a new mode of adaptation to the environment that is not available to nonhuman organisms—adaptation by means of culture. Organisms in general adapt to the environment by means of natural selection, by changing over generations their genetic constitution to suit the demands of the environment. But humans, and humans alone, can also adapt by changing the environment to suit the needs of their genes. (Animals build nests and modify their environment also in other ways, but the manipulation of the environment by any nonhuman species is trivial compared to humankind's.) For the last few millennia human beings have been adapting the environments to their genes more often than their genes to the environments.

In order to extend its geographical habitat, or to survive in a changing environment, a population of organisms must become adapted, through slow accumulation of genetic variants sorted out by natural selection, to the new climatic conditions, different sources of food, different competitors, and so on. The discovery of fire and the use of shelter and clothing allowed human beings to spread from the warm tropical and subtropical regions of the Old World to the whole earth, except for the frozen wastes of Antarctica, without the anatomical development of fur or hair. Human beings did not wait for genetic mutants promoting wing development; they have conquered the air in a somewhat more efficient and versatile way by building flying machines. People travel the rivers and the seas without gills or fins. The exploration of outer space has started without waiting for mutations providing human beings with the ability to breathe with low oxygen pressures or to function in the absence of gravity; astronauts carry their own oxygen and specially equipped pressure suits. From their obscure beginnings in Africa, human beings have become the most abundant species of mammal on earth. It was the appearance of culture as a superorganic form of adaptation that made humankind the most successful animal species.

Cultural adaptation has prevailed in humankind over biological adaptation because it is a more rapid mode of adaptation and because it can be directed. A favorable genetic mutation newly arisen in an individual can be transmitted to a sizable part of the human species only through innumerable generations. However, a new scientific discovery or technical achievement can be transmitted to the whole of humankind, potentially at least, in less than one generation. Moreover, whenever a need arises, culture can directly pursue the appropriate changes to meet the challenge. In contrast, biological adaptation depends on the accidental availability of a favorable mutation, or of a combination of several mutations, at the time and place where the need arises.

Erect posture and large brain are distinctive anatomical features of modern humans. High intelligence, symbolic language, religion, and ethics are some of the behavioral traits that distinguish us from other animals. The account of human origins that I have sketched above implies a continuity in the evolutionary process that goes from our nonhuman ancestors of eight million years ago through primitive hominids to modern humans. A scientific explanation of that evolutionary sequence must account for the emergence of human anatomical and behavioral traits in terms of natural selection together with other distinctive biological causes and processes. One explanatory strategy is to focus on a particular human feature and seek to identify the conditions under which this feature may have been favored by natural selection. Such a strategy may lead to erroneous conclusions as a consequence of the fallacy of selective attention; some traits may have come about not because they are themselves adaptive, but rather because they are associated with traits that are favored by natural selection.

Geneticists have long recognized the phenomenon of "pleiotropy," the expression of a gene in different organs or anatomical traits. It follows that a gene that becomes changed owing to its effects on a certain trait will result in the modification of other traits as well. The changes of these other traits are epigenetic consequences of the changes directly promoted by natural selection. The cascade of consequences may be, particularly in the case of human beings, very long and far from obvious in some cases. Literature, art, science, and technology, are among the behavioral features that may have come about not because they were adaptively favored in human evolution, but because they are expressions of the high intellectual abilities present in modern human beings; what was favored by natural selection (its "target") was an increase in intellectual ability rather than each one of those particular activities.

The Biological Roots of Ethical Behavior

I now will briefly explore ethics and ethical behavior as a model case of how we may seek the evolutionary explanation of a distinctively human trait. I select ethical behavior because morality is a human trait that seems remote from biological processes. My goal is to ascertain whether an account can be advanced of ethical behavior as an outcome of biological evolution and, if such is the case, whether ethical behavior was directly promoted by natural selection, or has rather come about as an epigenetic manifestation of some other trait that was the target of natural selection.

I argue that ethical behavior (the proclivity to judge human actions as either good or evil) has evolved as a consequence of natural selection, not because it was adaptive in itself, but rather as a pleiotropic consequence of the high intelligence characteristic of human beings. I will first point out that the question whether ethical behavior is biologically determined may refer either to (1) the *capacity* for ethics (i.e., the proclivity to judge human actions as either right or wrong) and which I will refer to as "ethical behavior," or (2) the moral *norms* or moral codes accepted by human beings for guiding their actions. My theses are that: (1) the capacity for ethics is a necessary attribute of human nature, and thus a product of biological evolution; but (2) moral norms are products of cultural evolution, not of biological evolution.

I have just noted that the question of whether ethical behavior is biologically determined may refer to either one of the following issues: (1) Is the capacity for ethics—the proclivity to judge human actions as either right or wrong—determined by the biological nature of human beings? (2) Are the systems or codes of ethical norms accepted by human beings biologically determined? A similar distinction can be made with respect to language. The issue whether the capacity for symbolic language is determined by our biological nature is different from the question of whether the particular language we speak (English, Spanish, or Japanese) is biologically necessary.

The first question posed is more fundamental; it asks whether or not the biological nature of *Homo sapiens* is such that human beings are necessarily inclined to make moral judgments and to accept ethical values, to identify certain actions as either right or wrong. Affirmative answers to this first question do not necessarily determine what the answer to the second question should be. Independently of whether or not human beings are necessarily ethical, it remains to be determined whether particular moral prescriptions are in fact determined by our biological nature, or whether they are chosen by society, or by individuals. Even if we were to conclude that people cannot avoid having moral standards of conduct, it might be that the choice of the particular standards used for judgment would be arbitrary, or that it depends on some other, nonbiological criteria. The need for having moral values does not necessarily tell us what these moral values should be, just as the capacity for language does not determine which language we shall speak.

The question whether ethical behavior is determined by our biological nature must be answered in the affirmative. By "ethical behavior" I mean here to refer to the urge *to judge* human actions as either good or bad, which is not the same as *good behavior* (i.e., choosing to do what is perceived as good instead of what is perceived as evil). Human beings exhibit ethical behavior by nature because their biological constitution determines the presence in them of the three necessary, and jointly sufficient, conditions for ethical behavior. These conditions are: (a) the ability to anticipate the consequences of one's own actions; (b) the ability to make value judgments; and (c) the ability to choose between alternative courses of action. I shall briefly examine each of these abilities and show that they exist as a consequence of the eminent intellectual capacity of human beings.

The ability to anticipate the consequences of one's own actions is the most fundamental of the three conditions required for ethical behavior. Only if I can anticipate that pulling the trigger will shoot the bullet, which in turn will strike and kill my enemy, can the action of pulling the trigger be evaluated as nefarious. Pulling a trigger is not in itself a moral action; it becomes so by virtue of its relevant consequences. My action has an ethical dimension only if I do anticipate these consequences.

The ability to anticipate the consequences of one's actions is closely related to the ability to establish the connection between means and ends, that is, of seeing a means precisely as a means, as something that serves a particular end or purpose. This ability to establish the connection between means and their ends requires the ability to anticipate the future and to form mental images of realities not present or not yet in existence.

The ability to establish the connection between means and ends happens to be the fundamental intellectual capacity that has made possible the development of human culture and technology. The evolutionary roots of this capacity may be found in the evolution of bipedal gait, which transformed the anterior limbs of our ancestors from organs of locomotion into organs of manipulation. The hands thereby gradually became organs adept for the construction and use of objects for hunting and other activities that improved survival and reproduction, that is, that increased the reproductive fitness of their carriers.

The construction of tools, however, depends not only on manual dexterity, but in perceiving them precisely as tools, as objects that help to perform certain actions, that is, as means that serve certain ends or purposes: a knife for cutting, an arrow for hunting, an animal skin for protecting the body from the cold. The hypothesis I am advancing, is that natural selection promoted the intellectual capacity of our biped ancestors, because increased intelligence facilitated the perception of tools as tools, and therefore their construction and use, with the ensuing amelioration of biological survival and reproduction.

The development of the intellectual abilities of our ancestors took place over two million years or longer, gradually increasing the ability to connect means with their ends and, hence, the possibility of making ever more complex tools serving remote purposes. The ability to anticipate the future, essential for ethical behavior, is therefore closely associated with the development of the ability to construct tools, an ability that has produced the advanced technologies of modern societies and that is largely responsible for the success of humankind as a biological species.

The second condition for the existence of ethical behavior is the ability to make value judgments, to perceive certain objects or deeds as more desirable than others. Only if I can see the death of my enemy as preferable to his or her survival (or vice versa) can the action leading to his or her demise be thought of as moral. If the alternative consequences of an action are neutral with respect to value, the action cannot be characterized as ethical. The ability to make value judgments depends on the capacity for abstraction, that is, on the capacity to perceive actions or objects as members of general classes. This makes it possible to compare objects or actions with one another and to perceive some as more desirable than others. The capacity for abstraction, necessary to perceive individual objects or actions as members of general classes, requires an advanced intelligence such as exists in human beings and apparently in them alone. Thus, I see the ability to make value judgments primarily as an implicit consequence of the enhanced intelligence favored by natural selection in human evolution. Nevertheless, valuing certain objects or actions and choosing them over their alternatives can be of biological consequence; doing this in terms of general categories can be beneficial in practice.

The third condition necessary for ethical behavior is the ability to choose between alternative courses of action. Pulling the trigger can be a moral action only if I have the option not to pull it. A necessary action beyond our control is not a moral action: The circulation of the blood or the digestion of food are not moral actions.

Whether there is free will has been much discussed by philosophers, and this is not the appropriate place to review the arguments. I will only advance two considerations based on our common-sense experience. One is our profound personal conviction that the possibility of choosing between alternatives is genuine rather than only apparent. The second consideration is that when we confront a given situation that requires action on our part, we are able mentally to explore alternative courses of action, thereby extending the field within which we can exercise our free will. In any case, if there were no free will, there would be no ethical behavior; morality would only be an illusion. The point that I wish to make here is, however, that free will is dependent on the existence of a well-developed intelligence, which makes it possible to explore alternative courses of action and to choose one or another in view of the anticipated consequences.

In summary, my proposal is that ethical behavior is an attribute of the biological make-up of human beings and, hence, is a product of biological evolution. But I see no evidence that ethical behavior developed because it was adaptive in itself. I find it hard to see how *evaluating* certain actions as either good or evil (not just choosing some actions rather than others, or evaluating them with respect to their practical consequences) would promote the reproductive fitness of the evaluators. Nor do I see how there might be some form of "incipient" ethical behavior that would then be further promoted by natural selection. The three necessary conditions for there being ethical behavior are manifestations of advanced intellectual abilities.

It rather seems that the target of natural selection was the development of these advanced intellectual capacities. This development was favored by natural selection because the construction and use of tools improved the strategic position of our biped ancestors. Once bipedalism evolved and tool-using and tool-making became possible, those individuals more effective in these functions had a greater probability of biological success. The biological advantage provided by the design and use of tools persisted long enough so that intellectual abilities continued to increase, eventually yielding the eminent development of intelligence that is characteristic of *Homo sapiens*.

The Ten Commandments: Beyond Biology

There are many theories concerned with the rational grounds for morality, such as deductive theories that seek to discover the axioms or fundamental principles that determine what is morally correct on the basis of direct moral intuition. There also are theories like logical positivism or existentialism, which negate rational foundations for morality, reducing moral principles to emotional decisions or to other irrational grounds. Since the publication of Darwin's theory of evolution by natural selection, philosophers as well as biologists have attempted to find in the evolutionary process the justification for moral norms. The common ground to all such proposals is that evolution is a natural process that achieves goals that are desirable and thereby morally good; indeed it has produced human beings. Proponents of these ideas claim that only the evolutionary goals can give moral value to human action: Whether a human deed is morally right depends on whether it directly or indirectly promotes the evolutionary process and its natural objectives.

Herbert Spencer[5] was perhaps the first philosopher seeking to find the grounds of morality in biological evolution. More recent attempts include those of the distinguished evolutionists J.S. Huxley[6] and C.H. Waddington[7] and of Edward O. Wilson,[8] founder of sociobiology as an independent discipline engaged in discovering the biological foundations of social behavior. I have argued elsewhere[9] that the moral theories proposed by Spencer, Huxley, and Waddington are mistaken and fail to avoid the naturalistic fallacy.[10] These authors argue, in one or other fashion, that the standard by which human actions are judged good or evil, derives from the contribution the actions make to evolutionary advancement or progress. A blunder of this argumentation is that it is based on value judgments about what is or is not progressive in (particularly human) evolution.[11] There is nothing objective in the evolutionary process itself that makes the success of bacteria, which have persisted for more than 3 billion years and in enormous diversity and numbers, less "progressive" than that of the vertebrates, even though the latter are more complex.[12] Nor are the insects, of which more than one million species exist, less successful or less progressive from a purely biological perspective than human beings or any other mammal species. Moreover, the proponents of evolution-grounded moral codes fail to demonstrate why the promotion of biological evolution by itself should be the standard to measure what is morally good.

Determining the morality of human actions on the basis of natural selection or the course of evolution leads, moreover, to paradoxes. Evolution has produced the smallpox and AIDS viruses. But it would seem unreasonable to accuse the World Health Organization of immorality because of its campaign for total eradication of the smallpox virus, or to label unethical the efforts to control the galloping spread of the AIDS virus. Human hereditary diseases are conditioned by mutations that are natural events in the evolutionary process. But we do not think it immoral to cure or alleviate the pain of persons with such diseases. Natural selection is a natural process that increases the frequency of certain genes and eliminates others, that yields some kinds of organisms rather than others; but it is not a process moral or immoral in itself or in its outcome, in the same way as gravity is not a morally-laden force. In order to consider some evolutionary events as morally right and others wrong, we must introduce human values. Moral evaluations cannot be reached simply on the basis that certain events came about by natural processes.

The most recent and most subtle attempt to ground the moral codes on the evolutionary process emanates from the sociobiologists, particularly from E.O. Wilson, who starts by proposing that "scientists and humanists should consider together the possibility that the time has come for ethics to be removed temporarily from the hands of the philosophers and biologicized."[13] The sociobiologists' argument is that morality is an epigenetic manifestation of our genes, which so manipulate human beings as to make them believe that some behaviors are morally "good" so that people behave in ways that are good for their genes, which they might not otherwise do because the genetic benefit is not apparent (except to sociobiologists after the development of their discipline).[14]

In my view, the sociobiologists' account of the evolution of the moral sense is misguided.[15] As I have argued above, we make moral judgments as a consequence of our eminent intellectual abilities, not as an innate way for achieving biological gain. Moreover, the sociobiologists' position may be interpreted as calling for the supposition that those *norms* of morality should be considered supreme that achieve the most biological (genetic) gain (because that is, in their view, why the moral sense evolved at all). This, in turn, would justify social preferences, including racism and even genocide, that many of us (sociobiologists included) judge morally obtuse and even heinous.

I submit that our biological nature may *predispose* us to accept certain moral precepts, but it does not constrain us to accept them or to behave according to them. The same eminent intellectual abilities that make ethical behavior possible and necessary, and in particular free will, also give us the power to accept some moral norms and to reject others, independently of any natural inclinations. A natural predisposition may influence our behavior, but influence and predisposition are not the same as constraint or determination. It may be that there are natural dispositions to selfishness and aggression. But human beings have the power to rise above these tendencies.

It seems to me apparent that some norms of morality are consistent with behaviors prompted by natural selection, but other norms are not so. The commandment of charity, "Love thy neighbor as thyself," often runs contrary to the fitness of the genes, even though it promotes social cooperation and peace of mind. If the yardstick of morality were the multiplication of genes, the supreme moral imperative would be to beget the largest possible number of children. But to impregnate the most women possible is not, in the view of most people, the highest moral duty of a man. Rather, the highest moral duties, as judged by cultural norms, have often been universal duties of justice and benevolence.

I will further point out that moral norms differ from one culture to another and even "evolve" from one time to another. Today, many people see that the biblical injunction "Be fruitful and multiply" has been replaced by a moral imperative to limit the number of one's children. No genetic change in human populations accounts for this inversion of moral value. An individual's biological fitness is still favored by having many children.

Moral codes must be consistent with biological nature, but biology is insufficient for determining which moral codes are, or should be, accepted. This may be reiterated by returning to the analogy with human languages. Our biological nature determines the sounds that we can or cannot utter and also constrains human language in other ways. But a language's syntax and vocabulary are not determined by our biological nature (otherwise, there could not be a multitude of tongues); they are products of human culture. Likewise, moral norms are not determined by biological processes, but by belief systems and cultural traditions that are products of human history.

The Essential Incompleteness of Scientific Knowledge

Science is a wondrously successful way of knowing. It seeks explanations of the natural world by formulating hypotheses that are subject to the possibility of empirical falsification or corroboration. A scientific hypothesis is tested by ascertaining whether or not predictions about the world of experience derived as logical consequences from the hypothesis agree with what is actually observed.[16] Science as a mode of inquiry into the nature of the universe has been successful and of great consequence. Witness the proliferation of science academic departments in universities and other research institutions, the enormous budgets that the body politic and the private sector willingly commit to scientific research, and its economic impact. The Office of Management and the Budget (OMB) of the U.S. government has estimated that fifty percent of all economic growth in the United States since the Second World War can directly be attributed to scientific knowledge and technological advances. The technology derived from scientific knowledge pervades, indeed, our lives: the high-rise buildings of our cities, thruways and long-span bridges, rockets that bring men to the moon, telephones that provide instant communication across continents, computers that perform complex calculations in millionths of a second, vaccines and drugs that keep bacterial parasites at bay, gene therapies that replace DNA in defective cells. All these remarkable achievements bear witness to the validity of the scientific knowledge from which they originated.

Scientific knowledge is also remarkable in the way it emerges by way of consensus and agreement among scientists, and in the way new knowledge builds upon past accomplishment rather than starting anew with each generation or each new practitioner. Surely scientists disagree with each other on many matters; but these are issues not yet settled, and the points of disagreement generally do not bring into question previous knowledge. Modern scientists do not challenge that atoms exist, or that there is a universe with a myriad of stars, or that heredity is encased in DNA.

Science is a way of knowing, but it is not the only way. Knowledge also derives from other sources, such as common sense, artistic and religious experience, and philosophical reflection. The validity of the knowledge acquired by non-scientific modes of inquiry can be simply established by pointing out that science dawned in the sixteenth century, but humankind had for centuries built cities and roads, brought forth political institutions and sophisticated codes of law, advanced profound philosophies and value systems, and created magnificent plastic art, as well as music and literature. We thus learn about ourselves and about the world in which we live and we also benefit from products of this non-scientific knowledge. The crops we harvest and the animals we husband emerged millennia before science's dawn from practices set down by farmers in the Middle East, Andean sierras, and Mayan plateaus.

It is not my intention in this essay's final section to belabor the extraordinary fruits of nonscientific modes of inquiry. I wish simply to state something that is obvious, but becomes at times clouded by the *hubris* of some scientists. Successful as it is, and universally encompassing as its subject is, a scientific view of the world is hopelessly incomplete. There are matters of value and meaning that are outside science's scope. Even when we achieve scientific understanding of a natural object of process, we are still missing matters that may well be thought by many to be of equal or greater import. Scientific knowledge may enrich aesthetic and moral perceptions, and may illuminate the significance of life and the world, but these are matters outside science's realm. In order to understand ourselves and our place in the economy of things, we need much more than scientific knowledge. We need psychology and sociology, as well as history, aesthetics and philosophy; if we seek religious understanding, we need theology. My purpose in this essay has been to provide what I see as a necessary dimension, the biological one, of any view of human nature that seeks to be relevant and complete. But I do not pretend that biology provides now, or will ever provide, a complete understanding of what we humans are and our place in the universe.

Notes

1. Charles Darwin, *On the Origin of Species,* 1st ed. (London: John Murray, 1859), 490.

2. Darwin, *Origin of Species,* 484–488. The text and pages cited are from the first edition, published on November 26, 1859. In the second edition, published on December 26, 1859, he wrote: "When the views advanced by me in this volume, and by Mr. Wallace in the Linnean Journal, or when analogous views on the origin of species are generally admitted." The *Origin*'s final sentence, which I cite as a leitmotif at the start of this essay, is also from the first edition. In the second edition, he added the phrase *by the Creator*: "originally breathed by the Creator into a few forms or into one."

3. F.J. Ayala, "The Myth of Eve: Molecular Biology and Human Origins," *Science* 270 (1995):1930–1936.

4. The genetic information is encoded in the linear sequence of the DNA's four nucleotide components (represented by A, C, G, T) in the same fashion as semantic information is encoded in the sequence of letters of a written text. Most of the DNA is contained in the chromosomes inside the cell nucleus.

5. H. Spencer, *The Principles of Ethics* (London, 1893).

6. T.H. Huxley and J.S. Huxley, *Touchstone for Ethics* (New York: Harper, 1947); J.S. Huxley, *Evolution in Action* (New York: Harper, 1953).

7. C.H. Waddington, *The Ethical Animal* (London: Allen & Unwin,1960).

8. E.O. Wilson, *Sociobiology: the New Synthesis* (Cambridge: Harvard University Press, 1975); *On Human Nature* (Cambridge: Harvard University Press, 1978).

9. F.J. Ayala, "The Biological Roots of Morality," *Biology and Philosophy* 2:235–252 (1987).

10. The "naturalistic fallacy" consists in identifying what "is" with what "ought" to be (G.E. Moore, *Principia Ethica*, Cambridge University Press, 1903). This error was already pointed out by Hume: "In every system of morality which I

have hitherto met with I have always remarked that the author proceeds for some time in the ordinary way of reasoning . . . when of a sudden I am surprised to find, that instead of the usual copulations of propositions, *is* and *is not*, I meet with no proposition that is not connected with an *ought* or *ought not*. This change is imperceptible; but is, however, of the last consequence. For as this *ought* or *ought not* expresses some new relation or affirmation, it is necessary that it should be observed and explained; and at the same time a reason should be given, for what seems altogether inconceivable, how this new relation can be a deduction from others, which are entirely different from it." (D. Hume, *Treatise of Human Nature* (Oxford: Oxford University Press [1740], 1978).

11. F.J. Ayala, "The Evolutionary Concept of Progress." In: G.A. Almond *et al.*, eds., *Progress and Its Discontents* (Berkeley: University of California Press, 1982), pp. 106–124.

12. See S.J. Gould, *Full House. The Spread of Excellence from Plato to Darwin* (New York, NY: Harmony Books, 1996).

13. Wilson, *Sociobiology*, p. 562.

14. M. Ruse, *Taking Darwin Seriously: A Naturalistic Approach to Philosophy* (Oxford: Basil Blackwell, 1986); M. Ruse, "Evolutionary Ethics: A Phoenix Arisen," *Zygon* 21:95–112 (1986); M. Ruse and E.O. Wilson, "Moral Philosophy as Applied Science," *Philosophy: Journal of the Royal Institute of Philosophy* 61:173–192 (1986).

15. F.J. Ayala, "The Difference of Being Human: Ethical Behavior as an Evolutionary Byproduct." In: H. Rolston, *Biology, Ethics and the Origin of Life*, 3rd ed. (Boston and London: Jones and Bartlett, 1995), pp. 113–135. See also note 9 above.

16. F.J. Ayala, "On the Scientific Method, Its Practice and Pitfalls," *History and Philosophy of Life Science* 16 (1994):205–240.

Chapter Eight

Human Life: Creation Versus Evolution?

WOLFHART PANNENBERG

Ever since its first publication by Charles Darwin in 1859, the doctrine of evolution of living forms and species by natural selection among individual variations within a given population in a struggle for survival has been a matter of dispute among scientists, and it has become an ideological controversy. The dispute among scientists, however, did not center on the issue of whether there is or can be a process of evolution of higher organized species from lower forms of life. Rather, the scientific discussions were mainly concerned with the question of whether the principle of natural selection is sufficient to explain the process of the emergence of ever new and more complex forms of life.

There are a number of difficult questions related to this issue. First of all: What is the standard requirement, according to which selection operates? Is adaptation to external conditions the standard of fitness for natural selection, as the mechanistic interpretation of Darwinism in the late nineteenth century assumed, or does the spontaneous productivity of genetic variation lead to the discovery of new natural "niches" for survival and consequently of new objects for adaptation? Furthermore, can a continuous and cumulative occurrence of small variants under the pressures of natural selection issue in the emergence of a new species, or do small changes tend to disappear because they don't fit in the overall system of the organism and of its functioning? Would, then, a "fulguration" of a complete new scheme of organization be required for a new species to emerge? Finally, how is the apparent direction of the evolutionary process toward ever more complex forms of organic life to be accounted for? These are but a few of the more important riddles that have plagued Darwinism from the start and still continue to vex its defenders. Nevertheless, the general perspective of the Darwinian theory has been victorious, even though it is still hypothetical and the evidence for it rests on a somewhat defective fossil record rather than on experiential demonstration. For all its difficulties, the theory of evolution still provides the most plausible interpretation of what is known about the history of organic life on this planet.

The resistance against the new theory from the side of the churches had been predictable, since it stood in clear contrast, if not contradiction, to the traditional concept of creation. For many centuries it had been taken for granted that, as according to the biblical account in the first chapter of Genesis, the species of plants and animals had been created by God on the fifth and the sixth day of creation and have remained unchanged ever since. It is the position that so-called "creationists" defend in the present day. Even among those, however, who do not cling to biblical literalism, it seems unacceptable that the theory of evolution could replace God's purposive action in bringing about the different forms of life by a mechanical process of nature. In this controversy, the point is that before Darwin the purposive action of the creator had been understood to provide the only explanation for the fact of different species of animal life. Therefore, the proposal of a natural explanation of the same result was taken as a denial of God's purposive action in the creation of living forms. In principle, of course, the assumption of God's purposive action need not have excluded the use of natural causes in the execution of the Divine purpose. In historical fact, however, in the situation after Darwin's book *On the Origin of Species* had been published, explanation by divine purposes and by the mechanical operation of natural causes were taken as alternatives.

Attempts at Theistic Evolution

Given the antagonistic climate of the early discussions on Darwin's theory, it is astonishing that in the beginning some leading British churchmen and theologians tried to reinterpret Christian doctrine in the light of the perspective of evolution. The most remarkable of these attempts was a book edited by Charles Gore in 1889 under the title *Lux Mundi: A Series of Studies in the Religion of the Incarnation*. As the title suggests, the book reinterpreted the incarnation of the divine Logos in Jesus Christ in terms of providing the culmination of the evolution of life. While the process of natural evolution culminates in the emergence of the human race, so the history of the human race reached its climax in the incarnation.

To a certain extent, such a theological scheme was suggested by early Church Fathers like Irenaeus. But now in post-Darwinian times the picture of a salvific history of humanity leading toward the event of the incarnation was being immensely broadened by including the process of natural evolution of life as a prehistory of that salvific history.

Interestingly, the authors contributing to *Lux Mundi* did not take Darwinian evolution to describe a mechanical process, but rather a historical process. That was hardly warranted by the situation in the development of evolutionary theory around 1890. *Lux Mundi* rather pointed beyond that situation to a future concept of "emergent" or "organic" evolution, as it was proposed in 1923 by Lloyd Morgan: Emergence means that in each step of the evolutionary process something new comes into existence. It does not merely "result" by mechanical necessity from past conditions. This concept of emergent evolution vindicated the positive evaluation of Darwinism by the group of *Lux Mundi*, who had celebrated the new theory for doing away with the God of deism who had been responsible for the beginnings only, while now God could be seen to be active in every new turn of the evolutionary process. The concept of emergent evolution overcame the mechanistic, reductionistic way of describing Darwin's theory, and the tendency to emphasize the element of the New in the sequence of evolving forms of life was further strengthened by the realization that major steps in the evolutionary process need "fulgurations" of new schemes of organization rather than a sequence of small steps of cumulative variations.

Evolution and the Biblical Witness

After providing the stage for a theological discussion of evolution, I now turn to the crucial issue of whether a theological appropriation of the doctrine of evolution can do justice to the biblical witness on the creation of animal species by God. In a subsequent section of this chapter the same question will be asked with regard to the human race. What has been said so far on the further development and refinement of the theory of evolution since Darwin will prove helpful in the attempt at answering both of these questions.

When we turn to the biblical witness on creation, the first thing must be to remind ourselves of the fact that the biblical texts are historical documents and have to be interpreted accordingly in terms of what they were trying to say at the time of their composition. This principle of the historical interpretation of the Bible is the core issue in all discussions with creationists. Historical interpretation reads the biblical affirmations relative to the context of their writing, to the concerns of their authors at the time of their writing, to the knowledge they had at their disposal. Such historical interpretation does not imply that the biblical affirmations, being limited to their own time, have nothing to tell readers of a much later period. But whatever they have to tell us, they convey it precisely through their historical particularity. To the degree that their affirmations have universal significance, it is inherent in their particularity. Otherwise it would not be the meaning of the biblical affirmations, but a meaning the modern interpreter reads into them. Furthermore, the historical reading of the biblical affirmations does not preclude their appreciation as the Word of God, the Word that addresses us as it does every generation of human persons. The Word of God expressed in the biblical affirmations is, however, a unified entity. It is the Word of God that became incarnate in Jesus Christ. To read or hear the Bible as the Word of God is to relate each particular biblical affirmation to the whole of the biblical witness and to interpret the detailed, historically distinctive affirmations in that light. Therefore, reverence for the Bible as the Word of God does not stand in opposition to a careful historical scrutiny of each individual sentence.

With regard to the biblical report on the creation of the world in the first chapter of Genesis, this means that we have to read its affirmations as witnessing to the God of Israel who is the creator of the world by using the natural science of the sixth century before Christ, i.e. Babylonian wisdom, in order to account for the sequence of creatures coming forth from God's creative activity. The relevance of this report in our present situation, then, is primarily the encouragement to use the science of our era in a similar way for the purpose of witnessing today to the God of the Bible as creator of the universe as we know it. This is the authority of the biblical report on the creation of the world. It calls us to try our own theology of nature, but in doing so to remain true to the peculiar and distinctive nature of the God of Israel, just as the authors of the priestly report on the creation of the world did in their own era.

The authority of the biblical report does not require us to consider every detail as the last word on the respective issue. Many statements are inevitably indebted to the limited knowledge about nature in the sixth century B.C. One example is the idea that the experience of rain is evidence of a huge supply of water in heaven above the clouds, comparable to the oceans down on earth. On this assumption, it is astonishing that the waters above the clouds normally remain separated from those beneath. This is explained by the idea (Genesis 1:6ff.) that God created a vault to keep the waters above from pouring down. This mechanism is completely rational, and yet this beautiful and important detail can no longer be part of our conception of nature.

The same applies to the assumption that all the different types of creatures, and especially all the different species of plants and animals, were created in the beginning and remain permanently unchanged. This idea is an example of the mythical attitude of mind in early cultures, where generally, as Mircea Eliade told us, the world order was conceived as having been built in the "original time," *in illo tempore*, without later change. By contrast, the modern knowledge of nature provides sufficient evidence for assuming that the natural world is in a continuous process of becoming. This means that there is a continuous emergence of new types of creatures, along with the disappearance of others. All this belongs to the picture of nature with which we work.

Contingency and Newness in Natural History

Does the modern picture of nature in terms of continuous change contradict the biblical doctrine of creation? It is certainly at variance with the image in the first chapter of Genesis that the whole order of creation was produced in six days and continues to exist unchanged. But within the Bible as a whole we find other pictures of God's creative activity. In the prophetic writings, for example, we learn that God is continuously active in the course of history and that once in a while he creates something quite new (Isaiah 48:6ff.). That is not to deny the creation of heaven and earth in the beginning. Yet Second Isaiah takes that as an example of God's continuously creative activity. This, then, is the model of a continuous creation which is coextensive with the course of the world's history. In this model the creation of heaven and earth is much closer to the modern understanding of nature in terms of a history of the universe than is the image of the six-day creation in Genesis. Such a conception of continuous creation does not have difficulties with a doctrine of evolution, according to which the different species of animals emerge successively in the long process of life's history on earth.

There is one requirement, however, which must be met if the concept of evolution is to be compatible with a theology of nature based on the biblical idea of God. This is the acknowledgment that something new occurs in each and every single event. Newness also occurs in the emergence of new forms of life in the process of evolution. This element of newness or contingency was not in the focus of the early mechanistic interpretation of Darwinism. However, it has been increasingly emphasized in the conception of epigenesis, which means the emergence of something new. Contingent newness belongs in the concept of *emergent evolution*.

Why is the element of contingency so important in a theological appropriation of the theory of evolution? The reason is that the Bible conceives of God's relationship to the world in terms of free creative acts in the course of history as well as at the beginning of this world. In the first chapter of the Bible, this concern for God's freedom in his creative activity is expressed in the concept of the divine word which brings about its effect in the most effortless way. In each creative act, God's freedom brings forth something new simply by his word. Therefore the history of the world is seen as an irreversible sequence of contingent events, notwithstanding all the regularities that can be observed in its course. Consequently, a concept of evolution in terms of a purely mechanical process would not be easy to reconcile with the biblical idea of God's creative activity; yet the concept of an epigenetic process of evolution with something new to occur in virtually every single event is perfectly compatible with it.

In addition, God's creative activity does not exclude the employment of secondary causes in bringing about creatures. In the priestly document on creation from the sixth century B.C., preserved in the first chapter of Genesis, the creator calls on the earth to bring forth vegetation (Genesis 1:11). And again it is the earth that is called upon to produce animals, especially mammals (Genesis 1:24). If our creationist friends today would adhere, in this case, to the letter of the Bible, they could have no objection to the emergence of organisms from inorganic matter, nor to the descent of the higher animals from those initial stages of life. In the biblical view, such a natural mediation does not contradict the affirmation that the creatures are the work of God. For in the next verse it is explicitly said that *God* made the beasts and the cattle and everything that creeps upon the ground (1:25).

Of course, the biblical text does not tell anything about the higher species of animals as having evolved from lower ones. But that is an issue of secondary importance, if compared with the question of whether the act of creation must be conceived of as an immediate action of God without any mediation by other creatures. This question, however, has been answered already. The immediacy of God's creative action with reference to its creatures is not impaired by secondary causes, since their activity is not on the same level with that of the creator.

The Appearance of the Human Soul

The case of the human being is a special one, because human persons are related to God in a special way. This fact is indicated by the importance of religion of one form or another in the history of the human race. Human self-consciousness seems closely connected with some form of awareness of the divine. In the Bible, this close relationship to the origin of the universe is expressed in the idea that the human person has been created in the image of God. Therefore, the human being represents the creator himself with regard to the rest of God's creation. Doesn't that require that the human being was created by God alone, without the cooperation of other, earlier creatures? In the first chapter of the Bible no such cooperation is mentioned. Does that mean it is excluded?

The older report on the creation of human beings in the second chapter of Genesis does not justify such a suggestion, because it says that the human body was formed of "dust from the ground" (Genesis 2:7). That seems to be roughly equivalent to the role of the earth in the first chapter of Genesis, when God addresses the earth to bring forth plants and animals. Therefore, our body is perishable, which is to say, it will return to the earth. Only the human spirit is said to come directly from God, as the second chapter of the Bible describes it: God breathes his breath into the figure he formed from the dust; he "breathed into his nostrils the breath of life" (Genesis 2:7). Correspondingly, with our last breath we return the gift of the spirit to God, like the psalm says which, according to the Gospel of Luke, Jesus quoted when he died on his cross: "Into thy hand I commit my spirit" (Psalm 31:5, Luke 23:46). In the moment of death the spirit or breath gets separated from the body, and as Ecclesiastes says, "the dust returns to the earth, as it was, and the spirit returns to God who gave it" (Ecclesiastes 12:7).

Does that mean that we are allowed to think of the human *body* as coming from the process of evolution of animal life, but not so of the human soul and spirit? This could seem to be required by the older creation story when it says that the creator breathes the breath of life into the figure formed from clay and that thereby the human creature became a living being (Genesis 2:7). The Hebrew term here is *nephesh hajah*, and *nephesh* was often translated as "soul." Thus God is presented here as creating the human soul by breathing the spirit of life into the nostrils of the human body. It was from this sentence that the old Christian creationism of the Patristic period derived its theory about the origin of the human soul: While the body of each new individual was considered to come from the chain of propagation, each individual soul was believed to be added to the body by the creator himself. But this Patristic creationism presupposed the independent status of the soul as compared to the body, an idea that is in keeping with Platonism, but not with the Hebrew Scriptures. In the Old Testament *nephesh hajah*, which we translated by the term *soul*, is not independent from the body, but the principle of its life, though it is not the origin of life itself. The *nephesh* is only the continuous hunger and thirst for life. The root meaning of the word is "throat." It is in constant need of the spirit of God, that productive breath or wind which animates the soul and through the soul its body. The origin of life, then, is finally the divine spirit and not the human soul. It is only through the spirit that the human being becomes a "living soul" as the phrase in the creation story goes.

To be a "living soul," however, is not a distinctive prerogative of the human being. According to the creation story in the first chapter of Genesis, the "breath of life" is in all the animals, the beasts on the ground, and the birds in the air (Genesis 1:30). This corresponds exactly to the idea in the earlier report on the creation of the human race, where God breathes the breath of life into the figure of clay so that it comes alive. If the animals have the breath of life within themselves, although they are products of the earth which was summoned by the creator to bring them forth, then there is no difference from the creation of the human being with regard to its description as "living soul," *nephesh hajah*. The difference of the human being from the other animals is not that the human being has a "living soul," but that it is destined to exist in a particular relationship to God, so that it is called to represent the creator himself with regard to the animal world and even to the earth (Genesis 1:26).

The excursion into biblical exegesis was necessary to meet the charge of modern creationists that the doctrine of evolution and especially the derivation of the emergence of the human race from the evolutionary process of animal life contradicts the biblical creation stories. When in the Bible animal life is seen as a product of the earth and the formation of human life as "living soul" is understood as analogous to animal life, then there is no reason why the human being should not have emerged from the evolution of animal life. The idea of evolution as such is a modern concept and cannot be derived from biblical conceptions. But it is not opposed to the basic concerns of the Biblical conceptions of the origin of animal and of human life. This can be affirmed as long as the modern idea of evolution does not exclude the creative divine activity within the entire process of evolution.

Beyond Mechanism to Emergence

The doctrine of evolution is open to a theological interpretation, when it is not conceived in terms of a mechanical process, based on the principle of natural selection, but as describing a process of emergence, in the course of which the productivity of life continuously produces something new. The element of contingency in this concept of emergent evolution secures its openness to the creative activity of God in this process. That each form of life can be understood as a creature of God is not dependent on the idea of purpose, the assumption of a purposeful adaptation of each species to the conditions of its survival in its environment. In earlier times it was assumed that such purposeful adaptation presupposes and demonstrates the intelligent will of the creator and is not reducible to other causes.

It was this assumption that Darwin destroyed by explaining the adaptation of a species to its environment as a result of natural selection. But the principle of natural selection does not exclude the continuous activity of the creator in the very productivity of life. The superabundant creativity of life and the creative action of God are not alternative notions—no more so than the productivity of the earth is which is called upon by God in the biblical creation story to bring forth vegetation and even animals. The spontaneous creativity of life is the form of God's creative activity.

In a modern perspective, self-organization is characteristic of life on all levels of its evolution. It accounts for the spontaneity in all forms of life, and it is in this principle of spontaneous self-organization that we have to perceive the roots of human subjectivity. Self-organization is the principle of freedom and of superabundance in the creative advance of the evolutionary process. Human self-consciousness is its highest manifestation as far as we can see, as it allows us to integrate all other consciousness into the unity of our individual self. Self-consciousness itself is not merely a given fact of nature, however. In each individual life history it arises from the early stages of the development of our consciousness. Self-consciousness itself is a product already of the creativity of life within each one of us, a product of the creative activity of the divine spirit.

Evolution and the Divine Spirit

The creative self-organization of life in the process of evolution since the transition from inorganic matter to the first organisms corresponds to the blowing of the divine wind, the Spirit of God that breathes life into ever new creatures and thus blows through the evolution of life until it overcomes all perishableness in the resurrection of Jesus Christ. The death of individuals is due, according to the biblical witness, to their limited share in the divine Spirit (Genesis 6:3). To Jesus, however, though a finite being himself, the Spirit of life was given "without measure" (John 3:34). Therefore he was raised from the dead by the power of the Spirit and transformed into a spiritual body (I Corinthians 15:44ff), which is to say: into imperishable life, which is imperishable because of its unbroken participation in the divine Spirit who is the source of all life.

A Christian account of the evolution of life as expression of the divine Spirit blowing through creation cannot avoid some reference to the eschatological resurrection of the dead, the climax of the creative activity of the divine Spirit that was first realized in the resurrection of Jesus, but is meant to embrace humankind in general by communion with Jesus and even, according to Paul, the world of other creatures, because "the creation itself will be set free from its bondage of decay and obtain the glorious liberty of the children of God" (Romans 8:21).

To the modern mind, the biblical description of life as created by the dynamic activity of the divine Spirit may appear as merely metaphorical. Such an appraisal becomes even more suggestive when one realizes that the Hebrew notion of spirit means breath or wind rather than intellect. The images of breath and wind seem to be just images, without providing rational explanation.

The people of ancient Israel, however, took breath and wind quite literally to be the cause of life. This seemed to be confirmed by everyday experience: Life begins when a baby starts to breathe, and it ends with the last gasp of a person. Modern people may no longer consider this intuitive evidence to provide a sufficient explanation for the beginning and end of human life. Yet breath is still more than an arbitrary image, because it indicates the dependence of life upon a flow of energy that enters our body from the outside and passes through ourselves. Like flame, our life is a process of exploiting a flow of energy by degrading the high-level potential energy of our food and the oxygen we breathe into a state of increased entropy. Life is an autocatalytic process of self-organization that exploits the gradient of energy in our environment, like the flame does by keeping its equilibrium at the price of slowly consuming a candle.

The Spirit and Human Development

The description of life by the phenomenon of breath that goes through us is an example, like the flame is, of taking advantage of a flow of energy by letting it pass through ourselves. This consideration is not specific to *human* life, of course, since it applies to all organic life even in its most primitive forms. But the wonder of life is in the abundance of increasingly complex forms that the principle of self-organization produces as it happens in the process of evolution. The human being is a very complex and specific example of such creative self-organization, in the development of an individual as well as in human culture. In an elementary way, self-organization takes place in the development of each individual, and there we can try to perceive a peculiar form of the work of the Spirit in human beings. This work of the Spirit is not yet the specific function of sanctification, but first the invigorating action of the Spirit in our personal development.

Human life is endowed with consciousness, memory and self-consciousness, but all these characterstics have to develop in the course of our individual life. In the beginning there is no self-consciousness, but only a disposition for its development. Even the acquaintance with our environment is a task that we can only meet by our own productive activity. Perception and consciousness of objects is something we share with the animals before us, but only to a modest extent do we react instinctively, like they do, to stimuli from the outside. Rather, we have to develop our own survey of our world in order to relate to the objects of experience, and we achieve that by the development of language. Language is a form of organization, an active organization of our world for ourselves. Though each individual person takes over language from the social context, the process of acquiring language is still a creative process of self-organization, as is the later appropriation of our cultural heritage. Yet such self-creative activity is not something we "make," but it is rather produced by some sort of inspiration that activates ourselves. It is only in the course of that process that we learn to distinguish our own body from the objects around, learn to give our own body its name like other objects and finally learn the use of the difficult word "I" and related words like "mine" or "my." Self-consciousness is developing along this line. It is not there and complete from the outset, but depends on the development of language, though later on it becomes the center of our personal life. The key to our human life is language. Nothing is independent of it. Even the use and development of tools beyond primitive stages depends on language.

The world of language is not the only, but the most distinctively human dimension of the activity of the Spirit in our lives. Therefore, we are not mistaken to use the word spirit in a special connection with consciousness and language. It activates us so that we actively develop our conscious life and language, but we do not "make" it in the specifically technical sense of that word. We are active in producing it, while we participate in our social context and in the language of our culture. Through and beyond that, we participate in a spiritual dynamic that does not originate with us, and also surpasses and comprises our society and world. A sense of the surpassing mystery of life belongs to the human condition, precisely because we organize the objects of experience with the help of language in encompassing totalities that are themselves transcended by the surpassing mystery. Where humans encountered that mystery, they usually called it by the name of God. The awareness of the religious dimension of life belongs very closely to the specifically human form of consciousness and self-consciousness. It belongs to the origins of language. In the Bible it is God who brings the animals to Adam "to see what he would call them" (Genesis 2:19). It serves the poetic purpose of that story that this episode is dealt with before the creation of the woman, but it seems, rather, that language is a social phenomenon, not a solitary product of solitary individuals, and furthermore it may have had ritual origins in its beginnings.

Our secular culture tends to underestimate the encompassing importance of religion in the early history of human culture. This also applies with regard to the period of transition from prehuman animal life to human life in the full sense of the word. Burials belong to the oldest documents of human life, and their occurrence since the paleolithic period, even before the early traces of visual art, serves as a criterion for when and where the transition from animal behavior to human culture has come to its conclusion (K.J. Narr, A.F.C Wallace). Thus religion is constitutive for the beginnings of humankind.

Whether this final step—from biological to cultural evolution—took place only once, is a matter of secondary importance. In the Bible, of course, all humans were understood to have come from a single pair of parents, Adam and Eve. But in the biblical creation story this is not a matter of special theological emphasis, but follows from the narrative's way of treating the creation of humankind in the form of one paradigmatic individual, Adam. In the Roman Catholic doctrine, the descendance of all human beings from the one Adam is still considered important because of the doctrine of original sin as inherited from Adam. If, however, the story of the fall is to be read as a paradigmatic description of human behavior rather than in terms of a unique event in the beginnings of human history, then the Christian doctrine of original sin depends more on the affirmation that all human beings repeat the paradigmatic pattern of Adam's and Eve's behavior in the garden of Eden, than on biological heritage. Therefore, the question of whether the transition from prehuman life to humanity took place in only one individual (or two individuals), or at several points within a larger group of individuals, is a matter of secondary importance as compared to the spiritual nature of life in general and of human life in particular.

Chapter Nine

Evolution and the Living God

POPE JOHN PAUL II

Evolution is an essential subject which deeply interests the Church, since revelation, for its part, contains teaching concerning the nature and origins of humanity. How do the conclusions reached by the various scientific disciplines coincide with those contained in the message of revelation? And if, at first sight, there are apparent contradictions, in what direction do we look for their solution? We know, in fact, that truth cannot contradict truth.[1] Moreover, to shed greater light on historical truth, research on the Church's relations with science between the sixteenth and eighteenth centuries is of great importance.

[The Pontifical Academy of Sciences is] undertaking a "reflection on science at the dawn of the third millennium," starting with the identification of the principal problems created by the sciences and which affect humanity's future. With this step we point the way to solutions which will be beneficial to the whole human community. In the domain of inanimate and animate nature, the evolution of science and its applications gives rise to new questions. The better the Church's knowledge is of their essential aspects, the more she will understand their impact. Consequently, in accordance with her specific mission she will be able to offer criteria for discerning the moral conduct required of all human beings in view of their integral salvation.

Before offering several reflections that more specifically concern the subject of the origin of life and its evolution, I would like to remind you that the Magisterium of the Church has already made pronouncements on these matters within the framework of her own competence. I will cite here two interventions.

In his Encyclical *Humani generis* (1950), my predecessor Pius XII had already stated that there was no opposition between evolution and the doctrine of the faith about humanity and human vocation, on condition that one did not lose sight of several indisputable points.[2]

For my part, when I received those taking part in the Academy's assembly on October 31, 1992, I had the opportunity, with regard to Galileo, to draw attention to the need of a rigorous hermeneutic for the correct interpretation of the inspired word. It is necessary to determine the proper sense of Scripture, while avoiding any unwarranted interpretations that make it say what it does not intend to say. In order to delineate the field of their own study, the exegete and the theologian must keep informed about the results achieved by the natural sciences.[3]

Evolution and the Church's Magisterium

Taking into account the state of scientific research at the time as well as of the requirements of theology, the Encyclical *Humani Generis* considered the doctrine of "evolutionism" a serious hypothesis, worthy of investigation and in-depth study equal to that of the opposing hypothesis. Pius XII added two methodological conditions: that this opinion should not be adopted as though it were a certain, proven doctrine and as though one could totally prescind from revelation with no regard to the questions it raises. He also spelled out the condition on which this opinion would be compatible with the Christian faith, a point to which I will return.

Today, almost half a century after the publication of the Encyclical, new knowledge leads us to the realization that evolution is more than a hypothesis. It is indeed remarkable that this theory has been progressively accepted by researchers, following a series of discoveries in various fields of knowledge. The convergence, neither sought nor fabricated, of the results of work that was conducted independently is in itself a significant argument in favour of this theory.

What is the significance of such a theory? To address this question is to enter into the field of epistemology. A theory is a metascientific elaboration, distinct from the results of observation but consistent with them. By means of it a series of independent data and facts can be related and interpreted in a unified explanation. A theory's validity depends on whether or not it can be verified; it is constantly tested against the facts; wherever it can no longer explain the latter, it shows its limitations and unsuitability. It must then be rethought.

Furthermore, while the formulation of a theory like that of evolution complies with the need for consistency with the observed data, it borrows certain notions from natural philosophy.

And, to tell the truth, rather than *the* theory of evolution, we should speak of *several* theories of evolution. On the one hand, this plurality has to do with the different explanations advanced for the mechanism of evolution, and on the other, with the various philosophies on which it is based. Hence the existence of materialist, reductionist and spiritualist interpretations. What is to be decided here is the true role of philosophy and, beyond it, of theology.

The Church's Magisterium is directly concerned with the question of evolution, for it involves the conception of humanity: Revelation teaches us that humanity was created in the image and likeness of God (cf. Gn. 1:27–29). The conciliar Constitution *Gaudium et spes* has magnificently explained this doctrine, which is pivotal to Christian thought. It recalled that the human being is "the only creature on earth that God has wanted for its own sake."[4] In other terms, the human individual cannot be subordinated as a pure means or a pure instrument, either to the species or to society; the human has value *per se*. With intellect and will, the human individual is capable of forming a relationship of communion, solidarity and self-giving with peers. St. Thomas observes that the human person's likeness to God resides especially in the speculative intellect, for the relationship with an object of knowledge resembles God's relationship with what he has created.[5] But even more, humanity is called to enter into a relationship of knowledge and love with God himself, a relationship which will find its complete fulfillment beyond time, in eternity. All the depth and grandeur of this vocation are revealed to us in the mystery of the risen Christ.[6] It is by virtue of the spiritual soul that the whole person possesses such a dignity even in his or her body. Pius XII stressed this essential point: If the human body takes its origin from pre-existent living matter, the spiritual soul is immediately created by God.[7]

Consequently, theories of evolution which, in accordance with the philosophies inspiring them, consider the mind as emerging from the forces of living matter, or as a mere epiphenomenon of this matter, are incompatible with the truth about humanity. Nor are they able to ground the dignity of the person.

With humanity, then, we find ourselves in the presence of an ontological difference, an ontological leap, one could say. However, does not the posing of such ontological discontinuity run counter to that physical continuity which seems to be the main thread of research into evolution in the field of physics and chemistry? Consideration of the method used in the various branches of knowledge makes it possible to reconcile two points of view which would seem irreconcilable. The sciences of observation describe and measure the multiple manifestations of life with increasing precision and correlate them with the time line. The moment of transition to the spiritual cannot be the object of this kind of observation, which nevertheless can discover at the experimental level a series of very valuable signs indicating what is specific to the human being. But the experience of metaphysical knowledge, of self-awareness and self-reflection, of moral conscience, freedom, or again, of aesthetic and religious experience, falls within the competence of philosophical analysis and reflection, while theology brings out its ultimate meaning according to the Creator's plans.

We Are Called to Enter Eternal Life

In conclusion, I would like to call to mind a Gospel truth which can shed a higher light on the horizon of research into the origins and unfolding of living matter. The Bible in fact bears an extraordinary message of life. It gives us a wise vision of life inasmuch as it describes the loftiest forms of existence. This vision guided me in the Encyclical which I dedicated to respect for human life, and which I called precisely *Evangelium vitae*.

It is significant that in St. John's Gospel life refers to the divine light which Christ communicates to us. We are called to enter into eternal life, that is to say, into the eternity of divine beatitude.

To warn us against the serious temptations threatening us, our Lord quotes the great saying of *Deuteronomy*: "Man shall not live by bread alone, but by every word that proceeds from the mouth of God" (Dt 8:3; cf. Mt 4:4).

Even more, "life" is one of the most beautiful titles which the Bible attributes to God. He is the *living God*.

Notes

1. Cf. Leo XIII, Encyclical *Providentissimus Deus*.
2. Cf. *Acta Apostolicae Sedis* 42 (1950), pp. 575–576.
3. Cf. *Acta Apostolicae Sedis* 85 (1993), pp. 764–772; Address to the Pontifical Biblical Commission, April 23 1993, announcing the document on *The Interpretation of the Bible in the Church*: *Acta Apostolicae Sedis* 86 (1994) pp. 232–243.
4. *Gaudium et spes*, n. 24.
5. *Summa Theologica*, I-II, q. 3 a.5, ad 1.
6. *Gaudium et spes*, n. 22.
7. "*Animas enim a Deo immediate creari catholica fides nos retinere iubet,*" Encyclical *Humanis generis*, *Acta Apostolicae Sedis* 42 (1950), p. 575.

Chapter Ten

Evolution and the Human Person: The Pope in Dialogue

GEORGE V. COYNE, S.J.

The scope of this essay is much more limited than one might be led to believe from the rather ambitious-sounding title. And yet I do intend to offer some reflections on each of the topics enunciated in the title and on their nexus. In order to appreciate the recent message of John Paul II on evolution[1] one must see it against both the general backdrop of the science-faith relationship over the past four centuries (since the birth of modern science), and more specifically in light of the opening towards science generated under the current Papacy. An evaluation of the immediate circumstances in which the message was delivered is also important for an understanding of the message itself. I would like to do each of these in turn. Then I will identify the crux issue with which the Pope wrestles, namely, the consonance or dissonance between an evolutionary account of the origin of the human person and the classical religious view that God intervenes to create each person's individual soul. I will share in the Pope's wrestling on this, and I will argue that further dialogue may eventually resolve the issue.

Four Centuries to Set the Large Context

The message of John Paul II on evolution, received by the members of the Pontifical Academy of Sciences on 22 October 1996 during the Plenary Session of the Academy held in the shadow of St. Peter's Basilica, stirred a vast interest among both scientists and the wider public. This interest went well beyond the usual attention paid to papal statements. Why? An attempt to answer why this was so will also help us, I believe, to appreciate the contents of the message. While the immediate circumstances in which the message occurred provide the principal reasons for the interest aroused, it requires, I believe, a return to about three centuries ago to find a full explanation. The Pope himself, in fact, introduces his message in this vein when he asks:

> How do the conclusions reached by the various scientific disciplines coincide with those contained in the message of revelation? . . . Moreover, to shed greater light on historical truth, your [the Pontifical Academy's] research on the Church's relations with science between the 16th and 18th centuries is of great importance.

The relationship between religion and science has, in the course of three centuries, passed from one of conflict to one of compatible openness and dialogue. We might speak of the following four periods of history: (l) the rise of modern atheism in the 17th and 18th centuries; (2) anticlericalism in Europe in the 19th century; (3) the awakening within the Church to modern science in the first six decades of the 20th century; (4) the Church's view today. The approach of science to religion in each of these periods can be characterized respectively as: (l) Trojan horse; (2) antagonist; (3) enlightened teacher; (4) partner in dialogue.

The Trojan Horse

In his detailed study of the origins of modern atheism,[2] Michael Buckley, S.J. concludes that it was paradoxically the attempt in the 17th and 18th centuries to establish a rational basis for religious belief that led to the corruption of religious belief. Religion yielded to the temptation to root its own existence in the rational certitudes characteristic of the natural sciences. This rationalist tendency found its apex in the enlistment of the new science by such figures as Isaac Newton and Rene Descartes. Although the Galileo case is typically recalled as the classical example of confrontation between science and religion, it is in the misappropriation of modern science to establish the foundations for religious belief that we find the roots of a much more profound confrontation. From these roots, in fact, sprung the divorce between science and religion in the form of modern atheism. Thus science served as a Trojan horse within religion.

Antagonist

As to the second movement in the dissonant symphony initiated by religion and science we turn to nineteenth century anticlericalism. The founding of the Vatican Observatory in 1891 by Pope Leo XIII is set very clearly in that climate of anticlericalism and one of the principle motives that Leo XIII cites for the foundation is to combat such anticlericalism. His words show very clearly his view of the prevailing mistrust of many scientists for the Church:

> So that they might display their disdain and hatred for the mystical Spouse of Christ, who is the true light, those born of darkness are accustomed to calumniate her to unlearned people and they call her the friend of obscurantism, one who nurtures ignorance, an enemy of science and progress.[3]

And so the Pope presents, in opposition to these accusations, a very strong, one might say even triumphalistic, view of what the Church wished to do in establishing the Observatory:

> In taking up this work we have become involved not only in helping to promote a very noble science, which more than any other human discipline, raises the spirit of mortals to the contemplation of heavenly events, but we have in the first place put before ourselves the plan . . . that everyone might see that the Church and its Pastors are not opposed to true and solid science, whether human or divine, but that they embrace it, encourage it, and promote it with the fullest possible dedication.[4]

The anticlerical climate of the nineteenth century made science appear to be an antagonist, while the Vatican in its own way was seeking to overcome the antagonism.

Enlightened Teacher

We now pass to a period of enlightenment, the awakening of the Church to science during the first six decades of the twentieth century, which is concretized in the person of Pope Pius XII, who was a man of a more than ordinary scientific culture and who even in his youth had become acquainted with astronomy through his association with astronomers at the Vatican Observatory. The Pope had an excellent knowledge of astronomy and he frequently discussed astronomical research with contemporary researchers. However, he was not immune from the rationalist tendency which I spoke about above; and his understanding of the then most recent scientific results concerning the Big Bang origins of the Universe led him to seeing in these scientific results a rational support for the doctrinal understanding of creation derived from Scripture.

Treating science as an enlightened teacher risks repeating the invitation to the Trojan horse. A specific problem arose from the tendency of Pope Pius XII to identify the beginning state of the Big Bang cosmologies with God's act of creation. He stated, for instance, that

> contemporary science with one sweep back across the centuries has succeeded in bearing witness to the august instant of the primordial *Fiat Lux*, when along

> with matter there burst forth from nothing a sea of light and radiation. . . . Thus, with that concreteness which is characteristic of physical proofs, modern science has confirmed the contingency of the Universe and also the well-founded deduction to the epoch when the world came forth from the hands of the Creator.[5]

Georges Lemaître, the father of the theory of the primeval atom which foreshadowed the theory of the Big Bang, had considerable difficulty with this view of the Pope. Lemaître insisted that the Primeval Atom and Big Bang hypotheses should be judged solely as physical theories and that theological considerations should be kept completely separate.[6]

The contrasting views reached a climax when the time came for the preparation of an address which the Pope was to give to the Eighth General Assembly of the International Astronomical Union to be held in Rome in September 1952. Lemaître came to Rome to consult with the Cardinal Secretary of State concerning the address. The mission was apparently a success. In his discourse delivered on September 7, 1952,[7] Pius XII cited many specific instances of progress made in the astrophysical sciences during the previous half-century, yet he made no specific reference to scientific results from cosmology or the Big Bang. Never again did Pius XII attribute any philosophical, metaphysical, or religious implications to the theory of the Big Bang.

A Partner in Dialogue

Up until the recent papal discourse on evolution, which we shall discuss shortly, the principal sources for deriving the most recent view from Rome concerning the relationship of science and faith are essentially three messages of His Holiness John Paul II: (1) the discourse given to the Pontifical Academy of Sciences on November 10, 1979, to commemorate the centenary of the birth of Albert Einstein;[8] (2) the discourse given October 28, 1986, on the occasion of the fiftieth anniversary of the Pontifical Academy of Sciences;[9] (3) the message written on the occasion of the tricentennial of Newton's *Principia Mathematica* and published as an introduction to the proceedings of the meeting sponsored by the Vatican Observatory and the Center for Theology and the Natural Sciences in Berkeley to commemorate that same tricentennial.[10]

The public acceptance of the first two discourses has focused on statements made by Pope John Paul II concerning the Copernican-Ptolemaic controversy of the seventeenth century, especially the place of Galileo in those controversies. This has been an excessive emphasis, in my opinion. The Galileo affair is important, to be sure. However, if one reads the three papal documents which I have referred to above, it will be clear that there are many matters of much more significance and much more forward-looking than a reinvestigation of the Galileo case. The newness in what John Paul II has said about the relationship consists in his having taken a position compellingly opposed to each of those three postures of Trojan horse, antagonist, or enlightened teacher. For instance, John Paul II clearly states that

> science develops best when its concepts and conclusions are integrated into the broader human culture and its concerns for ultimate meaning and value. . . . Scientists . . . can come to appreciate for themselves that these discoveries cannot be a substitute for knowledge of the truly ultimate. Science can purify religion from error and superstition; religion can purify science from idolatry and false absolutes. Each can draw one another into a wider world, a world in which each can flourish.[11]

Science and religion are distinct. Each has its own integrity. In dialogue, each can contribute positively to the welfare of the other.

The newest element in this new view from Rome is the expressed uncertainty as to where the dialogue between science and faith will lead. Whereas the awakening of the Church to modern science during the papacy of Pius XII resulted in a too facile appropriation of scientific results to bolster religious beliefs, Pope John II expresses the extreme caution of the Church in defining its partnership in the dialogue: "Exactly what form that [the dialogue] will take must be left to the future."[12]

The Immediate Context for the Evolution Allocution

The message on evolution is in continuity with the partner-in-dialogue posture. While the encyclical of Pope Pius XII in 1950, *Humani Generis,* considered the doctrine of evolution a serious hypothesis, worthy of investigation and in-depth study equal to that of the opposing hypothesis, John Paul II states in his message: "Today almost half a century after the publication of the encyclical, new knowledge has led to the recognition that the theory of evolution is no longer a mere hypothesis."[13]

The sentences which follow this statement indicate that the "new knowledge" which the Pope refers to is for the most part scientific knowledge. He had, in fact, just stated that "the exegete and the theologian must keep informed about the results achieved by the natural sciences." The context in which the message occurs strongly supports this. As the specific theme for its plenary session the Pontifical Academy of Sciences had chosen: *The Origin and Evolution of Life*, and it had assembled some of the most active researchers in the life sciences to discuss topics which ranged from "Molecular Phylogeny as a Key to Understanding the Origin of Cellular Life" to "The Search for Intelligent Life in the Universe" and "Life as a Cosmic Imperative"; from, that is, detailed molecular chemistry to sweeping analyses of life in the context of the evolving universe. Only months before the plenary session of the Academy, the renowned journal *Science* published a research paper announcing the discovery that in the past there may have existed primitive life forms on the planet Mars. Furthermore, within the previous two years, a number of publications had appeared announcing the discovery of extra-solar planets. This ferment in scientific research not only made the plenary session theme very timely, but it also set the concrete scene for the papal message. Most of the scientific results cited were very tentative and very much disputed (as is true of almost all research at its beginning), but they were very exciting and provocative. Only three months after the plenary session the Pope would receive in private audience a group of scientists from Germany, Italy and the United States who were responsible for the high-resolution observations being made by the satellite, *Galileo*, of the Jovian planets and their satellites. Within a few months of that audience NASA would announce the discovery of a huge ocean on Europa, a satellite of Jupiter.

These are the circumstances surrounding the papal message on evolution. Did they influence it? Normally the Pope receives the papal Academicians at the time of their Plenary Session in a solemn, private audience, at times even in the presence of the College of Cardinals and the diplomatic corps. On this occasion he did not receive them at all, but rather sent his message to them.

Why? There can, of course, be many reasons for this, unknown and perhaps even unknowable to the historian. I would like to suggest, nonetheless, that a contributing factor to the nature of this message may be found precisely in the circumstances of the plenary session and the accompanying milieu of scientific research. A careful reading of the message is consistent with this suggestion. The Pope wished to recognize the great strides being made in our scientific knowledge of life and the implications that may result for a religious view of the human person; but at the same time he had to struggle with the tentative nature of those results and their consequences, especially with respect to revealed, religious truths. In other words an openness in dialogue appeared to be the most honest posture to take. Let us examine the message in this respect.

Science vs. Revelation; Evolution vs. Creation

In order to set the stage for dialogue the message distinguishes in traditional terms the various ways of knowing. The correct interpretation of observed, empirical, scientific data accumulated to date leads to a theory of evolution which is no longer a mere hypothesis among other hypotheses. It is an established scientific theory. But since philosophy and theology, in addition to the scientific analysis of the empirical facts, enter into the formulation of a theory, we do better to speak of several theories. And some of those theories are incompatible with revealed, religious truth. It is obvious that some theories are to be rejected outright: materialism, reductionism, spiritualism. But at this point the message embraces a true spirit of dialogue when it struggles with the two possibly incompatible stories about the origin of the human person: the evolutionist story and the creationist story. By "creationist" here I am not referring to the American evangelical or fundamentalist view that Genesis constitutes a scientific account of the world's origin. Rather, in the context of the papal discussion, "creationism" refers to the view that at conception God intervenes to create a new and unique soul for the individual person. It appears that no room exists within evolutionary theory to account for the divine creation of the human soul. This amounts to dissonance between science and religion, not consonance. This is the crux issue in Pope John Paul II's message.

The dialogue progresses in the following way: The Church holds certain revealed truths concerning the human person. Science has discovered certain facts about the origins of the human person. Any theory based upon those facts which contradicts revealed truths cannot be correct. Note the antecedent and primary role given to revealed truths in this dialogue; and yet note the struggle to remain open to a correct theory based upon the scientific facts. The dialogue proceeds, in anguish as it were, between these two poles. In the traditional manner of papal statements the main content of the teaching of previous Popes on the matter at hand is reevaluated. And so the teaching of Pius XII in *Humani Generis* that, if the human body takes its origins from pre-existent living matter, the spiritual soul is immediately created by God. And so, is the dialogue resolved by embracing evolutionism as to the body and creationism as to the soul? Note that the word "soul" does not reappear in the remainder of the dialogue. Rather the message moves to speak of "spirit" and "the spiritual."

If we consider the revealed, religious truth about the human being, then we have an "ontological leap," an "ontological discontinuity" in the evolutionary chain at the emergence of the human being. Is this not irreconcilable, wonders the Pope, with the continuity in the evolutionary chain seen by science? An attempt to resolve this critical issue is given by stating that:

> The moment of transition to the spiritual cannot be the object of this kind of [scientific] observation, which nevertheless can discover at the experimental level a series of very valuable signs indicating what is specific to the human being.

The suggestion is being made, it appears, that the "ontological discontinuity" may be explained by an epistemological discontinuity. Is this adequate or must the dialogue continue? Is a creationist theory required to explain the origins of the spiritual dimension of the human being? Are we forced by revealed, religious truth to accept a dualistic view of the origins of the human person? Are we forced to be evolutionist with respect to the material dimension, and creationist with respect to the spiritual dimension? The message, I believe, when it speaks in the last paragraphs about the God of life, gives strong indications that the dialogue is still open with respect to these questions.

Consonance and Continuous Creation

I would like to use the inspiration of Pope John Paul II's address to suggest that reflections upon God's continuous creation may help to advance the dialogue with respect to the dualistic dilemma mentioned above. We might say that God creates through the process of evolution and that creation is continuous. Since we assume that ultimately there can be no contradiction between true science and revealed, religious truths, I propose that continuous creation is best understood in terms of the best scientific understanding of the emergence of the human being.

The concern for continuous creation arises in the following summary statement by the eminent evolutionary chemist, Christian de Duve, in his paper at the very Plenary Session of the Pontifical Academy of Sciences to which the papal message on evolution was directed:

> Evolution, though dependent on chance events, proceeds under a number of inner and outer constraints that compel it to move in the direction of greater complexity if circumstances permit. Had these circumstances been different, evolution might have followed a different course in time. It might have produced organisms different from those we know, perhaps even thinking beings different than humans.[14]

Does such contingency in the emergence of the human being contradict religious truth? No; it appears to me that we might find consonance if theologians could develop a more profound understanding of God's continuous creation.

God in his infinite freedom continuously creates a world which reflects that freedom, a freedom that grows as the evolutionary process draws us toward greater and greater complexity. God lets the world be what it will be in its continuous evolution. God does not intervene arbitrarily, but rather allows, participates, loves. Is such thinking adequate to preserve the special character attributed by religious thought to the emergence of spirit, while avoiding a crude interventionist creationism? Only a protracted dialogue will tell.

Notes

1. See Chapter 9 of this volume. The original message in French was published in *L'Osservatore Romano* for October 23, 1996, and an English translation in the Weekly English Edition of *L'Osservatore Romano* for October 30, 1996.

2. Michael J. Buckley, S.J., *At the Origins of Modern Atheism* (New Haven: Yale University Press, 1987).

3. *Motu Proprio, Ut Mysticam*, published in Sabino Maffeo, S.J., *In the Service of Nine Popes, One Hundred Years of the Vatican Observatory* (Vatican City State: Vatican Observatory Publications, 1991, translated by G. V. Coyne, S.J.), p. 205.

4. Maffeo, *In the Service*, p. 205.

5. *Acta Apostolicae Sedis* (Vatican City State: Tipografia Poliglotta Vaticana, 1952), vol. 44, pp. 41–42.

6. Georges Lemaître, "The Primeval Atom Hypothesis and the Problem of Clusters of Galaxies," in *La Structure et L'Evolution de L'Universe* (Brussels: XI Conseil de Physique Solay, 1958), p. 7.

7. *Acta Apostolicae Sedis*, p. 732.

8. *Discourses of the Popes from Pius XI to John Paul II to the Pontifical Academy of Sciences* (Vatican City State: Pontificia Academia Scientiarum, 1986), p. 151.

9. *Discourses*, p. 151.

10. The message was first published in *Physics, Philosophy, and Theology: A Common Quest for Understanding*, ed. R. J. Russell, W. R. Stoeger, S.J., and G. V. Coyne, S.J. (Notre Dame, IN: University of Notre Dame Press, 1988), pp. M3-M14. Comments on the papal message by a group of experts have been published in: *John Paul II on Science and Religion: Reflections on the New View from Rome*, ed. R. J. Russell, W. R. Stoeger, S.J., and G. V. Coyne, S.J. (Notre Dame, IN: University of Notre Dame Press, 1990).

11. *Physics, Philosophy, and Theology*, p. M13.

12. *Physics, Philosophy, and Theology*, p. M7.

13. The English translation of this sentence, published as cited in note 1, is incorrect when it says, "the recognition of more than one hypothesis . . . "

14. Christian de Duve, "Life as a Cosmic Imperative," *Pontifical Academy of Sciences*, October 1996; see also his book *Vital Dust: Life as a Cosmic Imperative* (New York: Basic Books, 1995).

Chapter Eleven

Biological Evolution and the Human Soul: A Theological Proposal for Generationism

ANNE M. CLIFFORD, C.S.J.

Three years ago Nobel Laureate Francis Crick, of DNA discovery fame, published *The Astonishing Hypothesis: The Scientific Search for the Soul*, in which he argued that "a modern neurobiologist has no need for the religious concept of soul to explain the behavior of humans and other animals."[1] Curiously, he begins his book with a diatribe against a Catholic Catechism on the soul[2] and concludes that for the scientist the human mind, which he equates with the behavior of the brain, is best explained as an extraordinarily intricate neuronal machine that evolved in a long process of natural selection.[3] Crick admits that there is much about the human brain that remains "mysterious,"[4] (by which he means a problem yet to be solved by scientists). Nevertheless he argues that, although at this time science has limitations where explaining human consciousness is concerned, evidence from the study of the brain makes it clear that there is no soul or whole, only interacting neurons or complex parts.

Crick acknowledges that his hypotheses about human consciousness are provisional, but they are at least based on evidence—which is more than he can say for the religious ones, developed in a pre-scientific era to fill the need for total explanations of nature and of ourselves.[5] From an evolutionary standpoint, religious explanations, like that of the human soul and the promise of an after-life in immortal bliss with a deity, are the secondary consequences of other adaptive tasks in which early humans engaged to insure their survival.

Since the soul is customarily regarded to be a metaphysical concept, Crick's project is logically odd and epistemologically confusing. He treats the soul as if it should be a substance that can be empirically verified.[6] Although he refers to the soul frequently, he provides no definition of what he means by the term in the text or its glossary of terms. Without explaining what he means by "soul," he judges it to be a meaningless concept because its existence cannot be verified scientifically and because it has played a role in religious faith. His study of the brain was conducted with the express purposes of 1) disproving the location of the soul there, and 2) dismissing religious belief in the soul, its immortality, and God. It is unclear what or who God is for him and what his understanding of an "afterlife" may be. His position may be affected by a God of judgment and an archaic spatial eschatology. His "astonishing hypothesis," therefore, is dictated by the narrow parameters of a reductionistic materialism and, quite possibly, an obsolete theology.

Pope John Paul II: On the Soul

In October 1996, the topic of evolution and the human soul became a front page story in news papers around the world, including the *New York Times*, because Pope John Paul II addressed it in his annual message to the Pontifical Academy of Sciences.[7] John Paul II noted that Pope Pius XII had already affirmed biological evolution to be "an open question, as long as it confines its speculation to the development, from other living matter already in existence, of the human body."[8] Pointing out that evolution has been given a much higher degree of acceptance by scientists since 1950, John Paul II recognizes that biological evolution is more than an open question and effectively accepts it as scientific fact. But he also argues that, since there is a plurality of theories about the mechanisms of evolution, caution is needed. Some theories are dependent on extra-scientific notions borrowed from natural philosophy.[9] Although he singles out no specific ones, the reductionistic and materialistic hypothesis of Crick is the type of position with which John Paul II's warning is concerned.

Citing Leo XIII's position that "[scientific] truth cannot contradict [revealed] truth,"[10] John Paul II contends that those theories that claim that the human spirit emerged from the forces of matter, or that it is a mere epiphenomenon of matter are incompatible with a fundamental truth of Christian faith expressed by Pius XII: "souls are immediately created by God."[11] At the same time, such theories reject the important divinely revealed truth about the conception of humanity, as the only creatures "created in the image and likeness of God" (Genesis 1:27–29) and thereby deny the proper dignity due to the human person.[12]

Drawing from Thomas Aquinas' *Summa Theologiae*, John Paul II gives content to the human "spiritual soul," the source of dignity of the human person. He notes that "the human person's likeness to God resides especially in the speculative intellect . . . "[13] To deny its existence is to fail to acknowledge "an ontological difference in humans."[14] This is a recurring theme: In 1989, John Paul II stated that it is the responsibility of scientists to "respect the ontological transcendence of the person over all other beings in the natural world."[15] In the 1996 message, the ontological transcendence of the human species is described from an evolutionary standpoint as an "ontological leap"[16] that makes humans distinct from the rest of Earth's life forms.

The sciences, limited to the observable, cannot account for this leap, this transition to spiritual transcendence, even though they can record observations of what is specific to the human species. For John Paul II, the ontological difference falls within the competence of philosophical analysis. Theology in turn builds on this analysis by articulating "its ultimate meaning according to the Creator's plans."[17]

On the one hand, John Paul II claims that the status of biological evolution for Christian faith has changed since 1950, yet on the other hand, in regard to the creation by God of the human soul, it has remained the same. He reaffirms *creationism*, a position that emerged early in Christianity and can be traced to Hilary of Poitiers (ca. 315–367) who argued that though flesh is always born of flesh, "the soul of the body [can] be from nowhere else than from God."[18] In the Middle Ages, Thomas Aquinas supported creationism and argued that the rational soul of humans could be made only by [direct] creation, even though other life forms [species] could come into existence by generation and presumably, therefore, by evolution (although evolution would have been very foreign to Aquinas's mindset).[19]

Is this message of John Paul II to the Pontifical Academy, affirming the human soul's immediate creation by God, made in the spirit of *Roma locuta, causa finita* ("Rome has spoken, the cause is closed")? Is John Paul II, the Pope who more than any of his predecessors has called for dialogue and supported "a common interactive relationship" between Christian theologians and scientists,[20] building a wall around a protected territory of unchangeable truth by reaffirming a pre-scientific creationism? Since John Paul II draws on Thomas Aquinas' thoughts on the "speculative intellect," it seems appropriate to recall that in the process of forming his theological positions Aquinas engaged in dialogue with many responses to questions concerning the nature of the human being. He did this with a commitment to discern the truth in the light of what the best "science" of his time (Aristotle and his commentators) had to offer. Aquinas believed that this project was of vital importance because error about creatures would result in a false knowledge of God and would, therefore, lead a person away from

God.[21] It is in this spirit that I believe the message on evolution and the creationist origins of the human soul should be interpreted.

At the end of the message to the Pontifical Academy, John Paul II affirms that the sciences, philosophy (in this case classical metaphysics), and Christian theology must maintain their own integrity. This requires that scientists be attuned to their own ideological presuppositions, such as the opinion that science is our sole cognitive relation to reality and therefore, can explain biological life, including *Homo sapiens*, in the most complete way. Yet, if there is to be fruitful interaction between theologians and scientists now and in the future, then theologians must also be open to examining their own presuppositions with the possibility of revising their positions in response to those of the scientific community. In the desire for fruitful interaction with biological evolutionists, I now undertake a brief examination of Christian theological presuppositions on the human soul.

The Platonized and Aristotelianized Soul

Biblical anthropology envisioned the human person as a unity, not in terms of soul and body. Yet, there were Jews in the intertestamental period who believed in Sheol, the world in which the dead reside until the final judgment. Humans who had died did not vanish into nothingness, rather they awaited resurrection. This belief, which became an article of faith in the last centuries before Jesus Christ, was taken over by the first Christians and given a christological center. The eschatological imagery of Judaism became infused with christological meaning.

As belief in Christ's imminent coming (*parousia*) faded, Christian teaching on the resurrection of the dead was explained with the help of Greek thinking. One of the earliest philosophical analyses of the human which manifests Christianity adaptation to Greek patterns of thinking was that of Justin Martyr (ca. 110–ca. 160) who described the human as "a rational animal composed of a body and soul."[22] Earlier Plato had articulated an anthropology with a distinction made between the transitory body and the rational soul, which possessed immortality due to its divine origin.[23] Gradually, Christianity accepted the immortality of the human soul. Augustine, for example, discussed it at length.

In classical Christian anthropology the symbol, *imago Dei*, to which John Paul II referred, early on became identified with the Platonic concept of rational soul.[24] The *imago Dei* symbol not only gave rise to thought about the human as unique among creatures, but also to eschatological hope in the promise of everlasting life with God. In the Christianized Platonic schema the human soul, the locus of *imago Dei*, became separated from the body at death which enabled Christianity to account for the revelation of the resurrection in a way that affirmed the soul's immortality and final destiny with God.

Contrary to his predecessors who adhered to a Platonic notion of the human being which depicted the soul as the self and the body merely as its instrument, Aquinas envisioned the composition of the individual human in Aristotelian terms. The soul was the form-giving life principle of the whole human person. The soul's form-giving was a substantial union. The composite was the human being, a psycho-somatic unity with indissoluble mental and bodily aspects. But Aquinas also argued that the human soul as self-subsistent was incorruptible and would survive after the death of the body.[25]

It is curious that John Paul II did not cite the *Summa Theologiae*, I-I, questions 75–93, which address the composition and origin of the human person. Rather than draw upon creation-related material, John Paul II looks to a question in the *Summa* that has eschatological implications. The question in which Aquinas reflects on the "speculative intellect" focuses on the attainment of human happiness.[26] Aquinas concludes that only the speculative intellect knows true happiness, because it alone, (in contrast to the practical intellect and the senses) can contemplate and delight in Truth. It alone can rest in God and be united with God for all eternity. The speculative intellect can attain these things because the contemplation of God requires no bodily organs. It logically follows, therefore, that the intellectual soul (in contrast to the souls that only give form to the bodies of the other living beings that are lower in the hierarchy of being) continues to exist after the body has perished.[27] The contemplative bliss of the beatific vision does not require embodiment.

Biological Evolution of *Homo Sapiens*

Part of John Paul II's argument for exempting the human soul from evolution is that in humanity we find an unmistakable "ontological leap" to transcendence. This leap resulting in *Homo sapiens* goes beyond the possibilities of ordinary evolutionary development. The term, "ontology," used in philosophical discussions in reference to the nature of being, is foreign to science. From the standpoint of biological evolution, *Homo sapiens* shares a common sixty million-year evolution in which certain trends by which primates are identifiable as distinct from other animal orders emerged on Earth. Chief among these are the development of grasping and manipulative hands; the dominance of sight over smell; an emphasis on mobility in the design of the joints of the forelimbs; the ability to hold the trunk of the body upright and to walk (or otherwise progress) on the hind limbs if necessary; the development of complex forms of social organization that depend on elaborate signaling systems between individuals and; the enlargement of the brain relative to body size. The twentieth century humans' closest genetic relatives are the chimpanzees with whom humans share ninety-nine percent of their genes.[28]

To more fully answer the question what is *Homo sapiens*, however, requires information about the origin of the human species and therefore demands the study of the fossil record. The fossil evidence, however, is sparse and difficult to interpret. At present, there are two major schools of paleoanthropology that interpret the available fossil evidence differently. One adheres to gradual change in hominids over a long period of development by natural selection.[29] This school highlights the small gradations in the human fossil evidence and proposes a "multi-regional" model of *Homo sapiens* evolution in which local populations of hominids were in enough contact with other groups to avoid separating into different species. At the same time, these populations were sufficiently isolated to accrue adaptations to local environments. In this way the varieties of modern humans would have evolved their differences over long periods of time, while remaining a part of one interbreeding population.

The other school focuses on discontinuities in the fossil record, noting the frequency with which species changes appear abruptly.[30] This position called "punctuated equilibria" argues that the emergence of new species is a short-term event associated with geographic (e.g., an earth quake occurs and a river changes course) and/or climatic changes (an "Ice Age" brought on by a shift in the Earth's axis, the shape of its orbit and the amount of gasses, such as carbon dioxide, in the atmosphere). The emergence of *Homo sapiens* was not world wide, but rather limited to a center of origin, likely Africa.

The latter position argues that *Homo neanderthalensis*[31] (sometimes referred to as *Homo sapiens neanderthalensis* by the first school) co-existed with the ancestors of modern *Homo sapiens* in some of the same areas. There is, however, no evidence for their interbreeding on any significant scale, if at all. Although the Neanderthals shared with *Homo sapiens* bipedal posture, technology for tool making (simple unadorned stone implements) and the practice of burying their dead, at least occasionally. They flourished in western Europe until about 35,000 years ago and then gradually died out.

The second school of thought does not believe that the evolution of *Homo sapiens* has anything directly to do with the Neanderthals. Something akin to a "leap" in the sense of major qualitative difference may be perceived if one compares *Homo sapiens* with Neanderthals. For one thing their body structures, especially their cranial bones are different. But the evidence of their patterns of behavior set them apart even more dramatically. The *Homo sapiens* known as the Cro-Magnons[32] of 25,000 to 30,000 years ago made more intricate tools not only of stone, but also bone, antler and ivory, some of which were decorated (a characteristic missing in the Neanderthal tools). Cro-Magnons and other ancestors of modern humans of the Upper Paleolithic period (between 35,000 to 10,000 years ago in western and central Europe) also buried their dead. Some burials were elaborate: the dead were clothed in garments decorated with hand made beads and provided with useful implements, indicating belief in an afterlife. Their cave homes were decorated with compositions of animal figures, usually accompanied by abstract symbols of some kind. Many were painted while others were carved in bas-relief. These humans left behind evidence of a creative spirit unprecedented in the record of the species of the Earth.

What caused the appearance on Earth of the first humans who exhibited these behaviors remains unexplained by science, as John Paul II has pointed out. This is due not only to the scarcity of fossil evidence, but also to the deep divisions among scholars about how the fossil evidence should be interpreted. The present state of affairs may not be the case for the next generation of scientists. Gene-based technologies for the analysis of relationships of species, for one thing, hold the promise of more thorough explanations of the relationship of hominid species in the future. John Paul II's creationism argument for the direct infusion of the soul by God, could therefore prove to be a "God of the gaps" argument that will be something less than fully in the service of productive dialogue between theology and biological evolution. The creationist God is an interventionist God breaking into an evolutionary process that appears to have functioned without God intervening in it prior to the evolution of the first human beings.

A Theological Proposal for Generationism

The creationist position that the human body has evolved but the soul has not is inconsistent with biblical anthropology which understood the human to be an undivided whole. It also ignores the fundamental unity of the soul and body affirmed in the Christian tradition since the Middle Ages.[33] Aquinas, although he gave considerable attention to the human soul in its rationality (and presumably he would locate the seat of rationality in the brain), argued on Aristotelian grounds that the soul was in every part of the body of any living being. As the body requires the soul, so the soul requires the body. But the body requires the soul in a different way: the soul's union with the body is life giving. Consequently, there is a very close and pervasive unity between the soul and the body.[34]

In addition, a creationist position on the origins of the human soul also promotes a dualism that can easily result in the denigration of the body and all material reality. The former, due to the identification of woman with the body, resulted in the subordination of women to men and a belief, long supported in the Christian tradition, that women did not image God as fully as did men.[35] The latter has effected a virtual divorce between human beings and the Earth. The intellectual inheritance of this division has set humans apart from nonhuman nature in a relationship of superiority, contributing to the ecological crisis of the twentieth century.

I believe that a more theologically fruitful position on human evolution than creationism is "generationism."[36] I propose a generationist interpretation of the origin of the human soul in the interest of being responsive to biological science.

Creationism fails in this regard because it holds that God directly intervenes, adding the soul, at a moment of time when the human reproductive cells unite (or possibly at some point shortly thereafter). At this moment the human spiritual and intellectual soul is inserted into the bodily material that comes from the parents. The creationist understanding, however, ignores the findings of geneticists that indicate that traits such as intelligence and mental aptitudes, e.g., for music and mathematics, develop within limits that are genetically inherited.[37] Are these things distinct from the human soul? To what then does the soul refer in a creationist understanding after modern genetics has pruned so much away?

Generationism, in contrast, is more consonant with the mechanisms of evolution, emphasizing that evolution is mirrored in *Homo sapiens* and that modern humans are inextricably bound to evolutionary processes. Members of the species *Homo sapiens* are derived from parents with whom they share a common genetic inheritance. Generationism also acknowledges the apparent "randomness" in a process in which one out of several hundred million sperm is selected to fertilize a single ovum. There is an element of contingency in the origins of each human person and of the human species as a whole.

Soul and Body Interaction

Generationism affirms that from the union of sperm and ovum, a human person, and not merely the body of the human being, results. The unity of the human person is such that occurrences in the body affect the soul and conversely soul "events" affect the body. For example, heat or the lack of it affects the body. In fact, the extreme heat of sub-Saharan Africa likely contributed to the upright bipedal structure of the first hominids as the forests receded. A quadruped absorbs heat over much of its body, but by standing and walking upright the area of the body that receives the vertical rays of the sun is greatly reduced.[38] The types of sensations received by the bodily sense organs of upright, bipedal humans affect the soul. In turn, the soul with its desires, creative thoughts, sense of empathy and responsibility affect the body. The survival of the human body, including its long evolution through adaptations to changes in the environment, cannot be separated from the mental processes that enhance that survival.

The soul of humans in contemporary parlance can best be explained as a metaphorical naming of the compilation of those elements that make each of us a unique individual with a capacity for transcendence. "Soul" names qualities affected by genetic inheritance but is not reducible to them. For example, human beings inherit linguistic areas in the brain, but genetic inheritance, an individual's unique DNA, does not determine the language(s) one speaks and, more importantly, the thoughts one forms into words, and how those thoughts affect one's life directions and behaviors. The human soul is also more than the product of genetic inheritance combined with neurological reactions to changes in the environment. The environmental differentiations that a person encounters in a lifetime do not determine one's individual uniqueness, but merely modify it. The human soul names the individual creativity—the imagination, intelligence and freedom—of which the extinct Neanderthals and existing primate species were and are incapable.

The Soul, Our Identity, and the Mystery of God

Although the interrelationship of soul and body is interpenetrating, it is the reality to which the human soul refers, and not the body, that is the center of human individuation. This is obvious if one considers identical twins who have the same genetic inheritance. Even if they are indistinguishable physically, each has a unique personality. In twins who share the same living environment during their younger years, there are manifestations of uniqueness expressed in the life questions each twin raises in the pursuit of truth and meaning, in personal creativity of all types, in the desires and loves of each, in the personal exercise of freedom and in so much more.

Part of this "more" includes properties of the "speculative intellect," that capacity of the human for contemplation, to which John Paul II referred in his citation from Aquinas. It is this capacity which enables humans to recognize that mystery need not be reduced to problems that science will solve (cf. Crick). Rather, mystery is an all-encompassing horizon of meaning to which humans can relate with an unlimited questioning openness.[39] It is the orientation to mystery with its inexhaustible depth that makes the individuals of the species, *Homo sapiens*, distinct from the other primates and all other animals.

It is also this orientation that enables humans to name the all-encompassing mystery and inexhaustible depth, "God," and to name the human capacity for a relationship with this God "*imago Dei*." Can more be said of God than God is all encompassing mystery and inexhaustible depth? In generationism, which accepts the facticity of evolution without negating the body-soul unity that is the human person, God is envisioned to be continuously acting creatively in the world through its natural processes, including the evolving cosmic history of which humans are a part. There is no need for an interventionist Creator to affirm that humans are a unique species with a capacity for relationship with God.

Conclusion: Soul-Life and Worldly Mysticism

Generationism, although attuned to the processes of biological evolution more than creationism, makes no claims to comply with the empirical canons of science. Generationism is an expression of religious faith informed by a contemplative stance vis-a-vis an evolving world that locates all in God as the ultimate author and giver of life.

In a generationist theology, the dignity of the human, affirmed in the metaphorical designation *imago Dei*, is not lost because God is not envisioned to intervene in the insertion of the human soul into the cells of a human embryo. *Imago Dei* is not a symbolic cognate for the rational soul of a dualistic Christian metaphysics. *Imago Dei*, however, does remain the primary Christian symbol for affirming the inviolable dignity of the human person. Naming the human "*imago Dei*" eliminates neither the rootedness of the human species within the evolutionary process, nor the kinship of humans with all of Earth's other species. It does, however, serve as a reminder that the image of God describes not a primordial state of the first human who evolved, but the destiny toward which each human and the human community, as a whole, are called.[40]

The human person, co-constituted by the union of soul and body, and named by the symbol *imago Dei*, is a reminder of humanity's eschatological destiny without being world denying. Rather, it is an invitation to a worldly mysticism. If the soul is not fed by contemplation, it shrivels and the perspective on being human is easily reduced to interacting neurons and bodily processes. Human soul-life is nurtured by intimacy with other humans and with God. But soul-life is also fed by a worldly mysticism of intimacy with nonhuman nature with whom humans share an evolutionary history. Human soul-life thrives in a spirit of kinship solidarity with nonhuman nature, and in an openness to discovering, in the words of Langdon Gilkey, "the power, life, . . . and redemptive unity bestowed on it by God."

Notes

1. Francis Crick, *The Astonishing Hypothesis: The Scientific Search for the Soul* (New York: Simon and Schuster, 1994), 6.

2. Crick, *Astonishing Hypothesis*, 3–4; Crick does not limit his criticism to Catholicism. Christianity as a whole, as well as Islam, are also included in his critique of the soul.

3. Crick, *Astonishing Hypothesis*, 10 and 256.

4. Crick, *Astonishing Hypothesis*, 257–259.

5. Crick, *Astonishing Hypothesis*, 262 and 267.

6. The notion of soul as it has been traditionally used by Christianity, however, is a philosophical concept; it refers to a metaphysical "substance" or component of reality that interacts causally with other components; e.g., the soul is that substance that gives form to the body.

7. See Chapter 9, "Evolution and the Living God," in this volume.

8. "Evolution and the Living God" (see page 150). The citation is from the encyclical *Humani Generis* ("Concerning Certain False Opinions") in *Acta Apostolicae Sedis* 42 (1950), 575–576.

9. "Evolution and the Living God" (see page 150).

10. "Evolution and the Living God" (see page 149). John Paul II here is referring to a position in Leo XIII's encyclical *Providentissimus Deus*, "On the Study of Sacred Scripture," November 18, 1893 (Washington, DC: National Catholic Welfare Conference; reprinted by the Catholic Biblical Association, 1964), 27.

11. "Evolution and the Living God" (see page 151). Once again John Paul II refers to *Humanae Generis, Acta Apostolicae Sedis* 42 (1950), 575.

12. "Evolution and the Living God" (see page 151).

13. "Evolution and the Living God" (see page 151); cf. *Summa Theologiae* I-II, q. 3, a. 5.

14. "Evolution and the Living God" (see page 151).

15. "The Links between Science and Faith," *Origins* 19 (1989), 339.

16. "Evolution and the Living God" (see page 151).

17. "Evolution and the Living God" (see page 152).

18. Hilary of Poitiers, *On the Trinity*, translated by Stephen McKenna (New York: Fathers of the Church, Inc., 1954), Bk. 10, #22, 413.

19. *Summa Theologiae*, I-I, q. 90, a. 2; see also Thomas Aquinas, *Summa Contra Gentiles*, Bk. 2, q. 87, 294. In this work he takes a creationist position to argue against the soul's source being semen of the father.

20. "The Message to the Reverend George V. Coyne, S.J., Director of the Vatican Observatory"(1988), in *John Paul II on Science and Religion: Reflections on the New View from Rome*, edited by Robert J. Russell, William R. Stoeger and George V. Coyne (Vatican City State/Notre Dame, IN: Vatican Observatory Foundation and The University of Notre Dame Press, 1990), M 9.

21. Thomas Aquinas, *Summa Contra Gentiles, On the Truth of the Catholic Faith* (Garden City, NY: Doubleday and Co., 1956), Bk. 2, Ch. 3, 32.

22. Justin Martyr, "Extant Fragments of the Lost Work on the Resurrection," Ch. 8, in *The Ante-Nicene Fathers*, Vol. I, 297. Justin envisioned the relationship of soul and body to be a unity.

23. The idea of an immortal soul was central to Plato's philosophy; it was a notion closely akin to his divine archetypal ideas. The soul is treated by Plato in the *Apology*, *Phaedo*, *Phaedrus*, *Republic*, *Symposium*, *Timaeus*, *Laws* and other dialogues. In Plato's reasoning it was logical to suppose, by analogy, that since the processes of nature are in general cyclical (e.g., night passes into day and day into night, winter passes into summer and summer into winter), life also is cyclical: the dead return to life, just as the living die. Therefore, the soul is immortal. If this were not the case, eventually life would vanish from the universe. Plato also argued that since the soul is simple (uncompounded) it could not disintegrate. It is simple because it participates in the very idea of life and, therefore, excludes death.

24. Athanasius, *Against the Heathen*, Ch. 34, *Nicene and Post-Nicene Fathers of the Christian Church,* Vol. IV, 22; Augustine, *Genesis ad literam*, VI, 12 and Thomas Aquinas, *Summa Theologiae*, I., q. 93.

25. *Summa Theologiae*, I-II, q. 76. Aquinas spoke of the incorruptibility of the human soul on the basis of Scripture and reserved immortality for the risen Christ, the first humans in paradise and human beings after the resurrection of the dead. In this regard, his position resonates with that of Protestant theologians who find fault

with the notion of the immortality of the soul because its origins are Greek philosophy and not the Bible.

26. *Summa Theologiae*, I-II, q. 3.

27. *Summa Theologiae*, I-II, q. 4, a. 5.

28. Ian Tattersall, *The Human Odyssey: Four Million Years of Human Evolution* (New York: Prentice Hall, 1993), 42–43.

29. Milford H. Walpoff, *Paleoanthropology* (New York: Knopf/random House, 1980).

30. Niles Eldredge and Stephen Gould, "Punctuated Equilibria: an Alternative to Phylectic Gradualism," in *Models of Paleobiology*, edited by T.J.M. Schopf (San Francisco: Freeman, Cooper), 82–115, and Niles Eldredge, *Time Frames: The Rethinking of Darwinian Evolution and the Theory of Punctuated Equilibria* (New York: Simon and Schuster, 1985).

31. The name "Neanderthal" is derived from the German site in the valley ("thal") of the Neander River where the first fossil of this hominid was found.

32. Cro-Magnons get their name from the site where they were first found in south western France in 1868.

33. The Fourth Lateran Council (1215) taught that God created the human person as a unity of the soul and body (DS 800).

34. The unity of soul and body is something that Crick neglects in his book. Perhaps the underlying influence on Crick's thinking is Descartes, whose conception of soul and body (consciousness and matter) was highly dualistic.

35. For a thorough treatment of this position in the Christian tradition from Genesis 2–3 to the writings of Luther and Calvin, see Kari Elisabeth Børresen, editor, *The Image of God: Gender Models in Judeo Christian Tradition* (Minneapolis: Fortress Press, 1991).

36. Generationism can be traced to Augustine and his position on the transmission of "Original Sin" which was affirmed by Luther. I am deliberately bracketing the question of original sin here.

37. For more on genetic boundaries, see David Cole's helpful essay, "Gene Predestination?" *Dialog* 33 (1994), 17–22.

38. Tattersall, *The Human Odyssey,* 80.

39. Karl Rahner of course calls this openness to all encompassing mystery "the transcendentality of the human subject." He develops this basic category of his theological anthropology in relationship to biological evolution in "Natural Science and Reasonable Faith," in *Theological Investigations* XXI, translated by Hugh M. Riley (New York: Crossroad, 1988), 41–46.

40. For more on this important point, see Mary Catherine Hilkert, "Cry Beloved Image: Rethinking the Image of God," in *The Embrace of God: Feminist Approaches to Theological Anthropology* (Maryknoll, NY: Orbis Press, 1995), 196–205.

Chapter Twelve

Biocultural Evolution and the Created Co-Creator

PHILIP HEFNER

Understanding the human being as the created co-creator is, in my judgment, central to an adequate anthropology that is both scientifically responsible and theologically coherent. In what follows I would like to provide a structural outline for the concept of the created co-creator, treating it in two ways: as a theory and as a metaphor. As a theory it affirms this: *Homo sapiens* is created co-creator, whose purpose is the stretching or enabling of the systems of nature so that they can participate in God's purposes in the mode of freedom. As a metaphor it describes the meaning of biocultural evolution and therefore contributes to our understanding of nature as a whole. The meaning of nature can be stated this way: the appearance of *Homo sapiens* as created co-creator signifies that nature's course is to participate in transcendence and freedom, and thereby nature is to interpret its own essential nature and take responsibility for acting accordingly. When we introduce the Christian concept of God into the discussion by asserting that the created co-creator is God's creation, the result is that the interpretation of human being and of nature is conditioned by the very character of God.

Biocultural Evolution and the Created Co-Creator

Two evolutionary concepts lay the foundation for a fundamental understanding of the human situation today and for a Christian theological interpretation of that situation, namely, biology and culture. *Biocultural evolution* refers to (1) the emergence, within the physical realm, of biological processes of evolution that themselves generate the phenomenon of culture; and to (2) the distinctive, non-Darwinian, dynamic processes by which culture proceeds, while at the same time it existing in a relationship of symbiosis with the physical-biological processes in which it emerged and in which it continues to operate. The appearance of culture is directly correlated to the central nervous system, and the dramatic increase in the significance of culture in the human species is correlated with the equally dramatic development of the human brain. Culture is defined as learned and taught patterns of behavior, together with the symbol systems that contextualize and interpret the behavior. The single most critical product of human culture today is technology.

The *created co-creator* refers to the emergence of a creature, *Homo sapiens*, (1) who on the one hand is thoroughly a creature of nature and its processes of evolution—hence the term *created*—and (2) who at the same time is created by those very processes as a creature of freedom. I define *freedom* in a very particular way, describing the condition of existence in which humans unavoidably face the necessity both of making choices that govern their behavior and of constructing the stories that contextualize and hence justify those choices. In technological civilization, decision-making is unavoidable. Since technological civilization has altered the circumstances of living so radically, this necessity of decision-making and story construction is intensified. I call this freedom, because finally only human beings (whether as individuals or as groups) can make the decisions and carry out the behaviors, and only human beings can construct the stories that justify them.

Since it is rooted in the basic structure of the human being, in both of its basic components: genetic and cultural evolution, we may say that freedom, as I have described it, is a fundamental source of the concept of the *co-creator*. Genes alone and their programs cannot make a human being apart from culture, while at the same time culture cannot exist apart from the biophysical host with which culture lives in symbiosis.

Created Co-Creator as a Theory that Interprets Human Being

The concept of the human being as created co-creator gives rise to a rather comprehensive theory that interprets human being in its world. Several ancillary concepts serve to fill out this theory.

Belonging and Receptivity

The created co-creator concept joins the multitude of attempts to overcome dualistic understandings of the human being. The idea of *belonging* figures large in this effort to overcome dualism. We can no longer tolerate understandings of human nature that insist upon separating us from our fellow human beings, from the natural ecosystem in which we live, or from the evolutionary processes in which we have emerged. Humans are by nature creatures constituted both by receptivity and belonging. Any concept of *Homo faber*, the aggressive technological operator, that overlooks these basic qualities is clearly inadequate and even perverse.

"Two Natures": Genes and Culture

I have emphasized that *Homo sapiens* is constituted by "two natures," genetic and cultural. This insight is the most important contribution that the evolutionary and human sciences make to our understanding of human being. The genetic component has its locus in the processes of genetic evolution in which humans have emerged and developed. The cultural dimension has its roots in the highly developed human central nervous system. These are best construed as two *systems of information* for the guidance of human life, and their evolution is the basis of what we are today. Both systems are required for the formation of human being. These two components, genetic and cultural, might be understood as co-adapted, existing together in the symbiosis we call the human being.[1]

Culture as Challenge

Recognizing this two-natured quality of the human being underscores how fundamental a challenge culture is to humans; they have always faced the task of constructing the systems of culture that will guide human life in ways that not only survive, but which do so in the manner that we believe is essential for genuine human being. I have already suggested a working definition of culture: learned patterns of behavior and the symbol systems that we construct to interpret those patterns. The challenge that faces our cultural construction is to fashion a system of information that interfaces with our world as meticulously and as adequately as our physico-biogenetic systems do. Most living creatures live their lives in ways that are more dependent on physico-biogenetic programming that requires less self-awareness or decision than is the case with *Homo sapiens*. Human beings must learn to meet the challenges of their world; they simply do not have the kind of automatic programming systems that can serve the requirements for adequate living. Technology is one of the ways that we have learned to live adequately; it has become one of the most dramatic elements of human culture today. Not only must we learn, but we must justify or explain our learnings. These explanations serve as motivators for the behavior we require.

Most of the crises that threaten the human race today can be traced to our incompetence in constructing adequately the cultural systems of information and guidance that we depend on. Family breakdown, hunger, poverty, homelessness, war/peace issues, education, racism, environmental collapse—all of these manifest the inadequacy of our learned behaviors to deal with the demands that our contemporary world places upon human living.

Technological Civilization

Contemporary life, in all parts of the planet, has reached the point where nearly every important day-to-day activity is dependent upon culture in the form of technology and decisions concerning technology. This may be understood as dependence upon human decisions and the competent execution of those decisions. Growing food, harvesting and distributing it, transportation, job selection and the conditions under which we work, health, family formation, energy—these and many more items of the common life are no longer "natural," if "nature" is defined as untouched by human hands, decisions, and processes. Since technology is a major cultural form that human decision and execution takes in our lives, we may say that our lives are dependent upon the technological overlay that we have placed upon the natural world. This overlay touches all of the non-human systems of the planet. Reasonable estimates are that 50% of the persons now living would die if our technological overlay were appreciably reduced and we were obliged to support ourselves in a natural world that lacked substantial technological enhancement. It is this set of conditions, under which we live today, that I term Technological Civilization.

Freedom as the Human Condition

Freedom, as I have already mentioned, is critical in two essential ways that pertain to the theories that I set forth here: making choices that govern our conduct of our culture and constructing the stories that give meaning to that behavior and justify it.

The first of these critical functions of freedom, the making of choices that create and conduct culture, is an essential component of the way that human beings actually spell out that capability in their nature by which they survive distinctively as humans. Human beings do not possess freedom over their genetic nature and the stream of information that it contributes to their nature. However, there is no element of the cultural stream that is not bathed in freedom of choice. We understand how this freedom is intrinsic to the human condition when we take note of the fact that the emergence of the human central nervous system at one and the same time makes culture at the human level of complexity possible and also necessary for the survival of the species. To reiterate what was said earlier, genetic information alone cannot sustain human being; the genetically sponsored human body, with its brain, cannot survive without the successful elaboration of that brain's greatest capability: culture. Culture is enacted in the space that opens up between the mutual necessities and possibilities on the interface of genes and environment. Culture is the vessel in which the human animal negotiates the passage afforded by genetic possibilities and constraints when they interact with the constraints and possibilities presented in the environment.

Even though we often hide the fact under honorific references to the "hoary tradition," human cultural moves and shapes are never preordained by either genes or environment, nor are they enacted apart from some element of freedom. Culture never *just happens*. Even when the genetic leash on culture is most obvious and the environmental space most limited, freedom and possibility characterize the culture that humans construct. The history of the ways in which humans have defined the genders, raised their offspring, obtained their food, and built their cities is full of examples of how genetic and environmental factors are interwoven on the loom of constraint and freedom. Under the pressure to survive, however, humans are never free from the constraint to shape their cultures in ways that will work as well as humans can make them work. Consequently, we may say that human survival is dependent on the ways in which we use our freedom to shape our culture.

The second aspect of freedom is the construction of symbol systems that contextualize and justify the behavior of culture. Baby birds may simply grow into adulthood, but human babies must be educated into adulthood and ushered into that state with rituals that not only describe and interpret adulthood, but which also justify its demands. Salmon may simply follow their programmed inputs to the proper times and places of spawning, just as robins may build their nests almost automatically on the basis of such inputs. Humans, however, must understand, interpret, organize, and justify their mating practices. On occasion, they must motivate more procreative activity, just as at other times they must motivate the opposite. Both motivations require interpretation and justification, and oftentimes also rigorous social organization. Humans also interpret and justify their culture of building homes. A home may be "every man's castle," just as it may be every person's inalienable right or the reward for those who succeed; its availability may also be construed as a litmus test of whether or not the "American dream is working."

These symbol systems that contextualize culture are evidence of the fact that freedom is a possibility, and the ways in which freedom to shape culture is actually exercised must be interpreted and justified if they are to win acceptance and acquire the motivation they need for their maintenance. The functions of interpretive contextualization and justification are even more necessary when cultural forms change, or when they require discipline and sacrifice, or when they are especially ambiguous. Changing gender roles require justification, since they throw conventional patterns from the past into disorder. Eliminating lifetime job security for the sake of promoting new economic patterns needs justification since it causes dislocation for workers. Technological manipulation of the environment requires justification in the face of possible ecological disaster, just as restraining technology must be justified in the face of potential economic loss.

The fashioning of this interpretation and justification is itself a consequence of human freedom to discern its situation, devise responses to that situation, and make sense of both situation and response. The human animal responds not only to a "real" environment, but even more to the concepts and images by which we perceive and interpret that environment. This freedom has evolved from within the world-system. Since on the one hand, the processes of evolution have worked by means of natural selection, while on the other hand, freedom exists with purposes that pertain to the conditioning evolutionary processes that have preceded its appearance in *Homo sapiens*, freedom is to be interpreted as nature's way of stretching itself toward newness.[2] "Stretching" is, of course, a simile. More literally, we mean that freedom is nature's way of creating new conditions under which the genes and their programs must exist. In the process, novelty is elicited from those programs. This freedom also pertains to the creation of social forms, technology, metaphysical and religious explanations, art, and the media of communications.

The Emergence of the Interactive Concept of Truth

An inescapable condition of human knowing must also be noted if we are to describe the current human situation adequately. Ancient and medieval ways of knowing understood truth in a hierarchical, immutable, perfectly ordered way. Humans interface with such truth simply by fitting themselves into it and conforming to its objective configurations.[3] Astrology is an example—we do not influence our planets, they influence us, and we conform our lives to them. Today, however, we are moving toward what might be called an interactive concept of truth. Truth reveals itself to us only as we interact with it; both our perceptions and our descriptions of it bear the marks of our interactions. When our knowing is said to be "relative" or "post-modern," such terms are often interpreted as diminishing the objectivity of truth and our knowledge of it. It is more accurate to say that they are redefining the conditions under which those concepts possess their objectivity.

The conditions of knowing that I have just described underscore what has been unstated thus far in my discussion, but which lurks between the lines: that human beings are continually in a quest for understanding the purpose and meaning of their existence.[4] The pressing challenges that confront our culture-construction, particularly in a technological civilization do in fact require that we operate as if we had a clear sense of our purpose, when in fact we do not. It is no longer possible for us to function wholesomely as a species unless we recognize this interactive character of truth. The interactive concept of truth indicates that we will have to construct the stories that convey our sense of meaning and purpose, and, as Weinberg indicates, we must do so "as we go along," because we are continuously interacting with the "truth" of the world and ourselves in it. It will be ever more urgent that we learn how to assess the adequacy of our representations of the truth, and this assessment will be simultaneous with our task of constructing stories that speak of truth.

The Experience of Transcendence

The emergence of the created co-creator, within the process of our interacting with "truth," reveals how human beings encounter transcendence. Although the human species has been unleashed, so to speak, within the ecosystem of terrestrial evolution as a species that is bounded by that ecosystem and also defined by its working, the species is also bestowed with self-awareness and the necessity to act upon that awareness. The human species must actively seek to *discover* its bounds and its definition. Consequently, the human species is driven to define itself within the context of its already having been defined. Human survival requires both the act of defining and the responsible action that flows from definition. This is what it means to be created co-creator.

This self-definition, itself both reflective and political in character, configures the encounter with transcendence in our lives. This encounter can be spoken of in five aspects. (a) The evolutionary process and the contemporary ecosystem are transcending themselves when they question their purpose through *Homo sapiens*. To be created co-creator is to engage in reflection and discernment, and this is done in behalf of the natural processes that have produced the co-creator. (b) The human act of naming the world and its elements and correlating sets of uses to those names brings a dimension of transcendence to the non-human world. (c) Defining individuals in relation to groups and groups in relation to their individuals carries with it a transcendence with respect to self-understanding and behavior. (d) The task of self-definition in the context of the global village requires that we bring together in our self-understanding nature, individual, group, and global humankind. This confluence brings with it still another dimension of transcendence, and we see ourselves both relativized and yet integral to even larger and more complex communities. (e) In our self-defining, we transcend our own future by opening up new futures.

We encounter transcendence in the self-defining process. In the attempt to know and to actualize ourselves we find that from within what is

MORE, the transcendent; and although the process is very much this-worldly, we find ourselves in touch with the MORE than this world. We are ourselves continually altered and enlarged as we define ourselves. We surpass ourselves, and thus we are pulled and pushed towards newness. This is an unsettling state. Yet, being unsettled by the push and pull of transcendence is also profoundly sustaining and consoling. This is because the disturbance that belongs to our attempt *to be who we are*, and the effort to be what we arc called to be, is the most comforting and sustaining moment of life. There is no greater comfort than to be struggling to actualize our self-definition in accord with what we feel moved to become.[5]

Summing up. We may summarize how the created co-creator theory interprets human existence in the following statement: *The concept of the created co-creator proposes that the purpose of human being and human culture is to be the agency for birthing the future of the nature that has birthed us—the nature which is not only our own genetic heritage, but also the entire human community and the evolutionary and ecological reality in which and to which we belong—at least the nature that constitutes planet earth.*[6] In the final section of this essay, we shall place this naturalistic statement of purpose within the ambiance of the Christian theological tradition in this form: *Homo sapiens is God's created co-creator, whose purpose is the "stretching/enabling" of the systems of nature so that they can participate in God's purposes in the mode of freedom, for which the paradigm is Jesus Christ, both in respect to his life and to his understanding of the world as God's creation.*

Created Co-Creator as Metaphor of the Meaning of Nature

Up to this point, I have proposed the concept of the created co-creator as a theory that illumines a broad set of phenomena—science, technology, cultural crisis, and the like. I now extend that argument with the proposal that the created co-creator also functions to interpret the meaning of all of nature, and it does so as a metaphor.

The concept of the created co-creator is in a position to interpret nature, because of a number of considerations that are woven into my discussion up to this point only in an implicit way. Now I will make these considerations explicit.

The created co-creator is a natural entity, and its placement is fully within nature.

This means that when we look at the created co-creator and reflect upon its character and function, we are reflecting upon nature. Knowledge concerning the human being is knowledge of nature.

The reference or context for the created co-creator and its activity is nature.

Whatever purposes we ascribe to humans, whatever goals we set for their activity are to be referred to the rest of nature. The purposes of human beings are purposes within and for nature. The goals of human activity are in the service of nature. The contribution that humans make is a contribution to nature. Any purposes, goals, and contributions that are ascribed to humans are simultaneously statements about nature, about what nature is, and about its possible purposes.

The fact that the created co-creator has appeared is a statement about what nature has come to, what nature is capable of, and what nature itself has produced or allowed to appear.

Here we encounter the question of whether awareness, intentionality, and even agency and personhood can be imputed to nature and its processes. We cannot pretend to deal with these issues here, but our discussion does set a clear direction for thinking about them: that since the human species *is nature*, whatever we impute to human beings is also thereby imputed to nature, at least potentially—and unavoidably so.

If transcendence and freedom are characteristics of human being, they are ipso facto characteristics of nature.

It is nature that encounters transcendence in human being, and it is nature that experiences freedom. It would be important here to ask whether the non-human sciences, such as physics, astrophysics, and cosmology could identify any correlates to transcendence and freedom as I have described them. Do relativity theory, chaos and complexity theory, and theories of biochemical autocatalysis, for example, involve pre- and non-human correlates to what I have called transcendence and freedom?

The appearance of the created co-creator inclines us to speak of nature as "project," and to ask what the appearance of this creature suggests concerning "nature's project."

Here we come upon a difficult boundary line between anthropocentrism, on the one hand, and human beings as a key to understanding the rest of nature, on the other. Anthropocentrism, as the term suggests, asserts that human beings are in some sense the "center" of all reality and therefore also the goal of natural processes. An anthropocentric viewpoint argues that since human beings are the *telos* of nature, all of nature is in the image of humans. I am arguing quite differently. In the perspective set forth here, human beings are said to be part of nature's intentionality or *telos*. Consequently, to understand any aspect of nature is to gain insight into that intentionality. Since human beings do in fact exhibit intentionality more clearly and complexly than other forms of nature, they offer a particularly useful window through which nature can be understood and interpreted. So, for example, if nature in the form of *Homo sapiens* exhibits intentionality, then it cannot be said that intentionality is foreign to nature. It also cannot be said that nature's intentionality is equivalent to human intentionality. The human species can serve as a metaphor for the meaning of nature, and its intentionality can be said to be metaphorical to nature's intentionality.

Summing up. When the created co-creator is understood as a metaphor for the meaning of nature, its meaning can be stated as follows: *The appearance of Homo sapiens as created co-creator signifies that nature's course is to participate in transcendence and freedom, and thereby nature enters into the condition in which it interprets its own essential nature and takes responsibility for acting in accord with that nature.*

The Created Co-Creator in a Christian Theological Framework

When the created co-creator concept is placed within a Christian theological framework, it becomes integral to what Christians believe about God, namely that God is the creator of all that is, redeemer, and sustainer. The doctrine of creation affirms both creation-out-of-nothing (*creatio ex nihilo*) and continuing creation (*creatio continua*). Creation-out-of-nothing sets a significant foundation on which to interpret nature as God's creation. This doctrine asserts that God is the sole source of all that is, and that God created freely and without coercion or limitation. As Gerardus van der Leeuw[7] has suggested, the Biblical concept of creation in effect operates with an equation of only three members: God, what God has created, and what future God makes for the creation.

The upshot is that there is no mediating barrier between God and the creation, nor is there any external limitation on God's work of creation. On the one hand, this sets the Biblical creation story off from myths such as the Babylonian *enuma elish* (which posits the necessity of a conquest of chaos before creation as such can happen) and the platonic *Timaeus* (which posits preexistent chaos as a prior constraint upon God, with the result that God cannot create freely). On the other hand, the Biblical view as interpreted by later theology speaks of creation that is not only the free act of God, but which is conditioned ultimately by the character of God itself. This character includes freedom, intentionality, and love. Saint Bonaventure, in the twelfth century, expressed this insight in his statement that nature is God's song (*carmina dei*).[8]

The Christian view, as a result, is that the creation is grounded solely in God and that it is the creation that God freely desired and brought into being. By bringing the creation into unmediated relation with God, Christian theology correlates in a striking manner the nature of nature and the nature of God. This unmediated relation should not be confused with a notion of pantheism, since it carries no implication that the world is divine; nor does it call into question the classical insight that there is an infinite qualitative difference between God and the world. On the contrary, it asserts in a forceful manner that whatever the relationship between God and the world, God's nature conditions the nature of creation.

This Christian theological perspective is immediately relevant to the concept of the created co-creator, and its function as an interpretation of human being and a metaphor of the meaning of nature. In the first place, the theological framework asserts that nature as creation is a realm of intentionality, God's intentionality. This places all of nature and human being within this larger realm of God's intentionality. Consequently, it is not surprising that nature should include evolutionary processes in which freedom and intentionality have emerged, with these emergents on a continuum from simpler animals through the primates and, at the current time, *Homo sapiens*.

Secondly, this theological framework illuminates the fact that human intentionality exists not for its own sake, nor only for the sake of the human species, but as the expression of and for the sake of the larger intentionality of God's creation, nature.

Thirdly, the biblical traditions speak of humans as created in the image of God (*imago Dei*). This symbol has a checkered and ambiguous history of interpretation. It has often been employed to buttress some assumed superiority of humans to the rest of nature. Here, I suggest that it be taken more straightforwardly as a statement that humans are, in some manner, created to be an explicit representation and presence of God's will in the creation. Humans have the created calling to articulate within the natural world what God's intentionality might be.

All of these theological interpretations are formal, however, with little or no indication of material content. Toward what is nature's and human intentionality directed? What is the shape of this intentionality? Jesus Christ as the Word of God (logos, as in John 1, and as elaborated in the dogma of the Trinity) is the central Christian symbol for discerning God's intentionality. Furthermore, Christ is traditionally affirmed as the normative image of God in the world, thereby articulating God's intention for humans. Jesus Christ can, therefore, be interpreted as the paradigm of the created co-creator. This interpretation still does not provide concrete content for the symbol of the created co-creator, but it does set certain directions for the co-creator's activity: Jesus dedicated his life to the well-being of the world, in obedience to God's will, and he was steadfast to the point of death. The created co-creator's life is defined by this paradigm set forth in Jesus Christ. Furthermore, the paradigm includes not only action for the benefit of the world, but also the spirit of gratitude and a sense of the divine graciousness that sustains the life of the created co-creator.

Freedom, intentionality, and love—which we have associated with the nature of God that conditions the nature of nature—are thus set forth as the character of the created co-creator, as they have taken shape in the life, death, and resurrection of Jesus Christ.

Summing up. When our naturalistic statement of the nature and purpose of the created co-creator is placed within the ambiance of the Christian theological tradition, it takes this form: *Homo sapiens is God's created co-creator, whose purpose is the "stretching/enabling" of the systems of nature so that they can participate in God's purposes in the mode of freedom, for which the paradigm is Jesus Christ, both in respect to his life and to his understanding of the world as God's creation.*

This statement stands not only as a possible way of relating Christian theology to scientific understandings, but also as a proposal for understanding human purposes in the world today and for shaping the ways in which we conduct our scientific and technological culture in the face of the contemporary crisis of technological civilization.

Alternative Metaphors of the Meaning of Nature

A conceptual proposal draws support from two directions: from its inherent cogency and appeal and from its ability to distinguish between itself and other proposals to which it is an alternative. This essay has been devoted to presenting the constructive substance of the created co-creator proposal, with the intention to render it both cogent and attractive. I will conclude my discussion with a brief sketch of alternative proposals that presently circulate in the contemporary marketplace of ideas, proposals that are ruled out by the created co-creator as I have conceptualized it.

I list these alternative, rejected proposals seriatim:

1. Nature exists for the purpose of serving humans. This proposal states an undesirable anthropocentrism, a concept that is widespread throughout the world and to be found in many different religious and philosophical frameworks that otherwise are in conflict with one another. This view tacitly underlies much of our technology and our medical practice. Inadequate as it is, this view is correlated to a certain realistic concern for human survival.

2. Nature and humanity exist in a dichotomous relationship, one of warfare and conquest. Much of what is called "development" of resources and popular medical research invokes this proposal, sometimes quite explicitly. On occasion, conflicts over policies to protect the natural environment are cast in the imagery of warfare "between trees (or endangered species) and people's jobs." This imagery may indeed be an accurate description of the local situation in which a given community finds itself, but it is not an adequate response to the problems posed.
3. Technology and humanity, or technology and nature, exist in an intrinsically dichotomous and hostile relationship. This view was given currency by the great existentialist philosophers at mid-century, particularly Martin Heidegger. These thinkers feared the "thingification" of the human self and the emergence of so-called "mass society." Although this view is an inadequate interpretation of technology as such, it does offer a much-needed critique of the often mindless use of technology.
4. The relationship of humans to nature is one of paternalistic stewardship or caring. This view is a variation of the anthropocentrism described above. It is espoused by many thoughtful, well-intentioned persons, as a defense against greedy exploitation of the natural environment. Its inadequacy lies in its essentially dualistic presupposition that humans are separate from the rest of nature; its paternalistic tendencies may actually be dangerous.
5. Nature is blind, without purpose, and humans are to be subsumed under that concept of nature in a reductionist fashion. Adherents of "scientism" in its many forms may propound this view. It threatens to destroy the dimension of the MORE, which is essential if we are to probe human existence, values, and the significance of the natural world.
6. Humans exist in a condition of isolation from nature. Their purposes are other-worldly or humanistic. They do not exist in behalf of nature. Religious philosophies may endorse this assumption, as well as secular philosophies such as Marxism. This view represents a variation on several of the proposals mentioned earlier. Its distinctiveness lies in its conviction that the essential destiny of human beings lies either in an other-worldly realm or in a domain of human culture and ideas that can be indifferent to or totally exploitative of the rest of nature. This view is understandable as a misguided effort to preserve the distinctiveness of human personhood and community.
7. The processes of nature and human existence are absurd. Again, the great existentialist philosophers articulated this view. Albert Camus was perhaps the greatest of these, in portraying the myth of

Sisyphus as the prototypical description of the human condition. His proposals can be appreciated as responses to scientific cosmology as it contrasts the vastness of the universe in time and space to the small and transient nature of human life, together with the absence of any teleology. This proposal may be the most forceful contender against the concept of the created co-creator.

Conclusion: Science as Resource and Challenge to Theology

Underlying this essay is the author's conviction that the engagement of science and religious faith (and the theology that religious faith entails) focuses above all on our attempts to make sense of the world in which we live and to gain a sense of what we as humans are here for. In this engagement, theology finds scientific knowledge to be both a resource and a challenge.

Science is a resource to religion in that it supplies insights and concepts that help religious faith to understand itself in richer and more vital ways. Scientific concepts of the genetic and cultural components of human nature, mediated through the human brain, for example, add immeasurably to our understanding of what it means that we are created from the dust of the earth and that God has created us with special gifts and responsibilities within the natural world. In the light of these and other scientific insights, religious faith and its theology can fashion more adequate and compelling interpretations of ancient traditions, interpretations that are accessible as important statements about the world and the human condition today. In sum: science can help religion make better sense of itself.

Religious faith also encounters a challenge from science, in that we face the enormous task of making sense of science, as well as of religion. Scientific knowledge and its technological applications have brought us to the brink of a civilizational crisis, characterized by our inability to conduct our scientific and technological culture in adequate and wholesome ways. This inability goes hand-in-hand with the realization that we do not understand just what science is about, in terms of its place in the human quest for meaning. The concept of humans as God's created co-creators is an attempt to make sense of science and technology. Humans are to employ their freedom of action and meaning-shaping to the end of committing their scientific and technological culture to the well-being of the creation, in the paradigm of Jesus Christ. In this respect, this essay has also been an attempt to make sense of science and technology.

This essay constitutes only one, very fallible attempt to fashion a theological response to science as resource and challenge. The author is deeply convinced, however, that such attempts are of great moment today. These attempts must be articulated, by humanists whose thinking finds its home within secular modes of thought, as well as by thinkers of all the world's religions. These attempts to make sense of both religion and science constitute one of our major resources for understanding human life today and expressing that understanding in ways of living that can make for more viable and richer life on our planet today.

Notes

1. See Ralph Wendell Burhoe, "The Source of Civilization in the Natural Selection of Coadapted Information in Genes and Culture," *Zygon: Journal of Religion and Science* 11 (1976): 263–303; and "Religion's Role in Human Evolution: The Missing Link between Ape-Man's Selfish Genes and Civilized Altruism," *Zygon: Journal of Religion and Science* 14 (1979): 135–62.

2. Philip Hefner, *The Human Factor: Evolution, Culture, and Religion* (Minneapolis: Fortress Press, 1987).

3. Max Wildiers, *The Theologian and his Universe* (New York: Seabury Press, 1982).

4. See my "Science-and-Religion and the Quest for Meaning," *Zygon: Journal of Religion and Science* 31 (1996): 307–22.

5. Philip Hefner, "The Foundations of Belonging in a Christian Worldview," in Hefner and Schroeder, eds., *Belonging and Alienation: Religious Foundations for the Human Future* (Chicago: Center for the Scientific Study of Religion 1976), 175.

6. Hefner, *The Human Factor*, 131–38.

7. Gerardus van der Leeuw, "Primordial Time and Final Time," in *Man and Time*, ed. J. Campbell, vol. 3 of *Papers from the Eranos Yearbooks* (New York: Pantheon Books, 1957).

8. Zachary Hayes, "Christology and Cosmology," in Thomas Gilbert, ed., *The Epic of Creation* (forthcoming).

Chapter Thirteen

A Map of Scientific Knowledge: Genetics, Evolution, and Theology

ARTHUR PEACOCKE

Can we honestly say: "It's all in the genes"? If in fact all the complexities and nuances that comprise human life as we experience it can be reduced to genetic determination, does that make genetics the queen of the human sciences? Or, if genetics can be reduced to chemistry, should this queen herself abdicate to chemistry? Should theological understandings about human nature submit to reductionism and scientism?

I would hazard the guess that one of the most influential catchphrases of our times that has influenced popular perceptions of the implications of biology, especially genetics, is Richard Dawkins's dubbing of genes as "selfish" in the title of his widely read book, *The Selfish Gene*.[1] Within the general academic community a close runner-up, if not as an influence but rather as a goad, had appeared the previous year in the first few defining pages of that seminal work of E.O. Wilson that launched the ship of sociobiology:

> Sociobiology is defined as the systematic study of the biological basis of all social behavior. . . . One of the functions of sociobiology, then, is to reformulate the foundations of the social sciences in a way that draws these subjects into the Modern Synthesis.[2]

But in the scientific world, especially that of molecular biology that developed with the discovery of the molecular basis of heredity in DNA, much more influential in shaping the stances of many scientists was an earlier remark of Francis Crick. He was, of course, one of the discoverers of the DNA structure, for which he shared the Nobel Prize with another Englishman,

Maurice Wilkins, and the American, James Watson. He had, some ten years before Wilson, thrown down the gauntlet by declaring that "the ultimate aim of the modern movement in biology is to explain *all* biology in terms of physics and chemistry."[3] Such an imperialistic challenge can, in fact, be mounted at many interfaces between the sciences other than that between biology and physics/chemistry. The ploy is called "reductionism" or, more colloquially, "nothing-buttery"—"discipline X (usually meaning yours) is really *nothing but* discipline Y (which happens to be mine)."

Before investigating the whole question of reductionism, there is an even more sweeping claim that is sometimes implicit in the writings of certain scientists, namely, that—not only is (scientific) discipline X *nothing but* (scientific) discipline Y—but also that the *only* knowledge worthy of the name is *scientific* knowledge. All else is mere opinion, emotion, subjective perspective, etc.. This is the belief system called "scientism" (hence the adjective "scientistic"), that the only sure and valid knowledge is that which is found in the natural sciences and is to be obtained by its methods. It is the belief system of only some scientists and of very few philosophers. Nevertheless scientism—together with reductionism—often underlies, as all-pervading assumptions, statements made by a number of influential biologists and geneticists that penetrate into the public consciousness of the Western world.

There has been a strong and often effectual response to these exaggerated claims mounted often by scientists as well as by philosophers of science. Yet their proponents have nevertheless succeeded in conveying to many thinking people in our Western society that those who work on genetics, especially human genetics, share their (apparently[4]) reductionist and scientistic stances. I would surmise it is this which often engenders suspicion of the whole Human Genome Project. The project is consequently believed to possess, over and beyond its avowed aims to counter human genetic disease, a hidden agenda to control the future of humanity through manipulating its genes.

In order to allay such suspicions, it is not enough simply to affirm the integrity and good intentions of the scientists and fund-providers involved. Encouraged by the "selfish gene" terminology and the philosophical stance of many sociobiologists (now called "evolutionary psychologists"), the suspicion arises that these scientists think it is the genes alone that are indeed the control centers of human behavior and even human thought. This involves an implicitly reductionist assumption. The whole question of reductionism as a philosophy of the relation between the sciences therefore needs clarifying.[5]

Clarifying the relation between knowledge gained from the various sciences is the aim of this essay. Such clarification is needed for examining the theological implications of genetic research. If reductionism reigns, then theology could make no genuine contribution to the interpretation of genetics, nor of any other natural science for that matter. Yet a closer look will show a widening horizon of understanding as we move from the physical sciences to the life sciences and to the social sciences, and then finally to the realm of human culture where religious apprehensions of a postulated transcendent and immanent Reality have influenced the cause of human development.

Reductionism, Emergence, and Reality

To give an indication of the kind of issue at stake here, let me recount how the discovery of the structure of the genetic material DNA led me—as a physical biochemist studying its behavior in solution in the early 1950s—to *anti*-reductionist conclusions, unlike Crick. What was impressive about this development (and it is a clue to many important issues in the epistemology and relationships of the sciences) was that for the first time we were witnessing the existence of a complex macromolecule, the *chemical structure* of which had the ability to convey *information*, genetic instructions, to the next generation to be like its parent(s). In my days as a chemistry student, I had studied the structure of the purine and pyrimidine "bases," which are part of the nucleotide units from which DNA is assembled. That was pure chemistry, with no hint of any particular significance in their internal arrangement of atoms of carbon, nitrogen, phosphorus, etc. Yet here in DNA, there had been discovered a double string of such units so linked together through the operation of the evolutionary process that each particular DNA macromolecule has the new capacity, when set in the matrix of the particular cytoplasm evolved with it, of being able to convey hereditary *information*. This was a capacity absent from the component individual nucleotides. Yet the *concept* of "information," originating in the mathematical theory of communication (C.E. Shannon), had never been part of the organic chemistry of nucleotides, even of polynucleotides.

Hence in DNA we were witnessing a notable example of what many reflecting on the evolutionary process have called "emergence"—the entirely *neutral* name[6] for that general feature of natural processes wherein complex structures, especially in living organisms, develop distinctively new capabilities and function at levels of greater complexity. Such emergence is an undoubted, observed feature of the evolutionary process, especially of the biological. It is in this sense that the term "emergence" is being used here and *not* in the sense that some actual entity has been *added* to the more complex system.

DNA itself proves to be a stimulus to wider reflections, both epistemological, on the relations between the knowledge that different sciences provide; and epistemological, on the nature of the realities that the sciences putatively claim to disclose. To clarify what I am referring to, let us look at Figure 13.1, which represents the relation between the different focal levels of interest and analysis of the various sciences, especially as they pertain to

FIGURE 13.1 A Hierarchy of Disciplines

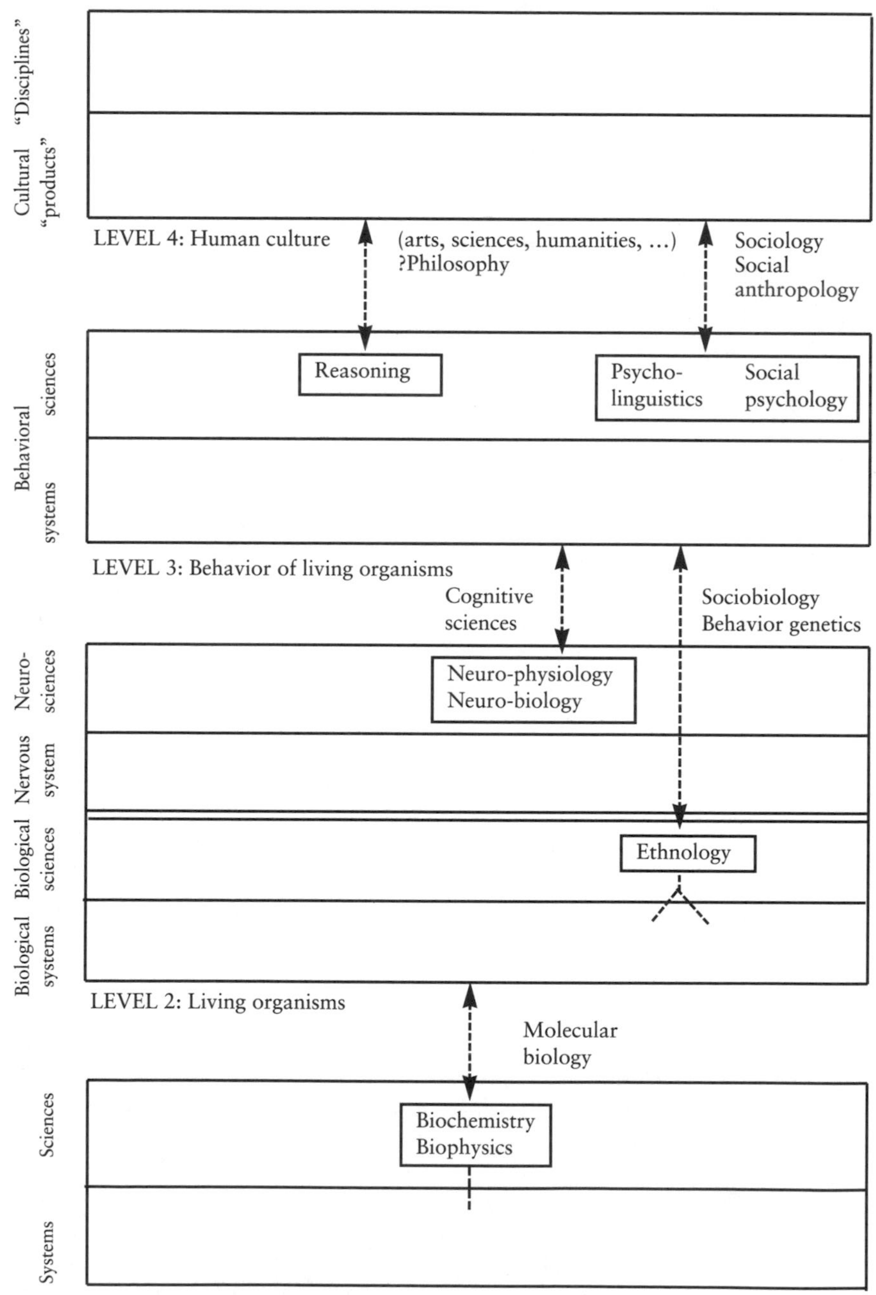

This figure is a simplified form of Figure 13.2

human beings. It functions rather like the different levels of resolution of a microscope.

The following four focal "levels" can be distinguished:

1. *The physical world*—whose domain can be construed, from one aspect, as that of all phenomena, since everything is constituted of matter-energy in space-time; the focus of the physical sciences.
2. *Living organisms*—the focus of the biological sciences (with a special "box" for the key neurosciences).
3. *The behavior of living organisms*—the focus of the behavioral sciences.
4. *Human culture.*

Although *within* some of these four levels of interest portions of part-whole hierarchies of complexity can be found (see the detailed Figure 13.2, attached as an Appendix, where the horizontal, solid arrows represent such sequences), this hierarchical whole-part character of the relationships of the natural world is more apparent in the relations *between* higher and lower levels in the figures. Within any particular analytical level of this scheme of disciplines, there are often subdisciplines that form a bridge with an adjacent level by focusing on the same events or domains. This allows for and shows the significance of interdisciplinary interactions. These "bridges" are indicated in both figures by the vertical, dashed arrows between the focal levels of interest.

This scheme is an epistemological presentation concerned with the foci of interest and analysis that naturally arise from the *methodologically* reductionist techniques of the sciences—the necessary breaking down of complex wholes into their smaller units for investigation. The figures illustrate "part-whole" hierarchies of complexity in which the sciences focusing on the more complex "wholes" are distinct from those focusing on the parts that constitute them.[7] As one goes up the figures, one finds the need to deploy distinctively new concepts and theories containing new referential terms in order to represent the observed capacities and functions and to describe accurately the structures, entities and processes that occur at those more complex levels (inevitably "higher" on the printed page).

The concepts and theories with their particular referential terms that constitute the content of the sciences focusing on the more complex levels are often (not always) not reducible to those operative in the sciences that focus on their components. This is an epistemological affirmation concerned with the nature of our knowing and knowledge. With particular reference to our concerns in this inquiry, it seems unlikely that the contents of level 3 and, even more, those of level 4 are likely to be reducible entirely to that of the science of genetics, which is located across the width of level 2.

Sometimes a variety of independent derivation, identification, or measurement procedures directed at a particular complex level find an invariance in the concepts and referential terms of the theories needed to account for the phenomena associated with them. W.C. Wimsatt at the University of Chicago has called[8] these "robust." I would argue that this indicates that what is yielded by the procedures appropriate to each level of investigation can then be said to be *real*, if only in the pragmatic sense that we cannot avoid taking account of them in our practical and experimental interactions with them. That is, when concepts and referential terms in theories turn out to be "robust" in Wimsatt's sense, there is then a *prima facie* case that the concepts and referential terms of the theories deployed in relation to the more complex levels actually refer to new realities distinctively emerging at those levels of complexity. There are (putatively) genuinely new realities to be observed in the behavior of living organisms (level 3) and in human culture (level 4) that are not subsumable under the concepts that refer to the genetic realities observed at level 2. In particular, human culture includes religious experience and the theologies that are the intellectual reflections upon it.

What I am saying here assumes some form of "critical" realist philosophy of science. This continues to commend itself to me as the appropriate account of the scientific enterprise for many reasons.[9] It also seems to be the working philosophy of most practicing scientists who infer from their experiments the best explanation, and thereby postulate provisional realities ("candidates for reality") based on the normal criteria of reasonableness—fit with the data, internal coherence, comprehensiveness, fruitfulness, and general cogency.

Such considerations allow us to infer from the map of knowledge depicted in the figure a kind of "scale" of being and becoming. Science has shown that the natural world is a hierarchy of levels of complexity. Each one operates at its own level, requires its own methods of inquiry and develops its own conceptual framework, in which at least some of the terms can refer to new nonreducible realities distinctive of the level in question. Moving up the figures from bottom to top also corresponds very closely to the sequence of the actual appearance in time of the entities, structures, processes, etc. on which the hierarchy of sciences respectively focus. There has been a successive appearance in time of new complex entities, etc., such that the natural world is today perceived as having evolved. The world manifests the natural appearance of new kinds of reality generated from within and by its own processes and by any addition of entities *ab extra*. Furthermore, on the basis of our considerations concerning the reality of what is referred to at different levels, one cannot say that, for example, atoms and molecules are *more* real than cells, living organisms, or ecosystems.

Moreover there are *social* and *personal* realities, too. As one moves up the figure, this recognition of the possibility of the emergence of new realities in the natural world gives a recognizable location within the map of knowledge for the emergence of the distinctively human, or all that is signaled by the use of the word "person." The language of personal experience, especially that of personal relations (including, for theists, relations to God and so the language of theology), thereby acquires a new legitimacy referring to realities that could be emergent in humanity. These realities are not to be reduced prematurely to the concepts applicable to the constituents of the evolved human body, in particular, its genes. They must be accorded a *prima facie* status of referring to realities until their respective terms and concepts have been shown unequivocally to be reducible totally to the sciences of the lower levels. So our particular concern in appraising the significance of genetic research, and concomitantly the implications and results of the Human Genome Project, must be to persist in asking whether or not a reduction of the personal to genetics is occurring with any elucidation of the human genome.

Structures, functions and processes pertinent to human beings are, of course, to be found at focal levels 1 to 3 of this scheme. No other part of the observed universe appears to include so many levels and to range over so much within these levels as do human beings, and level 4 is unique to them. Hence, a preliminary and initial purpose of this essay is to survey the gamut of the sciences that are relevant to understanding the human organism. Only then can the role of the gene—and of the social and scientific priority of genetics—be set in a context allowing judicious appraisal. This should then allow any excessive claims for genetics to be more accurately and suitably qualified. Even so, the level of operation of DNA, that of genetics, is certainly a key and influential one in the microcosm of the macrocosm that human nature transpires to be in this twentieth-century scientific perspective. However, genetics needs to be placed first in its scientific context before making any theological or ethical assessments of its consequences and implications. Such a survey of the sciences pertaining to humanity could also serve a more positive and wider purpose. For it is imperative that investigators in theology and ethics take seriously into account the multilayered complex entity that the sciences reveal human beings to be.

Levels of Human Being

The physical basis of human being (Focal level l): From time immemorial human beings have known that they are made up of the same stuff as the rest of the world—"dust thou art, and unto dust shalt thou return."[10] Today we would say that human bodies, like those of all other living organisms, are constituted of the same atoms as the rest of the inorganic and organic world and that, to varying extents, these atoms also exist throughout the universe and many of them originated in supernova explosions long before this planet formed.

A significant feature of the physical (atomic-molecular) level of natural reality pertinent to our existence is the capacity to form structures that can undergo replication in self-perpetuating processes and patterns. This is the focus of molecular biology, which grew explosively from the discovery of the structure of DNA in 1953 and now forms the *bridge between levels 1 and 2*. These scientific disciplines have entirely exorcised any ghostly remnants of the "vitalism" that was mooted in the earlier half of the twentieth century to account for the distinctive characteristics of living organisms and "living matter." But these developments equally do not warrant a reductionist interpretation of the functioning of biological systems, and in particular, a reduction to the DNA level. The pattern of "causal" relationships in biological evolution is interesting in this connection. We are dealing with a process in which a selective system "edits," as it were, the products of physico-chemical events (i.e., mutations, changes in DNA) over periods of time covering several reproductive generations.

Let us take the example of D. Campbell[11] to illustrate this: The surfaces and muscle attachments of the jaws of a worker termite are mechanically highly efficient, entirely conforming with the best engineering and physical principles. Their operation depends on the combination of properties of the particular proteins of which the jaws are made. Selection has optimized these. So, from the perspective of the whole organism's activity and its being only one in a series of generations of termites, it is the efficacy of the proteins in constituting jaws, whose efficiency has been enhanced by natural selection. This efficacy apparently determines the sequences of the DNA units here—even though when one looks at the development of a *single* organism, one observes with the molecular biologists only the biochemical processes whereby protein sequences and structures are "read out" from the DNA sequences.

Hence there is a sense in which the network of relationships that constitute the evolutionary development and the behavior pattern of the whole organism determines what particular DNA sequence is present at the controlling point in its genetic material in the evolved organism. Campbell called this "downward" or "top-down" causation insofar as specifying the higher levels of organization (the whole evolutionary system through time, in this instance) is necessary for explaining the lower level—in this case, the sequence in a DNA molecule.

Divine Delight in Evolutionary Diversity

Human beings as living organisms (Focal level 2): All the biological sciences depicted at this level in the figure can, in one way or other, include within their scope some aspects of human beings. This is not surprising in view of the evolutionary origins of humanity, as manifested particularly in the fact that approximately 98% of human DNA is the same (homologous in nucleotide sequence) as that of the DNA of chimpanzees. The evolutionary process itself is characterized by propensities towards increase in complexity, information-processing and storage, consciousness, sensitivity to pain, and even self-consciousness (a necessary prerequisite for social development and the cultural transmission of knowledge through succeeding generations). Successive forms are likely to manifest more and more of these characteristics. However, the actual physical forms of the organisms in which these propensities are actualized and instantiated is contingent upon the history of the confluence of disparate chains of events. There can, it seems to me (*pace* Stephen J. Gould[12]), be overall direction and implementation of purpose through the interplay of chance and law, without a deterministic plan fixing all the details of the structure of that which emerges as possessing personal qualities. Hence, the appearance of self-conscious persons capable, according to the Judeo-Christian tradition, of relating personally to God can still be regarded as an intention of God continuously creating through the evolutionary development. (It certainly must have been "on the cards" since it actually happened—with us!)

Remarkable and significant as is the emergence of self-conscious persons by natural processes from the original "hot Big Bang" from which the universe expanded over the last 10–20 billion years, this must not be allowed to obscure another fact about humanity, namely, how relatively recent is its arrival in the universe. If one takes the age of the earth as two days of 48 "hours" (1 such "hour" = 100 million years), *Homo sapiens* appears only at the last stroke of midnight of the second day. Our particular genetic constitution is a relatively recent arrival on the earth and is closely related to that of our nonhuman forbears. Theists must not underplay the significance of all other living organisms to God as Creator—even though they are able to depict only in extrapolated imagination the kind of delight that God may be conceived to have in the fecund multiplicity and variety of created organisms.

There are some other features of this history that any contemporary theological account of human origins and the nature of the human being must also take into account. Evolution can operate only through the death of individuals. New forms of matter arise only through the dissolution of the old; new life only through death of the old. We as individuals would not be here at all, as members of the species *Homo sapiens* if our forerunners in the evolutionary process had not died. Biological death was present on the earth long before human beings arrived on the scene, and is the prerequisite of our coming into existence through the processes of biological evolution whereby God, theists must assume, creates new species—including *Homo sapiens*.

Furthermore, the biological-historical evidence is that human nature has emerged only gradually by a continuous process from earlier "hominids." No sudden breaks of any substantial kind in the sequences have been noted by paleontologists and anthropologists. There is no past period for which there is reason to affirm that human beings possessing moral perfection existed in a paradisiacal situation from which there has been only a subsequent decline. Reference to human behavior brings us within the scope of level 3, but before this is examined we need to look at the bridge between levels 2 and 3.

Theological Response to Cognitive Science

Human beings in the perspectives of sciences bridging the biological and the behavioral (between focal levels 2 and 3): Sciences that bridge levels 2 and 3 include, on the one hand, cognitive science (or, "cognitive neuroscience") and, on the other hand, sociobiology (called by some "behavioral ecology") together with behavior genetics.

Cognitive science is concerned with relating meaningfully the different levels of analysis of information-processing to behavior (roughly, "cognition"). It thereby forms a bridge between the purely biological neurosciences and the sciences of behavior, and it is especially concerned with trying to understand how the mind-brain works, particularly in human beings. The detailed ways in which the various levels of analysis are applied and shape investigations concern us less here than the now widespread realization by cognitive scientists that, in order to understand the relation between the behavioral (at one pole) and the molecular (at the other), understanding of all levels of analysis, organization, and processing is necessary.

This pressure to integrate the study of different levels is, it seems, generated by the very nature of the problems that cognitive scientists address. Moreover, what applies to the operation of the nervous system also applies to the operation of the brain as a whole.[13] This is a clear example, in this instance from the cognitive sciences, of a general feature of biological systems. Because of their intricate complexity, especially that of nervous systems and *a fortiori* the human-brain-in-the-human-body, no one description at any one level can ever be adequate. Therefore, no one level has epistemological priority nor *a fortiori* (on a critical-realist reckoning) ontological priority. The emergent properties and functions at the more complex levels of analysis, organization and processing are emergent *realities*—and those of consciousness and self-consciousness are notably so (without any additions of new entities *ab extra*).

The question of whether or not the human brain operates as a digital computer (AI or "Artificial Intelligence") or by "parallel distributed processing (either PDP or "Connectionism") can only be settled by the ordinary processes of scientific research.[14] Recognition of the many-leveled foci of such research could now mean there is no necessary conflict between it and either the investigations of human mental activity by the behavioral sciences (level 3), or *a fortiori* those arising from the study of human culture. It may also turn out that the human brain is a nonlinear dynamic system, and so it is deterministic at the micro-level but will always be unpredictable by us in its succession of overall states at the macro-level. Might we not have here the physical correlate of the experience of consciousness, and so the warrant for giving an account in predominantly *mentalistic* terms of successions of what we experience as mental states?

It has been proposed by the brain scientist Roger Sperry[15] that the way the brain acts on the body through the operation of the central nervous system is best conceived as an instance of that "top-down causation" (or, better, or "whole-part constraint"), which we saw had earlier been postulated by D. Campbell in connection with the evolution of a DNA having a specific information content. Both are instances of the now widely recognized feature of many complex systems (whose complexity can be structural and/or functional and/or temporal), in which the macroscopic state and character of the system as whole is a constraint, effectively like a cause, upon what happens to the units of which it is constituted. These latter then behave in ways other than they would have done were they not part of that system.

In Sperry's account, the total state of the human brain-as-a-whole, a state describable to our self-consciousness only in mentalistic language, is a constraint upon the firing of individual neurons or groups of neurons in such a way as to trigger and actually be the specific action intended in the consciousness that was that brain state. This amounts to a contemporary scientific analysis of what is involved in personal agency in nonreductionist terms. This raises the question of whether past constraints—such as genetic constraints—can be regarded as a contemporary exposition of what is happening when human-brains-in-human-bodies are agents. The mechanism through which they act is based on structures genetically coded in their static form. However, the actions themselves cannot be accounted for by genetics alone, because total brain states are additional constraining factors in human actions and are only referable to and perhaps describable by mentalistic language, such as that of purposes or intentions. This places a fundamental limit on what we can expect genetics to explain.

None of this is inconsistent with the Christian anthropology stemming from the Bible, which regards human beings as psychosomatic unities displaying a many-faceted personhood uniting many properties, abilities, and potential relationships—rooted in materiality, and including DNA, we would add today. Nor need this material substructure of the human being, which arises *inter alia* from its genetic constitution, be regarded as a threat to the reality of subjectivity, of self-consciousness. Margaret Boden, in discussing the significance of AI (and the same could be affirmed of PDP) for the mind-body problem, points out that:

> Modeling a psychological phenomenon on a computer is a way of showing that—and how—it is *possible* for that phenomenon to arise in a physical system. . . . [AI] could (and should be) interpreted . . . as showing how it is possible for material systems (which, according to the biologist, we are) to possess such characteristic features of human psychology as subjectivity, purpose, freedom, and choice. . . . By analogy, then, it is no longer scientifically disreputable, as it has been thought for so long, to describe people in these radically subjective terms also.[16]

A Theological Response to Sociobiology

Sociobiology may be broadly defined as the systematic study of the biological, especially the genetic, basis of social behavior. In relation to human beings, it aims at exploring the relations between biological constraints and cultural change. In the ambitions of at least some sociobiologists, it thereby encroaches on level 4. Clearly this whole development is of theological concern. By thus encompassing in one theory human culture and the nonhuman biological world (especially in its genetic aspects), sociobiology must inevitably influence our thinking about what human beings are. This debate is not entirely a replay of the old nature-nurture dichotomy, for the subtlety and complexity of the strategies of gene perpetuation have undergone much revision; and the many-leveled character of humanity is becoming more and more apparent. The emphatically evolutionary outlook of sociobiology raises no new questions for Christian theology that have not been raised by the general idea of evolution, both cosmic and biological. However, because of the predominantly reductionist tone in the writings of many sociobiologists, there has been a tendency to interpret human behavior functionally only as a strategy for the survival of genes. In its general thrust, the theological response to such suggestions must be that made to any purely deterministic and reductionistic account of human behavior. But in making such a riposte, theologians should nevertheless recognize, far more explicitly than they have done in the past, that human nature is exceedingly complex and dependent on its shaping by genetic information—however much that is overlaid by nurture and culture.

It has indeed been the purpose of *behavior genetics* since 1960, when it first came to be recognized as a distinct discipline, to examine "the inheritance of many different behaviors in organisms ranging from bacteria to man."[17] Behavior genetics is predominantly concerned with explaining individual differences within species. As a discipline it represents a fusion of the interests of genetics and psychology, moving between the two poles of a genetics of behavior and a genetically-aware psychology[18] This new subdiscipline is currently being vigorously applied to human beings. The research proceeds and, like all scientific research, it both clarifies and at the same time generates new problems. Even in their present form such studies are producing evidence of the genetic underpinning of much in personal behavior and traits previously considered as entirely environmental and cultural.

Sociobiology and behavior genetics cannot but influence our general assessment of human nature and, in particular, the degree of responsibility assigned to societies and individuals for their actions. From a theistic viewpoint, the genetic boundaries that limit what we can do are what God has purposed to provide the matrix within which freedom shall operate. Furthermore, theologians should acknowledge that it is this kind of *genetically-based* creature that God has actually created as a human being through the evolutionary process. That genetic heritage cannot in advance itself determine the *content* of thinking and reasoning—even if it is the prerequisite of the possession of these capacities.

For example, to unravel the evolutionary and genetic origins of moral awareness is not to preempt its ultimate maturation in the moral sensitivity of self-aware, free, reasoning persons whose emergence in the created order God can properly be posited as intending. The vital question now becomes: What do we human beings make of these possibilities? The biological endowment of human beings does not appear to guarantee their contented adaptation to an environment that is inherently dynamic. They have ever-changing and expanding horizons within which they live individually and socially, physically and culturally, emotionally, intellectually, and spiritually. In particular, when one reflects on the balanced adaptation of other living organisms to their biological niche, the alienation of human beings from nonhuman nature and from each other appears as an anomaly within the organic world. Thus it is not surprising to find Lindon Eaves and Lora Gross, writing on behavior genetics, pointing out what they call the "possible gulf between the ecosystem in which human evolution occurred and the global environment into which humanity is now projected."[19] They go on to suggest that the basically unethical human favoring of genetic kin is a sign, at best, of tribal self-interest and "that humans bring into the world by virtue of their ancestry biological baggage which is ill adapted to the present world."[20] What constitutes the "world" for human beings transcends the purely biological.

Hence, as human beings widen their environmental horizons into ranges that are really more appropriate to level 4, they experience this "gulf" between their biological past out of which they have evolved and that in which they conceive themselves as existing, or that in which they aspire to exist. I think of such experiences as: contemplation of our own death, our sense of finitude, suffering, the realization of our potentialities, steering our path from life to death. The mere existence of this "gulf" between our experiences and our yearnings raises a problem for any purely biological account of human development. We may well ask, "Why and how has a process whereby there have successfully evolved living organisms finely tuned to and adapted to their environments failed, in the case of *Homo sapiens*, to ensure this fit between lived experience and the environing conditions of their lives?" It appears that the human brain has capacities that were originally evolved in response to earlier environmental challenges; but the exercise of which now engenders a whole range of needs, desires, ambitions, and aspirations that cannot all be harmoniously fulfilled. They are not compossible.

This provokes the further question of whether or not human beings have properly identified what their true "environment" really is—that "environment" in which human flourishing is possible. (We return to this paradox in the last section.) The complexity and character of the human predicament clearly involves more subtle levels of human nature than are the focus of level 2 or of the "bridge" sciences to the next level. We now turn to those sciences concerned with human behavior.

The Behavioral Sciences and the Social Sciences

The sciences and human behavior (focal level 3): Some of the principal behavioral sciences and the systems on which they focus are indicated in level 3 of the figures. This includes various forms of psychology, which is the study of the phenomena of mental life. In its usage since the eighteenth century, this study at first naturally included the (largely introspective) study of such human activities as perceiving, remembering, thinking, and reasoning. However, in the twentieth century until the mid-1960s, psychology was dominated by behaviorism and psychoanalysis. Although there was some continued interest in cognitive and other mental processes (e.g., the "Gestalt" school and Piaget and his successors), they were not in the forefront or in the public image of psychology.

This has now changed and mental processes have begun to be taken much more seriously. There has been a "cognitive," "consciousness,' or "mentalist" shift of emphasis in psychology that moves its focus of interest towards the content and activities of ordinary consciousness (sometimes neutrally denoted as "self-modification"). Consciousness is now much more frequently regarded as a theoretical term that refers to realities whose existence is inferred from observation. How it is to be a thinking and feeling human being have again come onto the agenda of many of the behavioral sciences (level 3). Sperry affirms[21] that there is a new openness in the behavioral sciences, not only in a "downwards" direction via cognitive science to the neurosciences, but also "upwards" to all those studies and activities that regard human consciousness and its content as real and worthy of examination and interpretation. Such suggestions also allow us to understand better that much larger transition from level 3 to level 4 that one recognizes intuitively but finds more difficult to explicate scientifically than that between levels 1, 2, and 3.

A rehabilitation thus appears to be occurring, from a scientific perspective, of the reality of reference of humanistic studies—in which theology should be included, if only because of its concern with religious experience. It also gives scientific credibility to what had never been doubted in theology—the pre-eminence of the concept of the personal in the hierarchy of our interpretations of the many-leveled structure of the world of which humanity is an evolved constituent. As the experimental psychologist M.A. Jeeves says, "we need a hierarchy of levels and their corresponding categories of explanation in order to do justice to the complexity and richness of what we find when we study man . . . we are trying to discover how the stories at different levels correlate[22]. All this has important implications for the relation of science and religion. Instead of a dichotomy between a dualism of "body" and "mind" (a common misapprehension of the Christian view of humanity) on the one hand, and a reductive materialism on the other, a new integrated "view of reality" could emerge. This, so Sperry hopes, "accepts mental and spiritual qualities as causal realities, but at the same time denies they can exist separately in an unembodied state apart from the functioning brain."[23] Thus, the situation looks more encouraging for a fruitful dialogue between religion and the sciences of human behavior than it has been for many decades.

The very multiplicity of psychological theories reminds us that focal level 3 theories are "underdetermined by the facts," a characteristic they share with the theories of the sciences of levels 1 and 2, though it is often less obvious with them. We have to tolerate the variety of theories in psychology as an inevitable consequence of the nature of their "subject-matter" (*mot juste* in this instance!). No one of the theories of psychology may claim to be so definitive and so established that theology must come to terms uniquely with it. All can throw light on human personality and need to be considered by theology—especially Jungian psychology, which is so sensitive to religious experience.

Furthermore, there is nothing static about the human condition. As Peter Morea puts it: "We are not so much human beings as human becomings."[24] He also points out the biological paradox of our lack of "fit" with our environment as we perceive it. Human beings are a problem to themselves and for themselves. For theists, this implies the apparent paradox of God seeming to create a misfit in a world wherein other living creatures are finely and appositely adapted to their environments. We are beings who comprehend and understand through the sciences vast tracts of the obscurities of the universe in which we find ourselves—only to be confronted with the most intransigent and unfathomable mystery when we face ourselves. Morea has expressed it thus: "Thrown into the world I become a puzzle to myself; scientific theory has failed to find a solution to [this puzzle of] St. Augustine. . . . If human beings are made in God's image it would explain why—at the boundaries of our scientific knowing of human personality—we sometimes sense beyond the mystery of human personality a much greater Mystery."[25]

Evolutionary Epistemology

The social sciences (between focal levels 3 and 4): The sciences variously designated as "social" form a bridge between the behavioral sciences and culture. The more the sciences are concerned with the mental life and behavior of human beings, the more they will impinge on the concerns of the Christian community. It is worth noting that the social conditioning of religious beliefs that the social sciences disentangle and reveal does not, of itself, settle any questions as to the truth of these beliefs.

The evolutionary process, however, introduces another dimension into this complex relation between religious belief and social setting, namely that of "evolutionary epistemology." This is the realization that cognition of its environment by a living organism has to be sufficiently trustworthy in its content to allow the organism to be viable under the pressures of natural selection. Cognition of its environment is "trustworthy" in this sense when the organism has to take account pragmatically of its content in its practical and experimental interactions with that environment in order to survive. This formulation of "trustworthiness" of cognition comes very close to the notion of "robustness" of Wimsatt to which we earlier referred. Those concepts and referential terms that were "robust" under scrutiny by the procedures appropriate to each level of investigation we then suggested could be regarded as "real," at least in the above pragmatic sense that we cannot avoid taking account of them in our practical and experimental interactions with them. The convergence of these two notions, of "trustworthiness" of cognition for survival and the "robustness" of higher-level concepts and theoretical terms, therefore helps in providing a pragmatic definition of "reality" for our present discourse.[26] It also indicates the significance of the evolutionary process for our understanding of "reality" so construed. Now the role of religious ideas and systems in evolution has begun to be taken seriously by social anthropologists and suggests that this might give some provisional warrant for the claimed reality of reference to such religious beliefs. By setting up norms related to the existence of a "transcendental reality" other than human authority, the cumulative wisdom of the religious traditions has, it has been suggested,[27] contributed crucially to the process of human social organization, wider and more complex than that of any other living organism. In other words, humanity could only survive and flourish if it took account of social and personal values that transcended the urges of the individual, embodying "selfish" genes.

In the light of our discussion of environmental realities that shape evolution (evolutionary epistemology), does not this imply that these social and personal values, enshrined in moral codes and imprinted in ethical attitudes, are part of the *realities* with which we humans have to deal and of which we have to take account or otherwise die out? This increasingly accepted role of the religions of humanity in socio-cultural evolution points to the existence of values as constituting a reality-system that human beings neglect to their actual peril:

> Nothing learned in social science forbids asking whether there is something transcendent to the human world, something sacred exerting its pull over society, and out of which the human natural worlds may be derived. What if there are some challenges and conflicts that a society can solve only religiously? . . . The fact is not so much that religion calls for an explanation outside itself in society. It is rather society that calls for an explanation outside itself in those realities to which religion points. Society, not just religion, is the effect.[28]

If this is so, religious beliefs are directly and causally pertinent to decisions relevant to the future of humanity, including its genetic future.

The Question of Transcendence and Human Origin

Human culture and its products (focal level 4): Such perceptions bring us to the domain of human culture, that of level 4 (Figure 13.2—see Appendix). The "cultural products" at focal level 4 are embodiments of human creativity in the arts, sciences, and human relations, including (theists would add) relations to God.[29] Those patterns of discernible meaning within the natural nexus of events in the world, which are the means of communication between human beings and between God and humanity, are generated through historical formation in continuous cultures, which invest them with meaning enabling such communication. Thereby, they have the unique power of inducting humanity into an encounter with the transcendence in the "other," whether in the form of another human person or of God—the Beyond within our midst.

George Steiner in his penetrating *Real Presences* has called such an encounter a "wager on transcendence": "The wager on the meaning of meaning, on the potential of insight and response when one human voice addresses another, when we come face to face with the text and work of art or music, which is to say when we encounter the *other* in its condition of freedom, is a wager on transcendence.[30] He does not hesitate to point to its theological import: "The wager . . . predicates the presence of a realness . . . within language and form. It supposes a passage . . . from meaning to meaningfulness. The conjecture is that "God" is, not because our grammar is outworn; but that grammar lives and generates worlds because there is the wager on God."[31] We can expect all such encounters with "cultural products" or such "wagers on transcendence" to communicate only in their own way and in their own "language" with an immediacy at their own level that is not reducible to other languages.

Such a robust assertion of the conceptual and experienced autonomy of what is communicated in human culture is reinforced by the rehabilitation of subjective, of inner experience, in cognitive science and in psychology, in fact, in the recovery of the personal, the recognition of the reality of personhood. We really do seem to be witnessing a major shift in our cultural and intellectual landscape, which is opening up the dialogue between the human spiritual enterprise (broadly, "religion") and that of science in a way long barred by the dominance of a reductionist, mechanistic materialism, thought erroneously to have been warranted by science itself. The human is undoubtedly biological, but what is distinctively human transcends that out of which and in which it has emerged.

This pressure for a wider perspective on humanity is being generated from within the sciences themselves (if not by all scientists) in attempting to cope with the many levels depicted in our figures. Is it too much to hope that we see here the first glimmerings of a genuine integration between the humanities, including theology, and the sciences? Are we seeing the beginnings of a breakdown of the dichotomy between the "two cultures" engendered by the absence of any epistemological map on which their respective endeavors could be meaningfully located?

The Paradox of Human Becoming

Even purely scientific perspectives raise more acutely than ever the paradox of a humanity that is a kind of misfit in its biological environment. "Evolution seems to have played a nasty trick, bringing into existence human beings vast in their desire and potential, but minute in their fulfillment and satisfaction," concluded the psychologist Morea.[32] Profounder and more extensive insights have been and still are forthcoming from novelists, poets, dramatists, historians, and social philosophers—all who have reflected on the enormities and degradations that mar our twentieth century history. They speak of "*Angst*," "alienation," "false self-consciousness," "one-dimensional humanity," "disintegration," and more.

Human beings possess a self-consciousness, which, by enabling them to be "subjects" over against "objects," ipso facto renders them out of harmony with themselves, with each other and (theists would affirm) with God—and so capable of thwarting the divine purposes. Self-consciousness, by its very character as self-consciousness, has made human beings aware of what they might become—and of their failure to fulfill their potentialities and satisfy their highest aspirations. It has made them aware of personal death and human finitude, as well as enhanced suffering.

The above modern descriptions of the human state, as "alienated," and so on, all reflect a sense of incompleteness, a felt lack of integration and a widespread judgment that the lives of human individuals in twentieth century society have failed to live up to the hopes engendered by scientific technology. These hopes have foundered on the rock of the obduracy of self-will operating in a humanity inadequate through its own inner paralysis of will to respond to the challenge of its newly won knowledge and power over the world. Our accounts of biology, genetics, and psychology incline one to ground at least some of this widely intuited individual and social malaise in the levels on which these sciences focus. But our perception of the multileveled character of the natural reality that is a human being concomitantly serves to warn us that no superficial palliatives can be expected to effect the fulfillment of human potentialities that must operate at the many levels of human existence in the individual and in society. For theists, these include supremely the relation of human beings to that all-encompassing, circumambient Reality that is named as "God,"—that eternal and transcendent "Environment" to which we need to "adapt" and to relate to harmoniously.

However much might be possible in remedying particular, localizable, and identifiable biological deficiencies, I conclude that it would be unwise to place too much hope alone on the possible future achievements of any directed genetic engineering for the amelioration of the general human condition, especially the psychological and spiritual. It would be irresponsible of all those engaged in the Human Genome Project if they ever gave the impression that it could do so.

Appendix

Legend to Figure 13.2

The relation of disciplines. "Focal levels" correspond to foci of interest and therefore of analysis (see text). Focal level 4 is meant to give only an indication of the content of human culture (cf. Popper's "World 3").

Solid horizontal arrows represent part-to-whole relationships of structural and/or functional organization. (N.b.: Molecules and macro-molecules in focal level 1 are also the constituent "parts" of the "wholes"' in focal level 2.) Dashed boxes represent subdisciplines in particular levels that can be coordinated with work at the next focal level in the scheme (the connections are indicated by vertical, dashed, double-headed arrows). In each of the focal levels 1–3, examples are given of the *systems* studied, which can be classified as being within these levels and also of their corresponding *sciences*. Focal level 2 elaborates additionally the part-whole relation of levels of organization and analysis of in the nervous system (after Figure 1 of Churchland and Sejnowski—see note 13).

In focal level 2, the science of genetics has relevance to the whole range of the part-whole hierarchy of living systems and, if included, would have to be written so as to extend across its entire width.

CNS = Central Nervous System

FIGURE 13.2 Relationships Within and Among the Disciplines

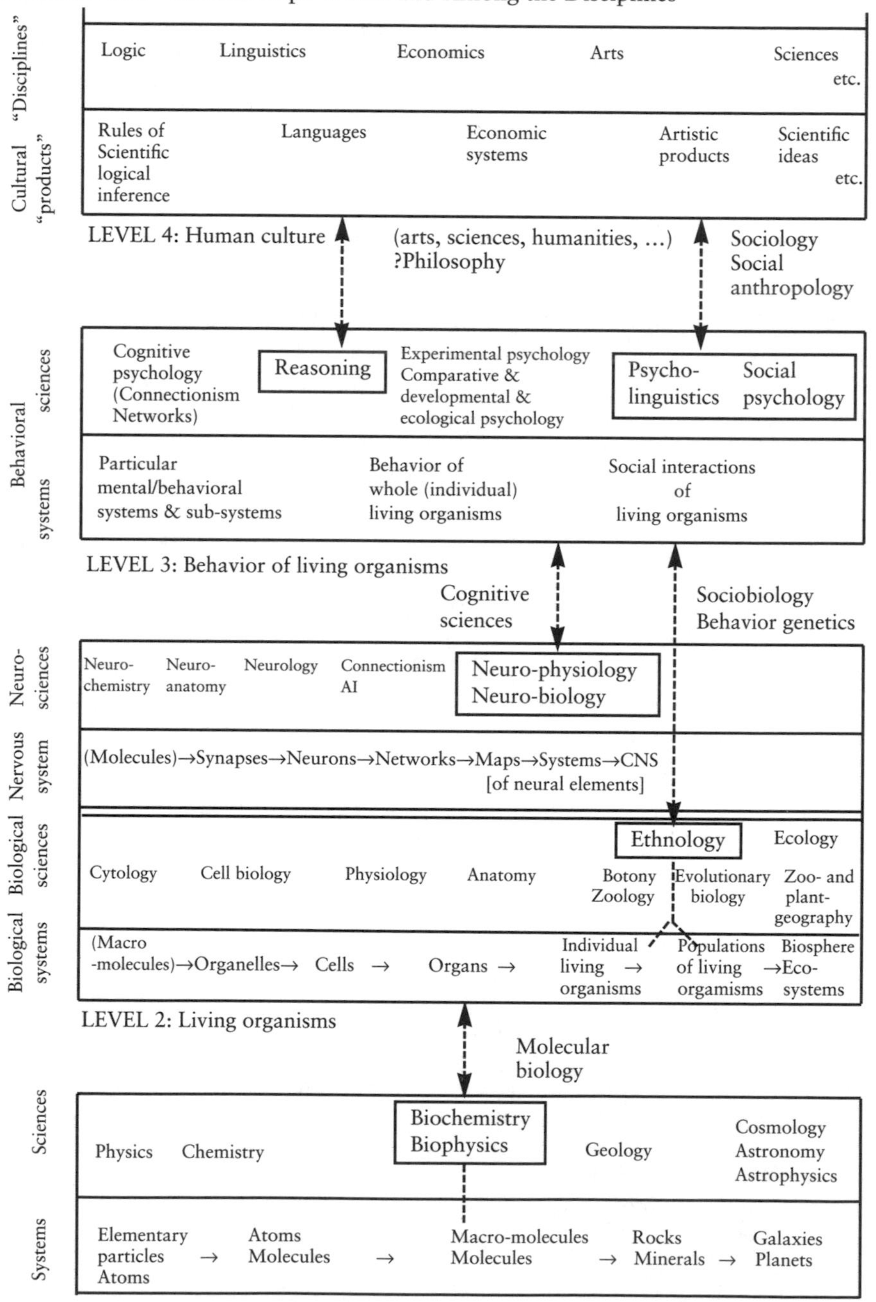

This figure is my elaboration of Figure 8.1 of W. Bechtel and A. Abrahamsen in *Connectionism and the Mind* (Oxford and Cambridge, Mass.: Blackwell, 1991).

Notes

1. Richard Dawkins, *The Selfish Gene* (Oxford: Oxford University Press, 1976), 21.

2. Edward O. Wilson, *Sociobiology: The New Synthesis* (Cambridge, Mass: Belknap Press, Harvard University Press, 1975), 4.

3. Francis C.H. Crick, *Of Molecules and Man* (Seattle: University of Washington Press, 1966), 10.

4. I say "apparently" because both R. Dawkins and E.O. Wilson, in the appropriate contexts, deny such intentions—in spite of their other emphatic statements. Thus Wilson sees the relation between different scientific disciplines as one of conflict and confrontation in which every discipline has its "antidiscipline" at the level below (in the sense of Fig. l of this paper, described later) and is an "anti-discipline" for that above. See "Biology and the Social Sciences," *Daedalus* 106:4 (Autumn 1977): 127–40. Yet the impression of a take-over bid by biology (as sociobiology) directed at sociology, anthropology and the behavioral sciences persists.

5. The broader issue of "scientism" will not be pursued here for it is less directly relevant to the assumptions implicit in the role assigned to genes by some authors. Needless to say, it is a major issue in our culture and can color many attitudes relevant to the application of scientific knowledge. However, it seems to me to be less widely assumed by scientists than the reductionism that, I believe, unwarrantedly underlies many discussions of genetics and its applications and is therefore the chief concern of the text at this point. For references to the literature on reductionism, see inter alia: Arthur Peacocke, *God and the New Biology* (London: Dent, and San Francisco: Harper and Row, 1986; reprint, Magnolia, MA: Peter Smith Publishing Co., 1994), chs. 1 & 2; Ian Barbour, *Religion in an Age of Science* (San Francisco: Harper and Row, 1990), 165–172.

6. This term need not (should not) be taken to imply the operation of any influences, either external in the form of an "entelechy" or "life force" or internal in the sense of a "top-down" causative influences. It is, in my usage, a purely descriptive term for the observed phenomenon of the appearance of new capabilities, functions, etc., at greater levels of complexity.

7. Such relations occur both horizontally, within the four broad categories of the boxes, and vertically, though it is these latter that are of most concern to us here.

8. W.C. Wimsatt, "Robustness, Reliability and Multiple-Determination in Science," in *Knowing and Validating in the Social Sciences: A Tribute to Donald Campbell*, ed. M. Brewer and B. Collins (San Francisco: Jossey-Bass, 1981).

9. See Arthur Peacocke, *Intimations of Reality: Critical Realism in Science and Religion* (Notre Dame: University of Notre Dame Press, 1984), ch. 1; idem, Theology for a Scientific Age, 11–14; Wentzel van Huysteen, *Theology and the Justification of Faith* (Grand Rapids: Eerdmans, 1989), ch. 9; Michael Banner, *The Justification of Science and the Rationality of Belief* (Oxford: Clarendon Press, 1990); and Barbour, *Religion in an Age of Science*, 41–5.

10. Genesis 3:19 (Authorized Version).

11. Donald T. Campbell, "'Downward Causation' in Hierarchically Organized Systems," in *Studies in the Philosophy of Biology: Reduction and Related Problems*, ed. F.J. Ayala and T. Dobshansky (London: Macmillan, 1974), 179–186.

12. Stephen J. Gould, *Wonderful Life: The Burgess Shale and the Nature of History* (London: Penguin Books, 1989), 51 and passim. For amplification of the brief reference to this work, see the discussion in my *Theology for a Scientific Age*, 220ff.

13. P.S. Churchland and T.J. Sejnowski, "Perspectives on Cognitive Neuroscience," *Science* 242 (1988): 744.

14. The very possibility of doing this at all has, of course, been called in question, most notably by Roger Penrose in *The Emperor's New Mind* (Oxford: Oxford University Press, 1989).

15. E.g., in his *Science and Moral Priority* (Oxford: Blackwell, 1983), ch.6, and subsequent writings.

16. Margaret Boden, article on "Artificial Intelligence," in *The Oxford Companion to the Mind*, ed. R.L. Gregory (Oxford and New York: Oxford University Press, 1987), 49–50.

17. D.A. Hay, *Essentials of Behavior Genetics* (London: Blackwells, 1985), 1.

18. Hay, *Essentials*, 4, quoting J.R. Vale in *American Psychologist* 28 (1973): 872.

19. L.J. Eaves and L.M. Gross, "Theological Reflection on the Cultural Impact of Human Genetics," *Insights* (Chicago CCRS, vol. 2, 1990): 17.

20. Eaves and Gross, "Theological Reflection," p. 17.

21. R.W. Sperry, "Psychology's Mentalist Paradigm and the Religion/Science Tension," *American Psychologist* 43 (1988): 608.

22. M.A. Jeeves, "Minds and Brains: Then and Now," *Interdisciplinary Science Revs*. 16 (1991): 70.

23. Sperry, "Psychology's Mentalist Paradigm . . . ," 609.

24. Peter Morea, *Personality* (New York: Penguin Books, 1990), 171.

25. Morea, *Personality*, 174.

26. An interesting analysis of this revival of "naturalism" in epistemology has been given by Philip Kitcher, "The Naturalists Return," *Philosophical Review* 101 (1992): 53–114. He is not unsympathetic to this "return" of naturalism in epistemology but rightly points out many of the unsolved philosophical issues it raises.

27. Donald T. Campbell, "On *the* Conflicts Between Biological *and* Social Evolution *and* Between Psychology *and* Moral Tradition," *Zygon* 11 (1976): 167–208.

28. Holmes Rolston, *Science and Religion* (New York: Random House, 1987), ch. 5, "Culture: religion and the social sciences," at 234.

29. I have argued elsewhere (in *Theology for a Scientific Age*, 1993 edition, ch. 11) that relations to God are expressed by their own distinctive means through meaningful patterns created in what is received initially through our senses.

30. G. Steiner, *Real Presences* (London and Boston: Faber and Faber, 1989), 4.

31. Steiner, *Real Presences*, 4.

32. Peter Morea, *Personality*, 171.

Chapter Fourteen

The Greening of Science, Theology, and Ethics

AUDREY R. CHAPMAN

More than three decades have passed since the publication of Lynn White's seminal article in *Science* magazine which played an important role in engendering ecological awareness in the religious community. In the article White implicates Christianity as a major contributor to the environmental crisis. According to White, the Christian worldview and the biblical mandate to dominate nature provided the context for an instrumental rather than a respectful approach to nature and an impetus to the development of an environmentally destructive science and technology.[1] In the past thirty years this has been a much debated subject.

In the last two decades religious thinkers have begun to respond in a meaningful way to a growing sense of the fragility, vulnerability, and interdependence of the creation. As Daniel Maguire notes, "If current trends continue, we will not. And this is qualitatively and epochally true. If religion does not speak to [this], it is an obsolete distraction."[2] A recent review of the literature concludes that the challenge to integrate ecology and justice concerns with the Christian faith has transformed Christian self-understanding in a relatively brief period.[3] Another survey of work by Christian ethicists contrasts the lack of attention to ecology prior to 1983 with the current situation: "In the last couple of decades, and especially the last few years, Christian ethicists have joined their secular counterparts in reexamining human obligations to plants, animals, and ecosystems in light of growing ecological devastation."[4] Whereas thirty years ago White considered Christianity to be a cause of the problem, today many secular environmental thinkers, scientists, and environmental activists look to the religious community with a sense of common purpose and commitment.[5]

Nevertheless, the monumental task of reevaluating and reformulating Christian theology and ethics in response to the environmental crisis is far from completed. While there has undoubtedly been a "greening" of religious thought since the first Earth Day in 1970, there are significant unresolved methodological, ethical, and theological issues. As a relatively young specialization struggling to do something new, for which there is no substantial heritage, eco-theology and eco-ethics are still "comparatively underdeveloped."[6] A study of the increasing influence on environmentalism on American Protestantism juxtaposes the considerable consensus on the need to address ecological issues with continuing conflicts and struggles over the appropriate orientation and direction. It characterizes Protestant environmental thought as internally divided, lacking philosophical and scientific rigor, and politically naive and uninformed,[7] and this assessment can be applied more broadly across the religious spectrum.

As this author has previously noted,[8] to date eco-theology and eco-ethics has tended to be inwardly focused. It has taken its primary task to be an evaluation of the role and responsibility of religion for the environmental crisis and a reinterpretation of various religious traditions to make them more environmentally sensitive. Much of the energy has been invested either implicitly or explicitly in responding to the challenge raised by Lynn White and other critics that Christianity and/or traditionally religious orientations more generally bear at least some responsibility for environmental abuses. Writers have variously sought to assess, amplify, or refute White's claim that Christian scripture and traditions are antiecological. Paralleling this effort, thinkers have reinterpreted Christian tradition to find resources for environmentally intentional theological reflection and engagement. As yet there has been little work to operationalize or apply a new ethic or vision to the various problems constituting the environmental crisis. Put in another way, thinkers argue from a variety of theological perspectives that we are responsible for good environmental stewardship or living in an ecologically sustainable manner, but this literature rarely offers concrete guidance on how to fulfill these obligations or evaluate the well-being of ecosystems.

Rationale for Interfacing Science, Theology, and Ethics

The constructive thesis of this article is that a greater integration of science into eco-theology and eco-ethics could contribute significantly to the development of ecological theology (eco-theology) and ecological ethics (eco-ethics). A multidisciplinary perspective could provide greater conceptual rigor, concreteness, and relevance to these specializations. A scientific grounding is essential if eco-theology and eco-ethics are to understand and come to terms with what is happening to the planet as a basis for formulating an appropriate theological and ethical response. Humanity's spiritual life and future depend, not so much on an exhortation to lead a sustain life and develop a sustainable society, but on learning what makes for sustainability and wrestling with the difficult theological, moral, social, and environmental issues it raises. Therefore, as philosopher Holmes Rolston III comments: "An environmental ethic is foolish not to be informed by the best (such) science available. The success of an environmental policy . . . depends on coupling (such) prescriptive values with an environmental science that is descriptively accurate and operationally competent.[9] This is not to argue, of course, that this reorientation and reconceptualization is the only valid approach to doing eco-theology and eco-ethics. And it also recognizes that, like all multidisciplinary work and perhaps even far more than most, it raises many methodological and conceptual challenges.

Other ecological thinkers have also called for a dialogue between science and religion at a more profound intellectual level and the development of a scientifically informed environmental ethic. Philosopher J. Baird Callicott envisions the emergence of a new international environmental ethic for the twenty-first century "based upon the theory of evolution, ecology and the new physics (the biological sciences, especially ecology and the theory of evolution, in tandem with the theories of special and general relativity and quantum theory) and expressed in the cognitive language of contemporary science."[10] Callicott observes that this ethic will have many conceptual affinities with various preindustrial natural attitudes and values, particularly of Asian origin. He anticipates that the revival of a multitude of traditional, cultural environmental ethics could resonate with and help to articulate a new scientifically grounded environmental ethic. The result, according to Callicott, will be one worldview and one associated environmental ethic corresponding to the contemporary reality of our shared origins, home, and environmental crisis expressed through a multiplicity of cultural and historical lenses.[11]

Several theologians have also recognized the need to promote greater interface between the scientific and religious communities on ecological issues. Rosemary Ruether's writings, for example, emphasize a need both for a continued critical evaluation of current scientific and societal paradigms from an ecological perspective and a dialogue and new synthesis between science and religion based on contemporary developments in the physical and biological sciences.[12] As she observes, "Only by understanding how the web of life works can we also learn to sustain it rather than destroy it."[13] Sallie McFague argues that just as theology has always conceptualized its central beliefs in terms of then current pictures of reality, contemporary theology must be congruent with the broad parameters of the late-twentieth-century scientific understanding of reality.[14] Like Ruether, McFague make a creative use of science as a resource for reconstructing theology from a feminist and an ecological perspectives. Process thought, a development of the work of Alfred North Whitehead, has gone the farthest in melding science and theology. Since the 1981 publication of Charles Birch and John B. Cobb, Jr.'s landmark work, *The Liberation of Life: From the Cell to the Community,*[15] various process thinkers, such as Jay McDaniel[16] and John Haught,[17] have utilized scientific data, particularly from biology and ecology, to offer a vision of a common creation in which we are radically united with all things living and nonliving.

Several religious ethicists have also been concerned with overcoming the historical divide between religion and science. In his 1982 book, *Forced Options: Social Decisions for the Twenty-First Century*, Roger Shinn underscores that the major issues confronting contemporary society, among them the ecological crisis, require decisions that combine ethical and technical judgments, religious commitment and specialized knowledge. Because ethical traditions are silent on many of the "forced options" of our epoch, Shinn acknowledges a need for new ethical theories arising out of practice, perplexity, and struggle with these issues.[18] Similarly, a major theme of Ian Barbour's *Ethics in an Age of Technology* is the need to redirect science and technology toward realizing human and environmental values on planet earth. Because the selection of technologies depends on value priorities and our vision of the good life, Barbour suggests that the biblical tradition could make a strong contribution to an ethic of respect for all creatures and concern for future generations.[19] Larry Rasmussen's *Earth Community, Earth Ethics* successfully integrates science, ethics, and poetry to render a vision of a "common creation in which we are radically united with all things living and nonliving, here and into endless reaches of space, and at the same time radically diverse and individuated, both by life-forms and within life-forms."[20]

The faith grounded and scientifically informed ecological theology and ethics that I am proposing builds on but also goes beyond some of the proposals and efforts cited above. It would entail far more than periodic dialogues between the two communities and envisions that at least some eco-ethics and eco-theology be done in a new way. It would use science as a resource to assure that a particular theological or ethical vision is consonant with the view of reality in contemporary physics, biology, and/or ecology. Rather than using scientific data as background to provide a setting, context, or rational for the religious community to deal with ecological issues, it anticipates a systematic interface. The goal is to meld an ecological worldview and a contemporary scientific understanding with religious categories of ethical and theological analyses. To do so, will require changes in the conceptualization of the task as well as the development of new methodologies and approaches.

I would like to clarify that I am proposing a new approach to eco-theology and eco-ethics and not abdicating the task to science or drawing theological and ethical conclusions directly from science. The interface I am advocating is to be guided by theological and ethical concerns and perspectives rather than science. As many theologians and ethicists note, it is not possible to make theological or ethical claims solely on the basis of scientific fact or to develop a theological perspective directly from a scientific theory. Here it is worth recalling James Nash's caution about not confusing technical judgments with moral claims.[21] The context of his statement is defining the competence of scientists. Nevertheless, it has equal applicability for theology and ethics. Scientific data, no matter how significant, cannot substitute for theological and ethical analysis.

Requirements for a Meaningful Interface

What would a more meaningful relationship between religion and science on ecological issues entail? On the side of religious thinkers, I believe that such an interface has four requirements: (1) comprehending the fundamentals of science, scientific methodology, and the changing views of nature emerging from twentieth-century science; (2) seeking the fullest possible consonance with contemporary biological and ecological sciences; (3) developing an in-depth scientific understanding of specific environmental subjects and issues; and (4) utilizing new methodologies and approaches to environmental ethics that can better integrate scientific analyses with a religious perspective. This section will deal with the first three of these needs.

If science is to serve as a resource for eco-theology and eco-ethics, it is necessary for environmental thought to be consistent with a contemporary scientific worldview. The objective is not to make religious thinkers into the equivalent of bench scientists, but for them to have a basic understanding of the nature of scientific methodology and the general structures and requirements of scientific reasoning. At a minimum this entails comprehending the relationship between particular observations and experimental data on the one side and general concepts, theories, and paradigms on the other. Relatedly, it is important for them to know something about the criteria and procedures for testing and evaluating theories in scientific research. Otherwise it will not be possible to evaluate the strengths and weaknesses of scientific data, theories, and extrapolations.

Scientific worldviews change over time, and it is therefore important that eco-theology and eco-ethics be based on late-twentieth-century scientific paradigms. Ian Barbour's *Religion in An Age of Science* provides a helpful overview differentiating post-modern or late-twentieth-century scientific models from the Newtonian worldview. According to Barbour, the Newtonian view imaged nature as a machine. Its approach to nature was reductionist and mechanistic, with uniform physical mechanisms and laws thought to determine all events, except those in the human mind. The Newtonian universe had an atomistic perspective claiming that separate particles or atoms were the most fundamental and basic reality. Change was understood as a rearrangement of these fixed basic particles. Nature was considered to be deterministic, with mechanical causes, not purposes, determining all natural events. Although the earth was no longer envisioned at the center of the cosmic universe, human beings, by virtue of their rationality, still had a unique status and significance.[22]

In contrast, twentieth-century science images nature as a community of interdependent beings. In Barbour's sketch of the twentieth-century scientific paradigm, nature is now understood to be evolutionary, dynamic, and emergent. In place of determinism, nature is characterized as shaped by a complex combination of law and chance, structure and openness. Reality is thought to be constituted by events and relationships rather than by separate substances and particles. Nature is viewed as relational, ecological, and interdependent. Attention is given to systems and wholes, as well as the analysis of the separate components. The perspective is less anthropocentric, and humanity is understood to be an integral part of nature. In place of the mind/body dualism, which was still prevalent in the Newtonian system, contemporary science supports a view of humanity as a psychosomatic unity.[23]

From the above, it is clear that differences between the classical Newtonian model and more contemporary images based on relativity theory, quantum mechanics, and ecology, the biological science of biotic communities, have significant implications for an understanding of nature. Theology and ethics that take the static Newtonian paradigm as a given or do not emphasize a dynamic and relational view of ecology misrepresent the world in which we live. One of the contributions of process and feminist thought has been to develop the theological implications of the worldview coming from contemporary science. Process thinkers view the universe as an evolving organism in which every aspect interpenetrates and interacts with others. As the name implies, process thought claims that interlinked momentary events that form a temporal process rather than tiny independently existing physical units of matter constitute the basic units of the physical universe. Charles Birch and John Cobb apply a process approach to environmental issues viewing nature as an evolving, infinitely complex, interconnected series of relationships in which every creature is endowed with intrinsic value and has some degree of self-creativity. They are also deeply critical of mechanistic models arguing that the conceptualization of nature as a machine has resulted in the oppression of humanity and nature.[24] Beginning with Carolyn Merchant's 1980 work on *The Death of Nature: Women, Ecology and the Scientific Revolution*,[25] many feminist thinkers similarly claim that mechanistic scientific models are complicit in patriarchal culture's domination of women and of nonhuman nature.

An ecologically relevant theological ethics also needs to be coherent with the orientation and findings of contemporary biological and ecological sciences. As James Nash notes, if Christian ethicists attempt to do ecological ethics without an adequate understanding of at least the fundamentals of ecological dynamics, Christian ecological ethics is likely to be reduced to romantic fluff or spiritual musings.[26] Seeking coherence with biological and ecological sciences requires more than being ecologically informed. According to Nash, "Faith itself must be interpreted in light of the best available evidence, the best and fullest interpretation of reality, that science can provide."[27] Otherwise, Nash warns, "bad" interpretations of biology will contribute to "bad" theology and ethics and may give rise to unnecessary conflicts between the fields.[28] Whether or not erroneous or inadequate understandings of biology will contribute to bad theology, it certainly will result in irrelevant ecological thought.

Perhaps most obviously, a scientifically informed environmental ethics requires knowledge and understanding of specific environmental issues and problems, including the causes, manifestations, projected trends, and policy implications. Moreover, these factors must be considered in relationship to particular locales and specific subgroups of people. This is because there is no such phenomenon as "the environmental crisis." Instead, there are a series of problems, sometimes interlinked, but each with its own underlying causes, manifestations, likely developments, and options for resolution. Nor do various problems have equal impact in all areas or similarly affect all peoples. To be more specific, an understanding of population pressure has a very different scientific basis than an understanding of climate change, ozone depletion, toxic exposure and storage or any of the other issues and problems with environmental implications. To be able to deal with the ethical issues related to the conservation of biodiversity requires knowledge that overlaps little, if at all, with the ethics of the production and storage of toxic waste disposal. Moreover, the manner in which a particular problem is manifested in different regions, the types of issues it raises, the populations it affects, and the available options will vary significantly and thus have disparate ethical implications. Without concrete scientific knowledge it is not possible to illuminate questions of responsibility, vulnerability, differential impacts, resultant human or societal effects, long-term prognosis, and/or policy options and trade-offs. Lumping these varied problems together, as many religious thinkers are want to do, confuses and confounds both the scientific and the ethical analyses.

The good news is that the findings of many of the scientific fields relevant to the environment are more accessible to nonscientists than physics, chemistry, genetics, or molecular biology. There is a considerable amount of relevant nontechnical scientific and policy literature available. Many sources written from the perspective of ecology, biology, public health, demography, and economics do not require advanced scientific training to understand. Moreover, many religious ethicists, as well as theologians working on environmental issues, are quite knowledgeable about environmental issues and grasp more of the scientific foundations of the environmental crisis than their writings sometimes convey.

Methodological Options and Potential Approaches

A major impediment to undertaking scientifically informed eco-theology and eco-ethics is the lack of clearly defined methodologies for how to do so. All cross-disciplinary research, analysis, and dialogues must cope with differences in methodological approaches, priorities, and vocabularies in the fields being interfaced. Distinctions in these regards between science and religion are particularly formidable to traverse. The two disciplines have very different orientations, approaches to framing and testing truth statements, terminologies, and worldviews.[29] Therefore there is a need to think through ways that science and religion can most effectively be brought into a more systematic ecological interface.

This chapter proposes integrating an ecological paradigm and relevant scientific data with theological and ethical analysis. Integration is more than merely using science as a background, context, or resource. How can we do this? Let us now consider potential approaches and methods for doing so. As noted in the examples discussed, each of these options has the potential of making a contribution but none are sufficiently simple to execute.

(a) Developing a theological or ethical framework based on a contemporary scientific understanding: Two works provide models of ways in which this task can be accomplished. The first is Larry Rasmussen's *Earth Community, Earth Ethics.*[30] Rasmussen's thesis is that the discovery that nature is a community is *the* scientific discovery of the twentieth century; but this needs to be accompanied by the further understanding that earth, human society included, is *also* a community.[31] Rasmussen turns to science, theology, and ethics to explicate and assess the implications of his holistic vision in which society and nature are understood as a single interrelated community. As he develops the vision, science illuminates theological and ethical analysis and theological and ethical norms provide the context for science. The book is arranged in three parts. The first section, "Earth Scan," undertakes an analysis of our global situation utilizing science, history, and policy debates as resources in order to bring the dangers threatening all life on our planet into relief. Part two, "Earth Faith," explores religion, ethics, and science to glean the resources so as to understand what makes for sustainability—social, environmental spiritual, and moral. Finally, the third part, "Earth Action," sketches a constructive ethic that can reorient the human vocation and role.

The Liberation of Life,[32] the joint work of a biologist (Charles Birch) and a theologian (John Cobb), offers a second approach. The initial sections of the book develop an "ecological model of life" based on the biological sciences, including molecular, organismic and population ecology, history, theology, and ethics. A middle portion draws the implications of the model for understanding animal rights, human rights, and biosphere ethics and interpreting what is meant by "faith in life." The final chapters apply the model to such issues as the biological manipulation of human life, justice and sustainability, and patterns of economic development.

While the pairing of a scientist and theologian appears to have promise, it does not necessarily assure the integration of science with theology or ethics in a meaningful way. Another multidisciplinary initiative which pairs John Cobb with economist Herman Daly results in a stimulating book on the topic of how to redirect the economy toward community, the environment, and a sustainable future, but, in contrast with *The Liberation of Life*, in *For the Common Good* ethical and theological analysis remain implicit until the final chapter.[33] And another work by philosopher and a geneticist entitled *On Behalf of God: A Christian Ethic for Biology* draws its model from biblical analysis rather than science and lacks the theological rigor and depth of *The Liberation of Life*.[34]

(b) Utilizing a topical focus: This article has advocated for redirecting at least some of the work of religiously based environmental thinkers from abstract and global issues to more defined and delimited topics. There is a "habit of thinking about 'humanity' and 'nature' as *en bloc* abstractions without internal structure or differentiation."[35] However, the scientific bases, theological implications, and ethical issues and alternatives differ very considerably depending on the subject being addressed. Biodiversity, climate change, and population issues, for example, have little in common other than being factors that affect ecological integrity.

The small but growing body of Christian ecological writings which does address specific issues underscores the ability of a more defined and limited focus to bring greater conceptual clarity and facilitate the use of scientific data. James Nash[36] and William Gibson[37] have written about global warming as a theological ethical concern. The World Council of Churches, which has had a long-term interest in global warming, has produced a document entitled *Accelerated Climate Change: Sign of Peril, Test of Faith*.[38] At the request of the Environmental Justice Program of the United States Catholic Conference, David DeCosse has undertaken a theological ethics analysis of issues arising from the proposed regulatory takings legislation that would require taxpayers to compensate a property owner whenever a federal government action reduced the value of that person's property based on Roman Catholic theology.[39] Drew Christiansen has explored the ecological dimensions of the concept of the common good as it is found in Catholic social teaching.[40] While he does not apply the norm to empirical data, Richard Randolph's forthcoming study utilizes the common good as a framework to assess and adjudicate environmental conflicts in the Amazon basin.[41]

Two Christian ethicists, Susan Power Bratton and James Martin-Schramm, have utilized a broadly multidisciplinary methodology to study population issues. Bratton's book, *Six Billion and More: Human Population Regulation and Christian Ethics*, considers various dilemmas from the combined perspective of biblical analysis, history, demography, economics, and Christian ethics. It conveys the scope and dimension of demographic trends while seeking to develop a Christian population ethic and applying it to concrete issues.[42] James Martin-Schramm has published a series of articles based on his doctoral dissertation that build on a scientific grounding while offering a consistently analytical and ethical approach to the interface between population-consumption issues.[43] His moral assessment of the final document issued by the United Nations 1994 International Conference on Population and Development from an ecojustice perspective provides a model on the way in which a religiously informed moral reflection can be brought to bear on population policies. He analyzes the Programme of Action from the perspective of four specific moral norms—sustainability, sufficiency, participation, and solidarity—as well as the adequacy of the document to accomplish its goals of reducing population growth while empowering women and improving the life of all people.[44]

(c) Taking ecological and human specificity into account: As noted, there is a need to have greater sensitivity as to differences in the manner in which ecological changes and problems affect different groups and their implications in particular settings. Although theologians and ethicists are sometimes critical of secular environmentalists for neglecting differences between how rich and poor, powerful and powerless, majority and minority, and female and male,[45] religious thinkers are just as prone to do so. Religious thinkers also tend to use abstract conceptual formulations that do not have clear empirical and scientific referents. As Susan Power Bratton observes in a perceptive article, two thousand years of western philosophical influence have kept Christian theology and ethics very abstract and global. The emphasis is on formulating the religious equivalent of empirical models and general theories. That theology and ethics are based on sweeping, first order principles, such as love of neighbor, and abstract concepts, such as the integrity of creation, further complicates the interface with science. Scientific research, particularly in the discipline of ecology, usually deals with specifics that cannot easily be generalized. The thrust of ecology is toward a "bottom-up approach" based on the detailed investigation of specific cases. Bratton concludes that one of the difficulties in developing a Christian environmental or demographic ethic is that Christianity, with its preference for

first-order ethics, is attempting to draw on scientific fields, such as ecology, which are most ethically productive when investigating specific cases.[46]

Bratton develops a methodology she terms a "diagnostic" approach that provides a way to integrate first order ethical principles with ecological and economic reality and, according to Bratton, enables an ethicist to actually "hear" the voices of the suffering, while "seeing" environmental degradation and understanding its roots.[47] She terms it a "diagnostic" approach because rather than attempting sweeping "first order" or global solutions, the topic that is addressed is first subjected to a diagnostic process to determine the appropriate scale, sub-issues, and information base. Due to the technical nature of case materials, ethical discussion should utilize a team approach, incorporating ecologists, sociologists, physicians, economists, policy analysts and others who can help in clarifying the sources and impacts of demographic change, in addition to theologians and ethicists, so that diverse perspectives, professional expertise, and sensitivities can be incorporated into the process. Bratton suggests that the diagnostic procedure include the following considerations: (1) At what level should an issue be properly addressed? How is it best defined both in space and time? (2) At what level should ethical analysis be undertaken? Ethical responses should be based on or tested through well-developed case histories. Most dependable ecological and economic analysis is likely to be second or third order, precluding sweeping statements about "all women" or "all families." For instance, it may be necessary to focus on "African farming women in semiarid lands." (3) What are the particular issues, and what types of information are relevant? (4) What are the specific environmental and demographic impacts of religious teachings, doctrines, activities, and social services? Do they address actual social realities? (5) What are the perceptions of their own church members and communities?[48]

(d) Operationalizing theological and ethical concepts: Paralleling these efforts, there is a need to "operationalize" theological and ethical concepts so that they can inform the collection and analysis of empirical data. By operationalizing I mean breaking down broad, abstract and sweeping concepts such as human dignity, sustainable societies, integrity of creation, and inter-species equity into component measurable parts. This requires clarifying their content and on that basis developing detailed criteria and determining the types of scientific data necessary for evaluating the realization of each dimension. Given the complexity of the task, it is likely to need several orders or layers of disaggregation. Like an onion, each level of disaggregation should be peeled away to achieve greater conceptual specificity and linkages to data. The task is more likely to be feasible when the subject being studied is focused in terms of subject matter and geographic locale.

Work within the religious community related to the "integrity of creation" illuminates both the potential contributions and the many problems in attempting to operationalize concepts. The phrase was first used in 1983 at the Vancouver assembly of the World Council of Churches to emphasize the inner connection between a commitment to justice and a concern for the environment. It quickly became a popular construct and served as the organizing theme for the WCC's "World Convocation of Justice, Peace and the Integrity of Creation" in Seoul in 1990 and other ecumenical meetings.[49] However the concept was not given a precise meaning.[50] It soon became popular as shorthand way of referring to a relationship of respect between human beings and other creatures but was open to a variety of interpretations. From the perspective of Catholic social teaching the integrity of creation requires transcending anthropocentrism while still affirming the unique dignity and value of the human person.[51] An Orthodox view emphasizes the microcosmic role of humanity in bringing about peace and justice, even with the non-human creation.[52] Other expositions variously emphasize a more egalitarian approach emphasizing the intrinsic rights of animals and/or the intrinsic value of all things in creation.

Larry Rasmussen offers one of the fullest and most adequate interpretations of the integrity of creation with the additional strength of building on a scientific understanding of the processes of nature. He defines the integrity of creation as having six dimensions: (1) it describes the integral functioning of endless natural transactions through the biosphere and geosphere that comprise the specific exchanges and cycles from which all nature lives; (2) it refers to nature's restless self-organizing dynamism; 3) it emphasizes that earth's treasures are a one-time endowment that our way of life is jeopardizing; (4) it underscores the integral relation of social and environmental justice; (5) it gives theological voice to the faith commitment that the creation has a divine source and an intrinsic dignity; and (6) it embodies an acceptance of a common moral citizenship and a view of existence as coexistence.[53] Despite his many contributions, Rasmussen fails to go the next step and offer standards or concrete indicators to measure any one of the dimensions or to serve at least as an elementary guide for assessing how specific policies or initiatives may contribute to or detract from the integrity of creation. It should be noted in Rasmussen's defense that he never takes on the assignment of fully "operationalizing" the integrity of creation in the manner that I am suggesting here, but such a goal seems fully consistent with his efforts to explicate "what might and ought to be" in a practical way.[54]

(e) Formulating middle axioms: Additionally, the formulation of middle axioms can facilitate the application of theological and ethical concepts and universal norms to concrete contexts, issues, and policies. Ted Peters is one of several theologians and ethicists who advocate the use of middle axioms as a way to translate and apply fundamental theological concepts to empirical data and thereby provide guidance in evaluating such issues as the envi-

ronmental crisis and economic injustice. He formulates seven middle axioms, calling them proleptic principles, to understand and give co-creative expression to the Christian imperative to love within the context of the contemporary world.[55] Instead of assuming that the way to determine what is right is to measure its degree of conformity or nonconformity to an already established law or moral precept, he suggests that the role of a proleptic ethic is teleological. Their evolving nature enables us to create new guidelines and positive laws consistent with agreed upon goals. In so doing, according to Peters, we are choosing the future of God—which he correlates with selecting what is best for a particular body politic.

Developing middle axioms as a linkage between abstract theological concepts and scientific research makes a great deal of sense, but only if the axioms themselves are capable of being operationalized. In many cases, including Peters' proleptic principles, the axioms are too broad, vague, and abstract to be measurable. Much like the effort to operationalize specific concepts, two further steps are required. Firstly, many of the axioms may need to be disaggregated into more specific conceptual components. Secondly, it will be necessary to translate each of the conceptual components into measurable standards. These steps may become clearer in the discussion of specific examples.

In *Loving Nature: Ecological Integrity and Christian Responsibility,*[56] James Nash offers principles analogous to middle axioms that come closer to the level of specificity that I have in mind. Nash concurs with the norm enunciated by the World Commission on Environment and Development that "all human beings have the fundamental right to an environment adequate for their health and well-being."[57] To make that general right meaningful, he subdivides it into seven specific environmental rights.[58] However, these constituent rights are still very broad and vague, and he does not define what such principles as sustainable productivity for present and future generations would entail.

Nash, who has a strong sense of the intrinsic value of all creatures, also argues that the concept of rights should be extended to nonhuman creatures, and to that end offers a bill of biotic rights that are meant to apply both to individual members and whole species. The general rights he proposes are as follows: (1) the right to participate in the natural competition for existence; (2) the right to satisfaction of basic needs and opportunity to perform their individual and/or ecosystemic functions; (3) the right to healthy and whole habitats; (4) the right to reproduce their own kind; (5) the right to fulfill their evolutionary potential with freedom; (6) the right to freedom from human cruelty, flagrant abuse, or frivolous use; (7) the right to redress through human interventions to restore a semblance of the nature conditions disrupted by human actions; and (8) the right to a fair share of the goods necessary for the sustainability of one's species.[59] These biotic rights are more specific and capable of being operationalized and evaluated through the application of scientific data. However, Nash does not go the next step and attempt to do so.

In addition to the discussion of biotic rights, Nash offers a set of principles to evaluate whether public policy is ecologically sound and morally responsible.[60] In several cases these principles or norms are further disaggregated into more specific norms. Responsibilities to future generations, for example, is broken down into seven subnorms. But even so, as Nash himself acknowledges, many of these overlapping rules or principles are "dysfunctionally vague." Yet it would be feasible to go beyond Nash's discussion of the policy implications of these norms to operationalize at least some of these guidelines. It would be possible, for example, to develop indicators for the principle of using no more than our "fair share" of nonrenewable resources and more specific measurable content for the norm of leaving the ecosphere to successors in as healthy a state as it was received. If these or other principles are to serve as guidelines for policy making or standards to evaluate the ethical adequacy of particular public policies, they will have to be translated into concrete and measurable standards.

Conclusion

For reasons noted in this chapter, we are still a long way from the development of scientifically informed ecological theology and ethics. Yet I recommend that we press on toward integrating the ecological paradigm with scientific methodology and relevant data. A cross-disciplinary perspective that integrates a scientific understanding and research to theological concepts and ethical norms can contribute to the conceptual clarity, rigor, concreteness, and relevance of eco-theology and eco-ethics. It is hoped that some of the recommendations in this article will prove useful for this effort. While this task is difficult and decidedly less glamorous than abstract theologizing, it will enhance the ability to protect and nurture God's creation.

Notes

This chapter is a further development of ideas in my paper "Developing Religiously Grounded Environmental Ethics from a Scientific Perspective," which will be published in Donald Conroy and Rodney Peterson, eds., *Creation as Beloved of God: Discovering the Creator's Love and Our Need to Care for Creation* (Humanities Press, forthcoming). I would like to thank Ted Peters and Jim Miller for their comments on an earlier draft.

1. Lynn White, Jr., "The Historical Roots of Our Ecological Crisis," *Science* 155 (1967): 1203–7. This article is reprinted in many collections.

2. Daniel C. Maguire, *The Moral Core of Judaism and Christianity: Reclaiming the Revolution* (Minneapolis: Fortress Press, 1993), 13.

3. Peter W. Bakken, Joan Gibb Engel, and J. Ronald Engel, "Critical Survey," in these authors' *Ecology, Justice, and Christian Faith: A Critical Guide to the Literature* (Westport, Connecticut, and London: Greenwood Press, 1995), 3.

4. Janet Parker and Roberta Richards, "Christian Ethics and the Environmental Challenge," in Dieter T. Hessel, ed., *Theology for Earth Community: A Field Guide* (Maryknoll, New York: Orbis Books), 113.

5. For example, in May 1992, 150 religious leaders and scientists, who gathered for a conference entitled the Mission to Washington, issued a joint declaration which affirmed a deep sense of common purpose and commitment to undertake bold action to protect the environment. The "Declaration of the Mission to Washington: Joint Appeal by Religion and Science for the Environment" affirms the possibilities, indeed the need for collaboration between two communities, who, for centuries, often have traveled different roads. "Declaration of the Mission to Washington: Joint Appeal by Religion and Science for the Environment." A copy of this document is reprinted in Roger S. Gottlieb, ed., *This Sacred Earth: Religion, Nature, Environment* (New York and London: Routledge, 1996), 640–642.

6. James A. Nash, "Ecological Ethics: Points of Engagement," a draft paper for the Interest Group on Environmental Ethics of the Society of Christian Ethics 1997 meeting and forthcoming in *The Annual of the Society of Christian Ethics*.

7. Robert Booth Fowler, *The Greening of Protestant Thought* (Chapel Hill, North Carolina: The University of North Carolina Press, 1995), 175–179.

8. Chapman, "Developing Religiously Grounded Environmental Ethics from a Scientific Perspective."

9. Holmes Rolston III, "Ecology: A Primer for Christian Ethics," Unpublished paper prepared for the Interest Group on Environmental Ethics of the Society of Christian Ethics at its 1997 meeting and forthcoming in *The Annual of the Society of Christian Ethics*.

10. J. Baird Callicott, "Toward a Global Environmental Ethic," in Noel J. Brown and Pierre Quiblier, *Ethics & Agenda 21: Moral Implications of a Global Consensus* (New York: United Nations Environmental Programme, 1994), 11.

11. J. Baird Callicott, "Toward a Global Environmental Ethic," in Mary Evelyn Tucker and John A. Grim, eds., *Worldviews and Ecology: Religion, Philosophy and the Environment* (Maryknoll, New York: Orbis Books, 1994), 31.

12. Rosemary Radford Ruether, *Gaia & God: An Ecofeminist Theology of Earth Healing* (San Francisco: Harper, 1992), and "Ecology in and of Theological Study," in Hessel, ed., *Theology for Earth Community*, 5–7.

13. Ruether, *Gaia & God*, 86.

14. Sallie McFague, *The Body of God: An Ecological Theology* (Minneapolis: Fortress Press, 1993), ix.

15. Charles Birch and John B. Cobb, Jr., *The Liberation of Life: From the Cell to the Community* (Denton, Texas: Environmental Ethics Books, 1981, 1990).

16. Jay B. McDaniel, *Of God and Pelicans: A Theology of Reverence for Life* (Louisville: Westminster/John Knox Press, 1989).

17. John F. Haught, *The Promise of Nature: Ecology and Cosmic Purpose* (New York/Mahwah, New Jersey, 1993).

18. Roger Lincoln Shinn, *Forced Options: Social Decisions for the Twenty-First Century* (San Francisco: Harper & Row, Publishers, 1982), 11–12.

19. Ian G. Barbour, *Ethics in An Age of Technology: The Gifford Lectures* (San Francisco: HarperSanFrancisco, 1993).

20. Larry L. Rasmussen, *Earth Community, Earth Ethics* (Maryknoll, New York: Orbis Books, 1996), 265.

21. James A. Nash, "Toward the Ecological Reformation of Christianity," *Interpretation* 50 (January 1996), 13.

22. Ian G. Barbour, *Religion in an Age of Science: The Gifford Lecture*s (San Francisco: HarperSanFrancisco, 1990), 219–220.

23. Barbour, *Religion in an Age of Science*, 220–221.

24. Birch and Cobb, *The Liberation of Life*, particularly 66–96.

25. Carolyn Merchant, The Death of Nature: *Women, Ecology and the Scientific Revolution* (San Francisco: Harper & Row, Publishers, 1980).

26. Nash, "Toward the Ecological Reformation of Christianity," 12.

27. Nash, "Toward the Ecological Reformation of Christianity," 12.

28. Nash, "Toward the Ecological Reformation of Christianity," 12–13.

29. See for example, Barbour, *Religion in an Age of Science*, 66–92, on the similarities and differences in scientific and theological/religious methodologies.

30. Rasmussen, *Earth Community*, particularly the preface, xi–xiv.

31. Rasmussen, *Earth Community*, 51.

32. Birch and Cobb, *The Liberation of Life.*

33. Herman E. Daly and John B. Cobb, Jr., *For the Common Good: Redirecting the Economy Toward Community, the Environment, and a Sustainable Future* (Boston: Beacon Press, 1989).

34. Bruce R. Reichenbach and V. Elving Anderson, *On Behalf of God: A Christian Ethic for Biology* (Grand Rapids: William B. Eerdmans Publishing Company, 1995).

35. Bakken, Engel, and Engel, "Critical Survey," 24.

36. James A. Nash, "In Quest of Ethical Adequacy on Global Warming," unpublished paper, Churches' Center for Theology and Public Policy.

37. William E. Gibson, in Dieter T. Hessel, ed., *After Nature's Revolt: Eco-Justice and Theology* (Minneapolis: Fortress Press, 1992), 109–121.

38. WCC Programme Unit III, *Accelerated Climate Change: Sign of Peril, Test of Faith* (Geneva: World Council of Churches, 1994).

39. David E. DeCosse, "Beyond Law and Economics: Theological Ethics and the Regulatory Takings Debate," *Environmental Affairs* 23 (Summer 1996): 829–849.

40. Drew Christiansen, S.J., "Ecology and the Common Good: Catholic Social Teaching and Environmental Responsibility," in Drew Christiansen, SJ. and Walter Grazer, eds., *And God Saw that It was Good: Catholic Theology and the Environment* (Washington, D.C.: United States Catholic Conference), 183–196.

41. Conversation with Richard Randolph.

42. Susan Power Bratton, *Six Billion and More: Human Population Regulation and Christian Ethics* (Louisville: Westminster/John Knox Press, 1992).

43. See for example, James B. Martin-Schramm, "The State of the Debate in Christian Ethics," in Hessel, ed. *Theology for Earth Community*, 132–142.

44. James B. Martin-Schramm, "Population, Consumption, and Eco-Justice: A Moral Assessment of the United Nations 1994 International Conference on Population and Development," unpublished paper presented at the Annual Meeting of the Society of Christian Ethics, Albuquerque, New Mexico, January 1996.

45. Larry Rasmussen, "Theology of Life and Ecumenical Ethics," in David G. Hallman, *Ecotheology: Voices from the South and North* (Geneva: WCC Books, 1994 and Maryknoll, New York: Orbis Books, 1994), 123.

46. Susan Power Bratton, "Christianity and Human Demographic Change: Towards a Diagnostic Ethic," *Biodiversity and Conservation*, 4 (1995): 871–872.

47. Bratton, "Christianity and Human Demographic Change," 876.

48. Bratton, "Christianity and Human Demographic Change," 874–876.

49. Denis Edwards, "The Integrity of Creation: Catholic Social Teaching for an Ecological Age," *Pacifica* 5 (June 1992): 189, 191.

50. On this point see Charles Birch, "Christian Obligation for the Liberation of Nature," in Charles Birch, William Eakin, and Jay B. McDaniel, eds., *Liberating Life: Contemporary Approaches to Ecological Theology* (Maryknoll, New York: Orbis Books, 1990), 61.

51. Edwards, "The Integrity of Creation," 203.

52. Stanley S. Harakas, "The Integrity of Creation: Ethical Issues," in G. Limoun, ed., *Justice, Peace, and the Integrity of Creation: Insights from Orthodoxy* (Geneva: World Council of Churches Publications, 1990), 24.

53. Rasmussen, *Earth Community*, 98–106.

54. Rasmussen, *Earth Community*, 5.

55. Ted Peters, *God—the World's Future: Systematic Theology for a Postmodern Era* (Minneapolis: Fortress Press, 1992), 357–376).

56. James A. Nash, *Loving Nature: Ecological Integrity and Christian Responsibility* (Nashville and Washington, D.C.: Abingdon Press in cooperation with The Churches' Center for Theology and Public Policy, 1991).

57. Quoted in Nash, *Loving Nature*, 171.

58. Nash, *Loving Nature*, 171.

59. Nash, *Loving Nature*, 186–189.

60. Nash, *Loving Nature*, 197–221.

Chapter Fifteen

Evolution, Tragedy, and Hope

JOHN F. HAUGHT

To generations of our fellow human beings the cosmos has often seemed to be almost like a book or a great teaching through which a transcendent meaning has become manifest.[1] Ancient Hebrew thought even claimed that "Wisdom" was already present at the world's foundation, and John's Gospel begins with the announcement that all of creation occurs in and through the eternal Logos, the divine Word and Wisdom incarnate in Christ. For Plato an eternal realm of ideas provides the template for cosmic intelligibility; and Taoism, Hinduism and Buddhism all make reference to a founding principle of "Truth" or "Rightness" after which the universe is patterned and human life given a meaning.

It is curious, therefore, that the age of science, which gives us unprecedented insight into nature's inherent order, has also brought with it so much suspicion that the universe may be no repository of meaning after all, and indeed that, considered as a whole, it may even be absurd. Although scientific inquiry has to assume, at some deep level of awareness, that nature is intelligible—for otherwise it could not even launch its voyage of discovery—many of its most noble and notable practitioners doubt that the universe has any ultimate or overall meaning to it.

Is There a Point to the Universe?

At the risk of overworking an oft-repeated citation, we need only call attention here once again to Steven Weinberg's grim proposal that the more comprehensible the universe has become to modern science, the more pointless it all seems.[2] Commenting on Weinberg's pessimism, astronomer Sandra Faber agrees that the universe is "completely pointless from a human perspective."[3] Physicist Marc Davis does also, even though he finds it "depressing." "Philosophically," he says, "I see no argument against [Weinberg's] attitude, that we certainly don't see a point. To answer in the alternative sense really requires you to invoke the principle of God, I think. At least, that's the way I would view it, and there's no evidence that He's around, or It's around."[4] And Harvard astronomer Margaret Geller thinks the subject is scarcely worth talking about at all: "why should [the universe] have a point? What point? It's just a physical system, what point is there?"[5]

How did we human beings ever arrive at this juncture in our spiritual and intellectual history when such sentiments can be delivered as though they were perfectly self-evident? We cannot trace here all the steps that led from the traditional sense of a meaningful cosmos to the now widely respected proposal that the universe may be pointless. It is enough for us simply to observe that this dramatic shift of perspective has emerged alongside of modern science. But does science inherently entail such cosmic pessimism? Or can we plausibly give another reading to the results of modern physics, biology, astronomy and other sciences?

Formerly it was the role of myth, religion and philosophy to decide whether we live in a friendly or an unfriendly universe. But today most of us would not venture to talk about the universe without also taking into account what natural science has to say. And what does science tell us? Albert Einstein thought that science's disclosure of the remarkable mathematical comprehensibility of the universe defies any cynical claim that the universe is unfriendly. But perhaps he was too caught up in the orderly idealism of mathematical abstraction and missed the concrete messiness of nature's actual unfolding. After all, those who study the story of life on Earth from an evolutionary perspective paint a much more troubling picture. They remind us of nature's random and reckless treatment of the weak, the enormous amount of struggle and waste during several billion years of life's unfolding, the previously unfathomed epochs of suffering and perishing. Especially since the days of Darwin sensitive scientific thinkers have been deeply affected by the indifference of nature, and for not a few this has made the ancient religious portraits of a meaningful cosmos completely unbelievable.[6]

Many others, of course, would be reluctant to draw any such sweeping conclusions. They would remind us that nature is not unambiguously cruel, but also cooperative and predominantly nurturing. Even more fundamentally they would instruct us that science as such—since it always abstracts to some degree from the full complexity of the actual world—cannot peer very far into the real depth of things. Natural science is simply not equipped to respond to such momentous issues as whether there is a point to the universe, or whether it is friendly toward us. If scientists such as Einstein and Weinberg undertake nevertheless to address such matters, they must surely realize that their opinions are not a part *of* science, but simply conjectures *about* science. In hazarding such guesses, each of us is inevitably influenced by tacit personal or social factors extraneous to science, and it is these unformalizable particulars, as much as the results of science itself, that lie behind our more philosophical musings.

Consonance or Dissonance Between Science and Theology?

Nevertheless, any beliefs we may hold about the universe, whether pessimistic or otherwise, cannot expect to draw serious attention today unless we can display their *consonance* with science. In other words, our metaphysical or theological commitments must blend harmoniously with the authoritative results of scientific discovery, even if they cannot be confirmed by science itself. However, it may not be immediately obvious that the visions of hope underlying our religions, and especially the prophetic traditions that claim Abraham as their common ancestor, can coherently contextualize some of the most important discoveries of modern science. In fact, the intellectual approval given to Weinberg's pessimistic reading of the cosmos by the scientists cited above would seem to indicate that science corresponds more intuitively with a tragic interpretation, one that finds in the physical universe no basis for the steadfast hope that an Abrahamic faith would require. As Alfred North Whitehead has reminded us, tragedy and science have been deeply intertwined throughout the modern period. And the predominantly pessimistic interpretation given to the cosmos by numerous modern intellectuals was molded not only by scientific insight, but also by the apparent correspondence between mechanistic models of nature and the persistent strain of tragic thinking passed down to our own times from the ancient Greeks.[7]

This synthesis of science with tragic mythology, a blend that we may call "cosmic pessimism," still poses a serious challenge to those of us who are religiously committed to an eschatological or hope-filled interpretation of reality, and whose faith forbids acquiescence in the seemingly more realistic stoicism onto which so much modern science has been grafted. How can we expect the scientifically trained contemporary mind to embrace faith's conviction that reality is fundamentally shaped by God's promises, especially in light of the respectable intellectual lineage that takes the results of science to be more consistent with tragedy than with hope?

One religious response to this question has been to tolerate a sense of despair about the physical universe, but to look toward a state of immortal personal survival after death in a spiritual heaven detached from the material world. Although this solution is quite unbiblical and barely conceals the strain of cosmic despair that underlies it, more than a few believers have found considerable solace in its dualistic segregation of a supernaturally perfect realm up above from the imperfect and finally futile natural world down here. Dividing reality into the spheres of spirit and matter—and humans into soul and body—powerfully answers to our personal longing for the eternal; and it apparently renders religiously innocuous the sober modern scientific conjectures about the destiny of nature, including the prospect that the material universe may be headed toward final catastrophe. Dualism, in other words, releases theology from the obligation of seeking a genuine consonance between religion and contemporary science.

However, any religious faith professing to abide within the framework of the biblical vision of hope for the future cannot be content with such a settlement. For the Bible clearly invites us to see *all of reality*, including the physical cosmos, and what we would now recognize as the entire sweep of its evolution, as profoundly stamped by the promises of God, participating along with humans in the quest for a future fulfillment. If St. Paul's words about *the whole* of creation "groaning" for redemption mean anything at all, it is that we can no longer religiously consign nature to the realm of futility.

If we are to envision a divine promise as so fundamental to the definition of the universe, however, doesn't this place theology in an even more intellectually tenuous position than ever? For modern science's long affair with tragic pessimism still persists, and we cannot expect that scientific culture will casually renounce so stable a union. Especially the Darwinian discovery of life's epochs of struggle, waste and suffering, along with contemporary physics' layout of a universe eventually dissolving into permanent deep freeze or collapsing into another black hole—all of this is hardly suggestive of a world whose fundamental being is informed by divine concern for its future. How, by any stretch of the theological imagination, can we seriously claim that the natural world may be viewed more realistically within the framework of God's love and promise than of tragic pessimism?

Before we can deal with this question we must indicate what we mean by God's love and promise. Curiously these two themes, though central to biblical faith, are often barely visible in formal discussions of science and theology. Too often, it seems to me, our conversations about science and God tend to drift vaguely along without much agreement on what kind of God we are talking about. Perhaps out of a spirit of openness to dialogue, theologians often allow scientific skeptics to define the terms of the debate, even though this generally means trimming off features that faith considers essential to its pictures of God. Moreover, in their efforts to find common ground with scientific skeptics theologians sometimes tend to concede ideas about divine power and intelligence that may be quite out of keeping with actual religious experience. This accommodation has led many articles and books on science and religion into lengthy and uninteresting defenses of religiously pallid notions of God as a designer or planner of the universe, while the richer and more nuanced images of God given to religious experience hover helplessly in the background.

For example, in Christian theologians' dialogues with scientists, it is easy to lose sight of faith's primordial experience of God as *self-emptying* love, and to focus instead on a much more abstract representation of the deity, such as intelligent designer. Unfortunately the experience of God that occurred in connection with the life and death of Jesus, an encounter with ultimacy that Hans Küng rightly calls a "revolution" in the whole human story of God-consciousness,[8] is taken only minimally into theological engagements with science. Especially in debates about the compatibility of religion with the randomness, struggle and suffering in life's evolution, theologians typically find themselves guarding some bleary notion of divine power and rationality rather than bringing patently to the front faith's more troubling images of the compassionate Mystery that pours itself out into the world in unrestrained and vulnerable love.

Likewise, our treatises on God and evolution can easily become so sidetracked by obsession with the notions of order and design that we may ignore altogether another fundamental feature of biblical faith, namely, the experience of God as One who makes promises and who relates to the cosmos not by compelling it from the past, but by opening it to an enlivening and unpredictable future.[9]

Evolution and Divine Kenosis

Steven Weinberg perceptively argues that it is useless to reconcile some vaguely construed and religiously uninformed concept of deity with modern science. Instead we must ask whether science is compatible with the idea of an interested God who captures the hearts and souls of devout believers. After all, it is always possible to redefine the concept of God, as Einstein himself did, in terms that will make it scientifically palatable. But if we are to be fully candid we must instead ask whether the sense of God *as operative in actual religious awareness* is consonant with contemporary scientific understanding. Weinberg claims that it is not. Contemporary physics and especially evolutionary science, he argues, point to an utterly impersonal and indifferent universe, one that rules out the interested God of religious faith.[10]

One does not have to accept Weinberg's conclusion in order to agree with him that we should connect our thinking about issues in science and religion to images and convictions about God as these are found in actual religious experience rather than in philosophically watered down versions of theism. Of course, we cannot speak seriously about God's relationship to the scientifically understood universe without using philosophical or metaphysical language. However, such discourse must remain closely tethered to the nuances of actual religious experience. For Christian theology this would mean seeking to understand the natural world, and especially its evolutionary character, in terms of the outpouring of compassion and the corresponding sense of world renewal associated with the God of Jesus the crucified and risen Christ.

Christians have discerned in the Christ-event the decisive self-emptying or *kenosis* of God. And at the same time they have experienced in this event a God whose effectiveness takes the form of a power of renewal that opens the world to a new and unexpected future. As a Christian theologian, therefore, when I reflect on the relationship of science to religion I am obliged to think of God as both *kenotic love* and *power of the future*. This sense of God as a self-humbling love which opens up a new future for the world took shape in Christian consciousness only in association with the Christ-event; and so, as we ponder the implications of such discoveries as those associated with evolutionary science, it would be disingenuous of Christian theologians to suppress the specific features of their own community's experience of divine Mystery. This means quite simply that in Christian theology's quest to understand the scientific story of life, it must ask how evolution might make sense when situated in a universe that faith claims to be shaped by God's kenotic compassion and an accompanying promise of new creation.

From science itself, of course, we have no right to expect any sweeping judgments about the meaning of evolution. Following its customary constraints, science must acknowledge that it is not equipped to discover the significance or value of anything. But from the perspective of a theological vision that takes seriously both biological science and what Christian faith understands as revelatory portraits of a vulnerable and faithful God, nature's evolutionary journey may exhibit levels of meaning that could never be illuminated apart from a prior commitment to such a revelatory framework.

Such an interpretative commitment, I would submit, is no more of an impediment to objectivity than is the equally a priori allegiance many scientists have to the myth of cosmic tragedy. It is now common knowledge, after all, that some kind of faith commitment is a condition of, and not inevitably an obstacle to knowledge. Even to begin scientific exploration, for example, a scientist must already be committed to such beliefs as "the universe is intelligible" or "truth is worth seeking." And these scientifically essential *faith* commitments, I believe, correspond much more approximately to religious visions such as the one I am presenting here than they do to the seemingly more realistic tragic modern envisagements of an ultimately pointless universe.

At the center of Christian faith lies the conviction (John 3:16) that "God so loved the world that He gave his only Son" to redeem and renew that world. Theologically translated, this text and many others like it imply that the very substance of the divine life is poured out into the creation, and that the world is now and forever open to an infinitely replenishing future. Those who envisage the universe as enfolded by such infinite love and promise, I am arguing, will be able to appreciate aspects of Darwinian evolution that a more tragic spin on things might take as a reason for cosmic despair. St. Paul (Philippians 2:5–11) portrays Christ as one who "though in the form of God" did not "cling" to his divine status, but instead "emptied himself" (*ekenosen seauton*) and took the "form of a slave." It is to this image that Christian theology must always repair whenever it thinks about God's relationship to the world and its evolution.

God, the One Who Lets Us Be

What has been especially troubling in Darwinian science is its picture of a world in which randomness mingles with the impersonal process of natural selection in such a way that evolution seems to have no direction or inherent meaning. A world that sponsors such a process may seem at first to be incompatible with the existence of a loving and truly effective God, but perhaps this is only because our notion of divine power is usually implicitly uprooted from its grounding in divine kenosis. Consequently it is easy to forget that intrinsic to divine kenotic love is its authorizing creation to strive for genuine independence vis-a-vis its creator. Love by its very nature cannot compel, and so any God whose very essence is love should not be expected to overwhelm the world either with a coercively directive power or an annihilating presence. Indeed, an infinite love must in some sense absent or restrain itself, precisely in order to give the world the space in which to be and become something distinct from the creative love that constitutes it as other. We should anticipate, therefore, that any universe rooted in an unbounded love would have features that appear to us as random and undirected.

Even in the original creation of the cosmos the divine infinity may be thought of—in our imperfect human concepts—as contracting itself, foregoing any urge to direct the creation forcefully or to absorb it into itself. Such a humble retreat on God's part would allow the cosmos to stand forth on its own and then to evolve as a relatively autonomous reality distinct from its creative ground. Conceived of in this way, creation and its evolutionary unfolding would be less the consequence of an eternal divine *plan* than of God's humble and loving *letting be*.[11]

If God is essentially self-giving love, and if love in turn entails "letting the other be," then, theologically speaking, both the world's original coming into being and its indeterminate evolutionary transformation through time would be completely consonant with the Christian experience of God. An unrestrained display of infinite presence or omnipotence would leave no room for anything other than God, and so it would rule out any genuine evolutionary *self-transcendence* on the part of the cosmos. Theologian Jürgen Moltmann explains:

> Through the space conceded by God, creation is given detachment from God and freedom of movement over against him. If God were omnipresent in the absolute sense, and manifested in his glory, there would be no earthly creation. In order to make himself endurable for his earthly creatures, God has to veil his glory, "since he who looks upon God must die." Remoteness from God and spatial distance from God result from the withdrawal of God's omnipresence and "the veiling of his face." They are part of the grace of creation, because they are the conditions for the liberty of created beings.[12]

The world can have its own being and its own evolutionary potential, therefore, only if God's creative power and love consist of a kind of self-concealment. As I have already noted, it is in its encounter with the crucified man Jesus—and not in philosophical reasoning alone—that Christian faith is given this key to God's relation to the world. The cross reveals to faith the self-absenting of a God out of whose limitless generosity the world is called, but never forced, into being and becoming. This *kenotic* image of God, even though inaccessible to philosophical and scientific rationality as such, nevertheless gives a surprising intelligibility to the cosmic whole in which Darwinian evolution turns out to have played so important a role.

Not surprisingly, those scientific skeptics and theists whose ideas of God center primarily on the notion of intelligent design have found Darwinian ideas unacceptable. Skeptics have rejected a divine planner as incompatible with the undirected course of biotic evolution, while many theists have contemptuously dismissed evolution as incompatible with their notion of a designing deity.[13] The reigning theory among today's biologists, as already noted, has two features that have made evolution especially disturbing to advocates of intelligent design. In the first place evolution implies that chance, contingency, or randomness is the raw material of nature's advance into novelty. And so if chance is real, this seems to place God's power and intelligence in serious question. A universe entertaining such a high degree of indeterminacy seems incompatible with a transcendent power and intelligence. God, the alleged divine designer, is apparently not in control after all. In the second place, evolutionary theory posits an impersonal process of *natural selection* which, by sifting through an array of chance variations and other contingencies, apparently accounts for much of the creativity in the biosphere. But a process that selects species only on the basis of their accidentally favorable reproductive traits seems to be incompatible with a rational creator. Evolution appears to be a mindless lottery rather than the mighty act of an omnipotent God.

However, the God given to a faith shaped by the Christ-event is not first of all an infinite embodiment of what we humans narrowly understand as rationality and order, but an outrageously irrational and mysteriously humble love which comes to meet the world from out of the realm of an open and incalculable future. A theology attuned to this very specific, even unique, image of ultimacy suggests to us a way of rendering theologically meaningful the very same scientific data that have led a more rationally based theism to repudiate Darwinian theory, and scientific skeptics to a tragic interpretation of nature.

The creator's power (by which I mean the capacity to influence the world) is paradoxically made manifest in the vulnerable defenselessness of a crucified man. And such an expression of divine power is not only consonant with, but ultimately explanatory of, the world that evolutionary science now presents to us. The randomness, struggle and seemingly aimless meandering which the evolutionary story of life discloses as the underside of its marvelous creativity is consistent with the idea that the universe is the consequence of an infinite love. The key to such an interpretation lies in faith's unanticipated discovery that a truly effective power takes the form of self-emptying compassion.

If God were powerful only in the very restricted sense of possessing the capacity to manipulate things coercively, then the facts of evolution might be theologically problematic. But an infinite love, as the Roman Catholic theologian Karl Rahner has made clear, will not manipulate or dissolve the beloved—in this case, the cosmos. For in the act of seeking intimacy with the universe, God forever preserves the difference and otherness of that beloved world. God's creative love forever constitutes the world as something ontologically distinct from God, and not as a simple extension of the divine being. Consequently, the indeterminate natural occurrences that recent physics has uncovered at the most elementary levels of physical reality, the random events that biology finds at the level of life's evolution, and the freedom that emerges with human existence—these are all features proper to any world that is permitted and even encouraged to be distinct from the creative love that grounds it.

In order for the world to be independent of God, and therefore to undergo a genuine *self*-transcendence in its evolution, a God of love would concede to the world its own autonomous principles of operation—such as the impersonal laws of gravity, natural selection, and self-organization. This self-distancing of God, however, is in no sense apathy, but paradoxically a most intimate form of involvement.[14] God's will is that the world become more and more independent, and that during its evolution its own internal coherence intensify.[15] But this *absent* God is *present* to and deeply united with the evolving world precisely by virtue of selflessly allowing it to achieve ever deeper autonomy—as occurs most obviously in the evolutionary emergence of human freedom. The God of self-giving compassion is in fact the only God that normative Christian faith can legitimately claim ever to have encountered; and yet this founding intuition about the nature of ultimate reality all too seldom enters into our thoughts about whether the universe has a point to it, or whether the evolution of life can be reconciled with religious hope.

God, Cosmos, and the Future

The God whom Christian faith identifies with infinite love is also one who—as a resurrection faith vividly attests—opens up a new future for humans and the whole of creation. Hope's intuition of the coming of an always new and creative future is no less central to Christian faith than is the paradoxical divine power that became manifest in the defenselessness of the Crucified. And so it is also to the sense of God understood as the world's future that we need to connect our understanding of nature evolving.[16]

From the perspective of theology, in fact, it is the "coming of God" in the mode of a renewing future that *ultimately* explains the novelty in evolution. Even though cosmic pessimism would view the random or contingent events that allow for evolutionary novelty as utterly devoid of meaning, to a biblically informed faith these indeterminacies are essential features of any universe open to new creation. The entire fifteen billion years of cosmic evolution now appear, in the perspective of faith, to have always been seeded with promise. From its very beginning this extravagantly experimental universe has been bursting with potential for surprising future outcomes.[17] And the undeniable fact that life, mind, culture and religion have emerged out of the barely rippled radiation of the primordial universe gives us every reason to suspect that the cosmos may still be situated no less realistically within the framework of promise than of tragedy. Even prospects of eventual cosmic doom are not enough to defeat the proposal that nature's present indeterminacies are the repository of promise. The so-called "heat death" that may be awaiting the universe is not inconsistent with the notion that each moment of the entire cosmic process is perpetually taken into, and everlastingly preserved in, the boundlessly redemptive future that faith names as God.[18]

To fit the whole of nature into the framework of a religious hope based on the sense of openness to surprising future outcomes is not nearly so great a stretch as it may once have seemed. For today we are beginning to notice just how much of nature's concrete complexity and indeterminate creativity the linear mathematical methods of modern science since Newton had left out. Scientific abstractions appealed greatly to the Cartesian ideal of complete and immediate clarity, and they gave us enormous power to analyze and manipulate our natural environment. But the full actuality of the natural world had meanwhile slipped through the wide meshes of scientists' mechanistic nets.[19] And we have only recently begun to realize that the intellectual appeal of cosmic pessimism is supported not so much by nature itself as by abstract mathematical representations that inevitably overlook the elusive complexity and indeterminacy that open the cosmos to a genuinely novel future.

What modern science had passed over is now emerging palpably in the so-called sciences of chaos and complexity. Nature, as we can now picture it (especially with the help of computer imaging), is comprised of intricate adaptive systems that cannot be adequately understood simply by dissecting them into their constituent law-bound particulars. The makeup of the universe, from immense galactic clusters all the way down to infinitesimal quantum events, exhibits an unpredictably self-creative and self-organizing character for which the linear mathematics of mechanistic science cannot account. Although materialist dreams are still around, significant doubts about the abstract ways of reading nature that previously had fueled our fatalism are now beginning to spread within the scientific community and even spilling out into public awareness. The prospect of precise scientific prediction of final cosmic catastrophe is shakier than ever. If, as physicist John Houghton notes, science cannot even tell us where a billiard ball will end up a minute from now without taking into account the motion of electrons in outer space,[20] it is hardly in a position to settle the question of cosmic destiny either.

Although it may not be prudent for us to draw any theological conclusions directly from the new sciences of chaos and complexity, we cannot but notice how severely they have challenged the quaint claims that impersonal laws of physics are running the universe to ruin or that we are condemned to making only pessimistic predictions about the final outcome of cosmic process. It seems entirely plausible that the universe of contemporary science is more congenial to promise than pessimism.

Story and Promise

Obviously neither science nor faith is in a position to project the actual details of the cosmic future, but it is of great interest that science now places the cosmos within a narrative setting in which the universe is a story open to a future that is not in every sense fully calculable. The universe, as it turns out, is not eternal, nor is it just a set of abstract laws, nor a mere backdrop for human history. Rather it is a creative project yet unfinished, and because it is unfinished it still has a future.

Currently most scientists agree that cosmic evolution began in a hot Big Bang, after which the universe began to expand and cool, giving rise to atoms, stars and galaxies. Eventually elements and compounds cooked up in some now burnt-out stellar ovens came together to form our own planet. After another billion years or so the Earth's surface cooled sufficiently to allow primitive forms of life to appear. Biological evolution on Earth, according to the most recent estimates, began about 3.8 billion years ago, but like most other episodes of cosmic process it was apparently not in a hurry. In its unfolding it was often hesitant, sometimes explosive, and almost always extravagant. After experimenting with less complex forms of life it eventually blossomed out into plants, reptiles, birds and mammals. Not long ago, in our own species, evolution was endowed with self-consciousness.

The story has not been linearly progressive. For vast periods of time very little happened, and much of the history of life's evolution can be captured in the image of a randomly branching bush. But all great stories have quiescent interludes, blind alleys and unintelligible shoots; and a more sweeping view of cosmic evolution clearly shows, at least to those who care to notice, a narrative trend toward increasingly complex forms of natural order. Without too much difficulty we can make out a kind of story-line along which nature has traveled from trivial to more intricate and eventually sentient, conscious and self-conscious states of being. Although neo-Darwinian biologists often highlight what they take to be the aimlessness of evolution, if we step back and survey the life process within its larger cosmic context, it is hard even for the most entrenched pessimist to discount altogether the obvious directionality retrospectively visible in the overall movement of the cosmos from simplicity to complexity. And to those of us who have been encouraged by faith to look for signs of promise in all things it would seem egregiously arbitrary not to remark at how, at any past moment in its history, the cosmos has remained open to surprisingly beautiful future outcomes.

Astrophysics, for example, has recently instructed us that an incredible number of stunning physical coincidences had to have been present in the earliest micro-moments of the universe in order for life eventually to appear and evolve. And while it would be imprudent for theology to take the physics of the early universe as the basis for a new natural theology, the current scientific information is remarkably consistent with faith's conviction that the physical universe had always held at least the *promise* of emerging into life.[21] Though known to us only retrospectively, the early phases of the universe clearly contained the prospect of evolving toward such indeterminate outcomes as life, mind and even spirituality. Cosmic pessimism, therefore, does not seem to provide a sufficiently comprehensive metaphysical format for organizing our current scientific understanding of the universe. Until not too many years ago it may have been considered scientifically acceptable to think of the physical universe as inherently hostile to life, and to view life and evolution as absurdly improbable eventualities toward whose accidental appearance on our small planet nature was intrinsically unfriendly. But today it is much more scientific to acknowledge that physical reality has always been positively disposed toward the emergence of life and consciousness, much more so than we had ever suspected prior to the emergence of contemporary scientific cosmology.[22]

Thus, if it is now evident that the ambiguous cosmic past held such enormous promise as the emergence of life and mind, can we confidently claim that the *present* state of the cosmic story is not also pregnant with potential for blossoming into still more abundant new creation? Science by itself cannot answer the questions most important to faith. But in the panorama of cosmic evolution disclosed by science, faith is still permitted, perhaps even encouraged, to think of the cosmos as being called into yet newer ways of being.

A tragic perspective, on the other hand, will simply assume that the world's future states have always been fatefully coiled up in the remote past, needing only the passage of time to unfurl. However, as Alfred North Whitehead insists, the possibilities for any truly novel outcomes must be present somewhere other than the past alone.[23] It is unthinkable that novel events, in the deepest sense of the term "novel," could arise only out of the fixed past. Novelty must arise, of course, *in connection with* what is and what has been, for otherwise we would not grasp it as truly new. But it would not really be new if it were simply the algorithmic unfolding of a fully deterministic past.

New possibilities can arise only out of the region of time that we refer to as the *future*. And since the future is such a boundless reservoir of novelty we cannot simply assume that, simply because it is not fully present to us now, it is reducible to bare nonbeing (as both Greek philosophy and modern science have often implied). Because of its faithful and inexhaustible resourcefulness we must concede to the future some modality of *being*. Indeed, the biblical vision of reality's promise even implies something like a "metaphysics of the future" according to which the future is the *most real* (though obviously not yet fully actualized) of all the dimensions of time. The future claims the status of being eminently real not only because it always shows up even after every present moment has slipped away into the past, but ultimately because it is the realm from which God comes to renew the world.[24]

However, the future in its overflowing abundance is always hidden. By definition it cannot be fully captured in any fleeting present experience, or become fully exhausted in the fixed past. In its perpetual transcendence of the past and present it inevitably hides itself. Thus we may envisage God's self-concealment in an unavailable future as coinciding with the paradoxically intimate and involved divine absence that we earlier associated with the notion of *kenosis*. God's humble self-withdrawal, in other words, takes the form of God's being the inexhaustible futurity whose continuous arrival into the present is always restrained enough to allow the cosmos to achieve *its own* independent evolution. As biblical faith makes clear, God's glory is at present kenotically veiled, and where it does manifest itself, at least according to John's Gospel, it is paradigmatically in the picture of the "lifted up" and crucified Christ.

From a biblical perspective, of course, the whole point of the universe is to manifest God's glory,[25] but for the present God's glory is revealed characteristically in a *kenosis* that endows the world with a surprising degree of autonomy. The self-emptying God refrains from overwhelming the universe with an annihilating divine presence, but in the mode of futurity nonetheless constantly nourishes the world by offering to it a range of relevant new possibilities—such as those depicted by evolutionary science. At the same time God's compassionate embrace redemptively enfolds and preserves everlastingly each moment of the cosmic evolutionary story.

Conclusion

Thus in theology's conversations with contemporary science, it is more helpful to think of God as the infinitely generous ground of new possibilities for world-becoming than as a designer or planner who has mapped out the world in every detail from some indefinitely remote point in the past. The fundamental difficulty implied in the notion of such a plan for the world is that it closes the world off from any real future. Referring to some often overlooked ideas of Henri Bergson, Louise Young insightfully comments on the openness of evolution to the future:

> As we view the groping, exploratory nature of the process—the many favorable mutations, the tragic deformities—it is apparent that we are not witnessing the detailed accomplishment of a preconceived plan. "Nature is more and better than a plan in course of realization," Henri Bergson observed. "A plan is a term assigned to a labor: it closes the future whose form it indicates. Before the evolution of life, on the contrary, the portals of the future remain wide open. . . . "[26]

We might also say that God is more and better than a planner. A God whose very essence is to be the world's open future is not a planner or designer, but an infinitely liberating source of new possibilities and new life. It seems to me that neo-Darwinian biology can live quite comfortably within the horizon of such a vision of ultimate reality.

Notes

1. See Jacob Needleman, *A Sense of the Cosmos: The Encounter of Modern Science and Ancient Truth* (New York: E. P. Dutton & Co., 1976), pp. 11–13.
2. Steven Weinberg, *The First Three Minutes* (New York: Basic Books, 1977), p. 144.
3. Alan Lightman and Roberta Brawer, *Origins: The Lives and Worlds of Modern Cosmologists* (Cambridge: Harvard University Press, 1990), p. 340.
4. Lightman and Brawer, *Origins*, p. 358.

5. Lightman and Brawer, *Origins*, p. 377.

6. See Richard Dawkins, *River Out of Eden: A Darwinian View of Life* (New York: Basic Books, 1995), p. 131.

7. Alfred North Whitehead, *Science and the Modern World* (New York: The Free Press), p. 10: "The pilgrim fathers of the scientific imagination as it exists today are the great tragedians of ancient Athens, Aeschylus, Sophocles, Euripides. Their vision of fate, remorseless and indifferent, urging a tragic incident to its inevitable issue, is the vision possessed by science. Fate in Greek Tragedy becomes the order of nature in modern thought."

8. Hans Küng, *Does God Exist*, trans. Edward Quinn (New York: Doubleday & Co., 1980), p. 676.

9. I have developed the themes of divine compassion and promise and their relation to the natural world in much more systematic detail in *Mystery and Promise: A Theology of Revelation* (Collegeville, Minnesota: The Liturgical Press, 1993).

10. Steven Weinberg, *Dreams of a Final Theory* (New York: Pantheon Books, 1992), pp. 244–45.

11. This kenotic view of creation is found especially in kabbalistic Judaism. Likewise it occurs occasionally in the writings of Simone Weil as described in detail in Geddes MacGregor's *He Who Lets Us Be* (New York: Seabury Press, 1975). It is even more prominent in the writings of the Christian theologian Jürgen Moltmann. See, for example, *God in Creation*, trans. Margaret Kohl (San Francisco: Harper & Row, 1985), p. 88. A Jewish reaffirmation of the view that creation is grounded in God's self-withdrawal may be found in Michael Wyschogrod's *The Body of Faith* (New York: Harper & Row, 1983), pp. 9–10. It is perhaps illuminating to apply what Wyschogrod says about God's creation of humans to the creation of the cosmos: "A world in which the divine light penetrates and fills all is a world in which there is nothing but God. In such a world no finitude and therefore no human existence [cosmos] is possible. . . . The creation of man [the cosmos] involves the necessity for God's protection of man [the cosmos] from the power of God's being. This protection involves a certain divine withdrawal, the *tsimtsum* of the kabbalists, who were also puzzled by how things other than God could exist in the light of the absolute being of God. To answer this question they invoked the notion of *tsimtsum*, by which they meant that the absolute God, whose being fills all being, withdraws from a certain region, which is thus left with the divine being thinned out in it, and in this thinned out region man [the cosmos] exists." Some such notion seems essential to resolve the theological difficulties, especially those regarding the indeterminacy in evolution and human freedom, resulting from the traditional habit of modeling God's creativity on the rather deterministic idea of efficient causation.

12. Jürgen Moltmann, *The Coming of God*, trans. Margaret Kohl (Minneapolis: Fortress Press, 1996), p. 306.

13. See, for example, Phillip Johnson, *Darwin on Trial* (Washington, D.C.: Regnery Gateway: 1991).

14. In other words, such a God is nothing like the otiose God of deism. For it is out of a longing to relate deeply to the world that God foregoes any annihilating presence to the world. This retracting of presence, however, is the very condition of dialogical intimacy.

15. Wolfhart Pannenberg, *Systematic Theology*, Vol. 2, trans. Geoffrey W. Bromiley (Grand Rapids: Eerdmans, 1994), pp. 127–36. "Theologically, we may view the expansion of the universe as the Creator's means to the bringing forth of independent forms of creaturely reality" (p. 127). "Creaturely independence cannot exist without God or against him. It does not have to be won from God, for it is the goal of his creative work" (p. 135). See also Elizabeth Johnson, "Does God Play Dice? Divine Providence and Chance," *Theological Studies* 57 (March, 1996), 3–18.

16. See Moltmann, *The Coming of God*, and Ted Peters, *God—The World's Future: Systematic Theology for a Postmodern Era* (Minneapolis: Fortress Press, 1992).

17. Louise Young's book *The Unfinished Universe* (New York: Oxford University Press, 1986) is an excellent example of such a reading.

18. Process theology, following ideas of the philosophers Alfred North Whitehead and Charles Hartshorne, has been particularly effective in portraying how the experiences of the temporal cosmic past can plausibly be preserved and meaningfully patterned in the everlasting empathy of God.

19. Whitehead argues that the seventeenth century's science was dominated by the "assumption of simple location," according to which we can understand things only by leaving out any consideration of the concrete and complex web of organic connections that tie them all together. This assumption in turn was the result of a logical fallacy, the fallacy of misplaced concreteness, that mistook mathematical abstractions for concrete reality. See *Science and the Modern World*, pp. 51–57; 58–59.

20. John T. Houghton, "A Note on Chaotic Dynamics," *Science and Christian Belief*," Vol. 1:1 (April 1989), p. 50.

21. And since (relatively speaking) we may still not be too far removed from the cosmic dawn, who knows what other surprising and unpredictable outcomes lie enfolded in this promising creation?

22. Such a claim seems defensible independently of the status of the so-called Strong Anthropic Principle.

23. Alfred North Whitehead, *Process and Reality,* Corrected edition, ed. David Ray Griffin and D. W. Sherbourne (New York: The Free Press, 1978), p. 46.

24. See Moltmann, *The Coming of God*, pp. 259–95

25. Moltmann, *The Coming of God*, p. 323.

26. Young, *The Unfinished Universe*, pp. 201–202.

About the Editor and Contributors

Francisco J. Ayala is the Donald Bren Professor of Biological Sciences and Professor of Philosophy at the University of California at Irvine. His research focuses on population and evolutionary genetics, the origin of species, genetic diversity in populations, and philosophical issues concerning epistemology, ethics, and the mutual interaction between science and theology. He is former president and board chair of the American Association for the Advancement of Science; and he serves on the U.S. President's Committee of Advisors on Science and Technology. He has authored more than 600 articles and twelve books, including *Tempo and the Mode of Evolution* (1995); *Modern Genetics* (2nd ed., 1984); and *Studies in the Philosophy of Biology* (1974). He was a CTNS–Templeton Foundation lecturer at the University of Pennsylvania on April 24, 1997.

Audrey R. Chapman is director of the Program of Dialogue between Science and Religion at the American Association for the Advancement of Science in Washington, D.C. She is author of *Faith, Power and Politics* (1991) and *Health Care Reform: A Human Rights Approach* (1994).

Anne M. Clifford, C.S.J., is associate professor of theology at McAnuity College and the Graduate School of Liberal Arts at Duquesne University in Pittsburgh, Pennsylvania. She is author of the chapter "Creation" in *Systematic Theology: Roman Catholic Perspectives*, edited by Francis Schussler Fiorenza and John P. Galvin (1991), and other articles on the interaction of evolutionary theory and Christian theology.

George V. Coyne, S.J., has been director of the Vatican Observatory (Specola Vaticana) since 1978. He has published extensively in the field of astrophysics. He has edited a number of works on theology and science, including *The Galileo Affair: A Meeting of Faith and Science* (1984); and *John Paul II on Science and Religion: Reflections on the New View from Rome* (1990).

Paul Davies is the Chair of Mathematical Physics at the University of Adelaide in Australia. He is the author of numerous books, including *God and the New Physics* (1983); *The Cosmic Blueprint* (1987); *The Mind of God* (1992); and *Are We Alone?* (1995).

John F. Haught is Landegger Distinguished Professor of Theology at Georgetown University. He is author of *The Promise of Nature: Ecology and Cosmic Purpose* (1993), *Mystery and Promise: A Theology of Revelation* (1993), and *Science and Religion: From Conflict to Conversation* (1995). Dr. Haught is also director of the newly founded Georgetown Center for the Study of Science and Religion.

Philip Hefner is professor of systematic theology at the Lutheran Theological Seminary at Chicago and director of the Chicago Center for Science and Religion. He is editor of *Zygon* and author of the Templeton Prize–winning book, *The Human Factor* (1993).

Nancey Murphy teaches Christian philosophy at Fuller Theological Seminary in Pasedena, California. She is author of *Theology in an Age of Scientific Reasoning* (1990); *Beyond Liberalism and Fundamentalism* (1996); *Anglo-American Postmodernity: Perspectives on Philosophy, Science, and Religion* (1997); and coauthor with George Ellis of *on the Moral Nature of the Universe* (1996).

Wolfhart Pannenberg is professor emeritus of systematic theology at the University of Munich and director of the Ecumenical Institute there. He is author of *Theology and the Philosophy of Science* (1976); *Toward a Theology of Nature* (1993); and *Systematic Theology*, 3 volumes (1991–1998).

Arthur Peacocke is former senior lecturer in biophysics and chemistry at the University of Birmingham and later at Oxford and Cambridge Universities. He is now emeritus director of the Ian Ramsey Center in Oxford and Warden Emeritus of the Society of Ordained Scientists (SOSC). He coauthored *The Molecular Basis of Heredity* (1965) but is best known for his pioneering work in the dialogue between theology and science as reflected in such works as *God and the New Biology* (1986) and *Theology for a Scientific Age* (1990, 1993).

Ted Peters is professor of systematic theology at Pacific Lutheran Theological Seminary and the Graduate Theological Union in Berkeley, California. His research and teaching center on Christian doctrine, theology of culture, and the mutual interaction of theology and natural science. He is editor of *Dialog, a Journal of Theology*, and author of *Playing God? Genetic Determinism and Human Freedom* (1997); *For the Love of Children: Genetic Technology and the Future of the Family* (1996); and *GOD—The World's Future: Systematic Theology for a Postmodern Era* (1992). As a research scholar at the Center for Theology and the Natural Sciences, he directs the CTNS–Templeton Foundation University Lectures.

John Polkinghorne, formerly professor of mathematical physics at Cambridge, is now president of Queens College, Cambridge. He is author of *The Faith of a Physicist* (Princeton, 1994, the Gifford Lectures 1993–1994), and *Scientists as Theologians* (1996).

Pope John Paul II began his pontificate in 1979 and through the Pontifical Academy of Sciences and the Vatican Observatory has supported the dialogue between theology and natural science.

Robert John Russell is professor of theology and science in residence, the Graduate Theological Union, Berkeley, and founder and director of the Center for Theology and the Natural Sciences, Berkeley. He has published articles both in physics and in theology, and is coeditor of *Physics, Philosophy and Theology: A Common Quest for Understanding* (1988) and *Quantum Cosmology and the Laws of Nature: Scientific Perspectives on Divine Action* (1993).

Charles H. Townes is university professor of physics emeritus in the Graduate School at the University of California at Berkeley and pursues research in the fields of microwave spectroscopy, nuclear and molecular structure, quantum electronics, radio astronomy, and infrared astronomy. He received the Nobel Prize for his role in the invention of both the maser and the laser.

Credits

Chapter 1 is revised from an article originally published in *Dialog,* 34:4 (Fall 1995) as "Theology and Science: Where Are We?" It was republished in *Zygon* 31 (1996) and as "Theology and the Natural Science" in *The Modern Theologians,* ed. David F. Ford, rev. ed. (Oxford, UK: Basil Blackwell, 1996), 649–688.

Chapter 2 is adapted from the inaugural address of the CTNS–Templeton Foundation University Lecture Series in the Physics Department at the University of California, March 19, 1996.

Chapter 3 was originally published in *Dialog* 35:2 (Spring 1996).

Chapter 5 is adapted from an article published in *Theology Today*, April 1997.

Chapter 6 is adapted from her CTNS–Templeton Foundation University Lecture at Baylor University, April 12, 1996, previously published in *Dialog* 36:3 (Summer 1997).

Chapter 8 is adapted from a CTNS–Templeton Foundation University Lecture delivered as the University of Pennsylvania's Boardman Lectureship, April 24, 1997.

Chapter 9 is adapted from an address to the Pontifical Academy of Sciences on evolution of October 22, 1996, originally published in *L'Osservatore Romano*, Weekly English Edition, no. 44 (October 30, 1996), 7–8. This translation has been altered slightly to reflect gender inclusivity.

Chapter 11 was originally published in *Dialog* 36:3 (Summer 1997).

Chapter 12 was originally published in *Dialog* 36:3 (Summer 1997).

Chapter 14 was originally published in *Dialog* 36:4 (Fall 1997).

Figure 13.2 is reprinted from Arthur Peacocke, *Theology for a Scientific Age: Being and Becoming—Natural, Divine and Human* (London: SCM Press, 1990; and Minneapolis: Fortress Press, expanded edition, 1993). © 1990, 1993 Arthur Peacocke. Used by permission of Augsburg Fortress.

Index